Contents

HOW TO USE THIS COURSE

Following this course will help you to understand, speak and read most of the Russian you are likely to need on holiday or business trips. The course is based on recordings made in Moscow. You will hear ordinary Russians and other Russian-speakers in everyday situations. Step by step you will learn first to understand what they are saying and then to speak in similar situations yourself.

Before producing the course we talked to many people about why and how they learn languages. We know how important it is for learning to be enjoyable – and for it to be usable from the beginning. There is not a lot of point in knowing all the complexities of Russian grammar if you can't ask for a cup of coffee! There is a grammar section in each unit, but its main function will be to help you to understand and use the language.

We have introduced the Cyrillic alphabet in the first five units. Do remember that it is difficult to learn an entirely new alphabet, and that it takes time. The exercises in each unit will help you to learn the letters, as will writing out the new words and phrases you meet.

In the first five units we have transliterated all the words, that is, we have provided the nearest equivalents in Latin script to the Russian sounds. You will see that the spelling and pronunciation of Russian words do not always correspond! A few guidelines are given on pages 5 and 6, but our best advice would be to listen as much as possible to the native speakers on your recording and follow their pronunciation.

General hints to help you use the course

- Have confidence in us! Real language is complex and you will find certain things in every unit which are not explained in detail. Don't worry about this. We will build up your knowledge slowly, selecting only what is most important to know at each stage.
- Try to study regularly, but in short periods. 20–30 minutes each day is usually better than 4 hours once a week.
- To help you learn to speak, say the words and phrases out loud whenever possible.
- If you don't understand something, leave it for a while. Learning a language is a bit like doing a jigsaw or a crossword puzzle; there are many ways to tackle it and it falls into place eventually.
- Don't be afraid to write in your book and add your own notes.
- Do revise frequently. (There are revision sections after every three units.) It also helps to get somebody to test you – they don't need to understand Russian.
- If you can possibly learn with somebody else, you will be able to help each other and practise the language together.
- Learning Russian may take more time than you thought. Just be patient and above all don't get angry with yourself.

Suggested study pattern

Each unit of the course consists of approximately thirteen pages in the book and around ten minutes of recordings. The first page of each unit will tell you what you are going to learn and you will also find our Study guide there. The Study guide tells you the best way (we think) to tackle a unit. As you progress with the course you may find that you evolve a method of study which suits you better. That's fine, but we suggest you keep to our pattern at least for the first three units, or you may find you are not taking full advantage of all the possibilities offered by the material.

The book contains step-by-step instructions for working through the course: when to use the book on its own, when to use the recording on its own, when to use them both together, and how to use them in each case. On the recording our presenter Andrei Bell will guide you through the various sections. Here is an outline of the study pattern proposed.

Dialogues

Listen to the dialogues, first without stopping, and get a feel for the task ahead. Then go over each dialogue or suggested group of dialogues in conjunction with the vocabulary and the notes. You should get into the habit of playing the recording repeatedly to give yourself time to think, listen to sentences a number of times, and repeat them after the speakers. Don't leave a dialogue until you are confident that you have at least understood it.

Key words and phrases

Study this list of the most important words and phrases from the dialogues. If possible, try to learn them by heart. They will be practised in the rest of the unit.

Practise what you have learned

After each group of dialogues there are some listening and speaking exercises. To do them, you will need to work closely with the book. You will, for instance, often be asked to listen to a piece on the recording and then fill in answers or mark off boxes in the book. Or you will be asked to write an exercise and then check the answers on the recording. Use your PAUSE/STOP and REWIND or REPEAT buttons to give yourself time to think. Normally in the last exercise you will have an opportunity to practise the most important language in the preceding dialogues.

Grammar

At this stage in a unit things should begin to fall into place and you are ready for the grammar section. If you really don't like grammar you will still learn a lot without studying this part, but most people quite enjoy finding out how the language they are learning actually works and how it is put together. In each unit we have selected just one or two major grammar points.

Alphabet and *Read and understand*

In these sections you will practise reading and using the Cyrillic alphabet, and, later, understanding signs, menus and so on which you may come across in Russia.

Did you know?

In this section you will be given some practical background information about Russia.

Your turn to speak

Finally back to the recording for some more practice, this time using the main words and phrases of the whole unit. The book only gives you an outline of the exercises, so you will be listening to the recording and responding. For the first half of the units you will usually be asked to take part in a conversation where you hear a question or statement in Russian, followed by a suggestion in English as to how you might reply. You then give your reply in Russian and listen to see if you were right. You will probably have to go over these spoken exercises a few times. In the later units, as you become more confident, we will suggest situations which you might expect to encounter in Russia. Try these first yourself, and then turn on your recording to see how a Russian might talk on the same theme.

Answers

The answers to all the exercises (except those given in the recording) can be found on the last page of each unit.

At the back of the book

p.211 a grammar summary which covers the main rules of Russian grammar for those who wish to study them in greater detail than the main part of this course provides

p.214 a Russian–English vocabulary list containing all the words in the course, plus a short index of words and topics

Symbols and abbreviations

For cassettes: If your cassette recorder has a counter, set it to zero at the start of each unit and then note the number in the headphone symbol at the beginning of each dialogue. This will help you to find the right place on the tape quickly when you want to wind back.

For CD players: Your player will locate each unit as a track number. Note the number from your display at the beginning of each dialogue. This will help you find the right place on your disk when you want to repeat play.

➧	This indicates an important word or phrase in the dialogues.		
m.	masculine	sing.	singular
f.	feminine	pl.	plural
n.	neuter	lit.	literally

The Cyrillic alphabet and the transliteration used in this course

а	[a]
б	[b]
в	[v]
г	[g]
д	[d]
е	[ye]
ё	[yo]
ж	[zh]
з	[z]
и	[i] or, sometimes, [ee]
й	[y]
к	[k]
л	[l]
м	[m]
н	[n]
о	[o]
п	[p]
р	[r]
с	[s]
т	[t]
у	[u]
ф	[f]
х	[kh]
ц	[ts]
ч	[ch]
ш	[sh]
щ	[shch]
э	[e]
ю	[yu]
я	[ya]
ь	[']
ы	[y] or, sometimes, [i]
(ъ	– not transliterated in the course)

All letters given in square brackets reflect pronunciation.

As you can see, such a list is only useful for reference, since it can only approximately give the Russian pronunciation. Furthermore there are features of Russian which make our transliteration, based as it is on actual pronunciation, deviate from this norm. Most importantly:

(i) o is pronounced [o] when it is the stressed syllable and closer to [a] when not stressed.

A similar change occurs with я [ya] which can sound like [i] the further it is from the stressed syllable. It must, in fact, be acknowledged that any vowel sound which is not in stressed position may become blurred and even indistinguishable from other vowel sounds. Since this applies especially to the many different noun endings, such a situation can be *very* convenient for the learner!

(ii) Certain consonants sound more like others in particular combinations or at the end of a word. For example: в [v] will be closer to [f] before с [s] and some other consonants. We would stress that this is not a rule as such, but simply what the vocal chords force us to do (compare the English *absorb* v *absorption*).

Stress

From the above examples, you have seen how important stress – where you put the emphasis on a word – is in Russian. The stress can often change in accordance with a word's *role* in a sentence. Unfortunately there are no simple rules to help the learner. This need not inhibit you in speaking: a word wrongly stressed will probably be understood. However it is crucial to be *aware* of these possible changes, since pronunciation is sometimes radically altered. Most of the stresses are marked in this book, so that you can become accustomed to them. Russians do not, however, normally mark them in the written script.

1

TALKING ABOUT YOURSELF

You will learn

- common greetings in Russian
- to introduce yourself and people you are with
- to ask somebody's name
- to ask and reply to simple questions about nationality, etc

and you will read about the different forms a Russian name can take and when each is used

Before you begin

Always listen to the dialogues at least once before following them in your book. Don't worry if you can't make out every word. Try to follow the gist without being distracted by unfamiliar words. The more accustomed you are to the *sound* of the Russian language, the easier it will be to read the script. So don't hurry, and above all do not despair – all *will* fit into place!

In Unit 1 you will hear people greeting each other, introducing themselves and asking about others. We will be introducing the Cyrillic alphabet over the first five lessons with all dialogues in both Cyrillic and Latin scripts. Before turning to the first dialogues in your book, you will find it useful to read the section on the alphabet on page 15. See how many of the Russian words you can make out.

And now: желáем успéха! [zhiláyim uspyékha] we wish you success!

Study guide

To help you check your progress, mark off the *Study guide* list as you complete the tasks in each unit.

	Dialogues 1, 2: listen without the book
	Dialogues 1, 2: listen, read and study one by one
	Practise what you have learned
	Dialogues 3, 4: listen without the book
	Dialogues 3, 4: listen, read and study one by one
	Practise what you have learned
	Dialogues 5–7: listen without the book
	Dialogues 5–7: listen, read and study one by one
	Practise what you have learned
	Study the **Key words and phrases**
	Read and practise writing the **Alphabet**
	Study the **Grammar** section carefully
	Read **Did you know?**
	Do the exercises in **Your turn to speak**
	Listen to all the dialogues once again straight through

Dialogues

1 *Tanya greets a woman in the service bureau*

Tanya	Здрáвствуйте.	Zdrástvuytye.
Woman	Дóбрый день.	Dóbry dyen'.

> **здрáвствуйте** [zdrástvuytye] is the most common way of saying hello in Russian.
>
> **дóбрый день** [dóbry dyen'] good day
> At different times of the day one can also say:
> **дóброе ýтро** [dóbraye útra] good morning
> **дóбрый вéчер** [dóbry vyécher] good evening

2 *Katya arrives at Anna Sergeevna's house*

Katya	Здрáвствуйте, Áнна Сергéевна.	Zdrástvuytye, Ánna Sergéevna.
Anna Sergeevna	Здрáвствуй, Кáтя.	Zdrástvuy, Kátya.

> **здрáвствуй** [zdrástvuy] is the familiar form of 'hello' used with people you know well or with children.

Practise what you have learned

The exercise below is to help you become accustomed to the various forms of greeting. Concentrate on listening and clearly distinguishing each one.

1

Listen to the recording and see if you can match the voices to the pictures below. (Answers on page 20.)

(i) ....

(ii) ....

(iii)..

(iv)..

(a) (c) (b) (d)

Dialogues

3 *Irina introduces herself, then asks Anna Ivanovna her name*

Irina	Здра́вствуйте.	Zdrástvuytye.
Anna Ivanovna	Здра́вствуйте.	Zdrástvuytye.
Irina	Меня́ зову́т Ири́на. А как вас зову́т?	Minyá zavút Irína. A kak vas zavút?
Anna Ivanovna	Меня́ зову́т А́нна Ива́новна.	Minyá zavút Ánna Ivánovna.
Irina	О́чень прия́тно.	Óchin' priyátna.

меня́ зову́т... [minyá zavút...] my name is... (the Russian in fact means 'they call me'). This would answer the question **как вас зову́т?** [kak vas zavút?] 'how do they call you?' i.e. what is your name?

You may have noticed that in the word **зову́т** [zavút] the first vowel is not pronounced as it looks. It's not a mistake! In Russian **o** when not stressed sounds much closer to [a] than to [o]. (It's called '*a*kanye'!)

The **a** which begins Irina's question means 'and' in a contrastive sense, as in 'That's my name. And (but) what's yours?'

4 *Maria Dmitrievna introduces herself to her new students*

Maria Dmitrievna	Здра́вствуйте, ребя́та!	Zdrástvuytye, ribyáta!
Students	Здра́вствуйте!	Zdrástvuytye!
Maria Dmitrievna	Меня́ зову́т Мари́я Дми́триевна. А как вас зову́т?	Minyá zavút María Dmítrievna. A kak vas zavút?
Olya	Меня́ зову́т О́ля.	Minyá zavút Ólya.
Maria Dmitrievna	А тебя́ как зову́т?	A tibyá kak zavút?
Lena	Меня́ зову́т Ле́на.	Minyá zavút Lyéna.
Maria Dmitrievna	А тебя́?	A tibyá?
Volodya	Меня́ зову́т Воло́дя.	Minyá zavút Volódya.
Maria Dmitrievna	А тебя́?	A tibyá?
Kolya	Меня́ – Ко́ля. Извини́те, а как вас зову́т?	Minyá – Kólya. Izvinítye, a kak vas zavút?
Maria Dmitrievna	Меня́ зову́т Мари́я Дми́триевна.	Minyá zavút María Dmítrievna.

- **ребя́та** [ribyáta] is an informal way of addressing a group of children or teenagers.
- Maria Dmitrievna has used **здра́вствуйте** [zdrástvuytye] because she is addressing a group (while the children use this form because she is their teacher!)
- **как тебя́ зову́т?** [kak tibyá zavút?] what is your name? You would use **тебя́** [tibyá] addressing a child.
- **извини́те** [izvinítye] excuse me. More often than not you will hear **извини́те, пожа́луйста** [izvinítye, pazhálsta] excuse me please.

Practise what you have learned

2 A journey by train through the Russian Federation gives ample time to become acquainted! Listen to the snatches of conversation on your recording, then decide which corresponds to each of the pictures below.
(Answers on page 20.)

(i) ....

(ii) ....

(iii) ....

(iv) ....

Dialogues

5 *Misha wants his mother to meet a friend*

Misha	Ма́ма, э́то мой друг.	Máma, éta moy druk.
Dima	Здра́вствуйте, меня́ зову́т Ди́ма.	Zdrástvuytye, minyá zavút Díma.
Anna Sergeevna	О́чень прия́тно. А́нна Серге́евна.	Óchin' priyátna. Ánna Sergéevna.

➧ **э́то...** [éta...] this (is)... Introducing somebody can be very simple in Russian. You just need **э́то...** [éta...] and then a name or description of the person. To find out *who* somebody is, you ask **кто э́то?** [kto éta?] who is this?

➧ **мой друг** [moy druk] my friend. If Misha's friend was a woman, he would say **э́то моя́ подру́га** [éta mayá padrúga]. Note that **мой** [moy] is used talking about a man and **моя́** [mayá] about a woman.

Remember what was said above about **о** when not stressed. When written down, **мой** and **моя́** are obviously closely related, unlike their transliterated versions!

6 *Tamara asks Pavel his surname and where he's from*

Tamara	Па́вел, как ва́ша фами́лия?	Pável, kak vásha família?
Pavel	Моя́ фами́лия – Величе́нко.	Mayá família – Velichénko.
Tamara	Вы ру́сский?	Vi rússky?
Pavel	Нет, я украи́нец. Э́то украи́нская фами́лия.	Nyet, ya ukrayínets. Éta ukrayínskaya família.

➧ **как ва́ша фами́лия?** [kak vásha família?] what is your surname? **Фами́лия** [família] may not be a person, but it *is* a feminine noun (see the grammar section on page 17).

➧ **вы ру́сский?** [vi rússky?] are you Russian?
нет, я украи́нец [nyet, ya ukrayínets] no, I'm Ukrainian. If he was Russian, he would answer: **да, я ру́сский** [da, ya rússky].

A few more nationalities:
англича́нин [anglichánin] Englishman, **англича́нка** [anglichánka] Englishwoman; **францу́з** [frantsús] Frenchman, **францу́женка** [frantsúzhinka] Frenchwoman; **америка́нец** [amerikányets] American (male), **америка́нка** [amerikánka] American (female); **не́мец** [nyémets] German (male), **не́мка** [nyémka] German (female).

➧ **э́то украи́нская фами́лия** [éta ukrayínskaya família] it's a Ukrainian surname.

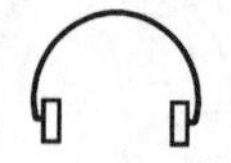

7 *At the end of an evening*

Tamara	До свида́ния, Па́вел.	Da svidánya, Pável.
Pavel	До свида́ния. Всего́ вам до́брого.	Da svidánya. Fsivó vam dóbrava.

всего́ вам до́брого [fsivó vam dóbrava] all the best.

➧ **до свида́ния** [da svidánya] goodbye (lit. 'until our next meeting')

Practise what you have learned

3 Tanya is in a very cosmopolitan hotel. Can you work out the nationalities of the people she speaks to? (Answers on page 20.)

(i) ....

(ii) ....

(iii) ....

(iv) ....

(a) **англича́нка** [anglichánka]	(b) **ру́сский** [rússky]
(c) **италья́нка** [ital'yánka]	(d) **францу́з** [frantsús]

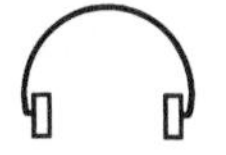

4 This time listen for the *professions* of each of the four people. (Answers on page 20.)

(i) Sergei ....

(ii) Tanya ....

(iii) Pavel ....

(iv) Larisa ....

(a) **матема́тик** [matimátik]	(b) **студе́нт** [studyént]
(c) **журнали́стка** [zhurnalístka]	(d) **студе́нтка** [studyéntka]
(e) **экономи́ст** [ekanamíst]	

Key words and phrases

Here are the words and phrases you have met so far. Do make sure you're confident with them before going further. The best way to learn them, we think, is to say them aloud as often as possible. The transliterated forms are as close as we could get to the Russian, but you should listen to how they *sound* on the recording, paying particular attention to where the stress falls. This can make an enormous difference to how a word is pronounced and spelled.

здра́вствуйте [zdrástvuytye]	hello
здра́вствуй [zdrástvuy]	hello (to a friend, or child)
до́брый день [dóbry dyen']	good day
до́брое у́тро [dóbraye útra]	good morning
до́брый ве́чер [dóbry vyécher]	good evening
как вас зову́т? [kak vas zavút?]	what is your name?
как тебя́ зову́т? [kak tibyá zavút?]	what is your name? (to a child)
меня́ зову́т... [minyá zavút...]	my name is...
о́чень прия́тно [óchin' priyátna]	pleased to meet you
извини́те (пожа́луйста) [izvinítye (pazhálsta)]	excuse me (please)
э́то... [éta...]	this is... / it is...
мой друг [moy druk]	my friend (male)
моя́ подру́га [mayá padrúga]	my friend (female)
как ва́ша фами́лия? [kak vásha famíliya?]	what is your surname?
моя́ фами́лия... [mayá famíliya...]	my surname is...
вы ру́сский? [vi rússky?]	are you Russian?
да, я ру́сский [da, ya rússky]	yes, I am Russian
нет, я украи́нец [nyet, ya ukrayínets]	no, I'm Ukrainian
э́то украи́нская фами́лия [éta ukrayínskaya famíliya]	it's a Ukrainian name
я бизнесме́н [ya biznismyén]	I am a businessman
до свида́ния [da svidánya]	goodbye

The Russian alphabet

The Cyrillic alphabet is named in honour of St Cyril (in Russian *Kyrill*), a 9th-century Macedonian monk, who, with his brother St Methodius, is credited with creating a writing system for the Slavonic languages. The two monks worked as missionaries, bringing Christianity to Slavs outside the Byzantine empire, and an alphabet was required to translate liturgical books and the Bible into Slavonic. Two original writing systems are known to have existed and whether in fact Cyril and Methodius' alphabet is the one we now call 'Cyrillic' is a matter of some conjecture among scholars.

The alphabet which developed into present Cyrillic shares many letters with the Greek and Latin scripts. Among its 33 letters there are, however, some which are quite different. You may find it useful to practise writing them out (try your name, and your friends' names!). Try also to follow as much as possible of the dialogues in Cyrillic, though there will be a transliterated version for the first five units while the alphabet is being introduced.

Beside each letter you will find the character, or characters, in Latin script which most closely correspond. They will seldom correspond entirely, so listen to Andrei as he pronounces the Russian letters.

There are five letters in Russian which need no introduction:

а	[as in *car*]
к	[k]
м	[m]
о	[as in *from*]
т	[t]

One letter is almost the same:

з	[z]

Some letters are deceptively familiar:

е	[ye as in *yet*]
в	[v]
н	[n]
с	[s]
р	[r]
у	[oo as in *good*]

And then there's **я** [ya] – an extremely important letter to remember since it can also mean 'I' or 'I am' in Russian.

Can you recognise these words?

ТАКТ	**КÓСМОС**	**ТРÁКТОР**
МОСКВÁ	**НЕТ**	**РЕСТОРÁН**
ТЕÁТР	**КОСМОНÁВТ**	**ВÁЗА**
МЕТРÓ	**НÓМЕР**	**ОРКÉСТР**
ТОСТ	**АТÁКА**	

Now listen to Andrei as he reads the letters aloud. You will notice that some letters, in particular **o**, do not always sound as they look. Mostly this is a question of stress, but we will explain particular discrepancies along the way.

Try writing the words printed at the foot of page 15. If you feel confident with those, see if you can fill in the missing letters in the next exercise.

как в.....с зо.....ýт?	what is your name?
мен..... зовýт В.....ра	my name is Vera
вот ре.....торáн	here is a restaurant
вот Сé.....а	here is Syéva (a man's name)
вот мет.....ó	here is the metro (subway/underground)
мо..... м.....ма рýсская	my mother is Russian

And now a little passage to read through.

— **Как вас зовýт?**
— **Меня́ зовýт Вéра.**
— **А как вас зовýт?**
— **Меня́ зовýт Сéва.**

Would you be able to write down the reply if the people's names were Anna and Zoya? What about Olya and Vanya? Svyéta and Kátya? (You'll find the names in Cyrillic upside down at the foot of the page.)

Áнна, Зóя, Óля, Вáня, Свéта, Кáтя

Grammar

One can talk about Russian grammar a lot, some people do it endlessly! However you can *communicate* in Russian without knowing *all* the 'rules' and we have therefore kept discussion of complexities to a minimum. The notes here and in the following units will give you the basic structure of the language. They will help you to understand and build on what you hear in each lesson.

Please don't worry if something baffles you, or if you can't remember it all. You can leave it, and still understand the unit. You'll probably find later that you can't remember why you were confused!

Grammar should be an aid, a tool in learning Russian. Remember though that very few grammatical mistakes will be serious enough to prevent you from being understood.

Nouns

In Russian nouns have a gender – masculine, feminine or neuter. Sometimes the choice will seem obvious – **ма́ма** [máma] can hardly be anything but feminine! More often, however, there seems to be no reason, good or otherwise, for the gender of a particular noun.

Fortunately in Russian the gender is normally clear from the ending of a noun.

- Masculine nouns most often end in a consonant:
  друг [druk] a male friend
- Feminine nouns usually end in **-а** or **-я**:
  подру́га [padrúga] female friend
  фами́лия [famíliya] surname
- Neuter nouns end in **-о** or **-е**:
  вино́ [vinó] wine

We will leave neuter nouns for the moment since they don't crop up so often. The reason for mentioning anything about gender is that any word describing a noun has to 'agree' with it.

мой **друг** [*moy* druk] my (male) friend
моя́ **подру́га** [*mayá* padrúga] my (female) friend

Any word describing a noun changes, for example:

украинская **фами́лия** [*ukrayínskaya* famíliya] a Ukrainian surname

You could have ***украинский*** **друг** [*ukrayínsky* druk] and ***украинская*** **подру́га** [*ukrayínskaya* padrúga]

If that seems complicated, it may be some consolation that you now know enough to construct full Russian sentences. The verb 'to be' ('I am', 'you are', etc.) is not used in Russian. To say that he is Ukrainian, Pavel simply uses the word for 'I' – **я** [ya] (not capitalised in Russian) and **украинец** [ukrayínets].

And a statement can be made into a question by simply changing one's intonation ('putting a question in the voice'):

Э́то украинская фами́лия? [Éta ukrayínskaya famíliya?]
Is it a Ukrainian name?
Да, э́то украинская фами́лия. [Da, éta ukrayínskaya famíliya.]
Yes, it is a Ukrainian name.

Did you know?

The polite way of addressing somebody older or whom you don't know very well is by name and patronymic. The patronymic is formed from one's father's name with different endings for a man or woman. In the dialogues you met Anna Sergeevna. Sergeevna indicates that she is 'the daughter of Sergei'. Her brother Nikolai would be Nikolai Sergeevich.

There are titles like our 'Mr' or 'Mrs' in Russian. However, these have traditionally been used when addressing foreigners. Other titles, some in common usage before the 1917 revolution, are beginning to reappear, but it is too early to judge whether these will endure.

You will probably have noticed that the patronymic is not always used. It would not be used in addressing a child or young adult, and probably only used on formal occasions about a person in his or her 20s or 30s. Instead the first name only, or, more probably, a shortened form, is used (Katya for example is the short form of Yekaterina).

It all depends very much on the situation and on how well you know a person. This may not be of great comfort to beginners, but in fact you shouldn't have much problem. Listen to how a person introduces him or herself. And if you can't make it out the first time, you can always ask them again:

Извини́те, пожа́луйста, как вас зову́т? [izvinítye, pazhálsta, kak vas zavút?]
Sorry, what is your name?

Бандура
Юрий Николаевич

Заместитель главного редактора
газеты «Московские новости»

Москва, Тверская ул., 16/2 229-82-18

Yuri BANDOURA

Deputy Editor-in-Chief
"Moscow News"
newspaper

16/2 Tverskaya St., Moscow **tel: 229-82-18**

Have you ever tried reading a Russian novel and had the strange sensation that characters are multiplying before your eyes? They're not! Since it is not always easy to match up a name with its short form, here are some of the more common Russian names.

	Full name	*Short form*
Women's names	Yeléna	Lyéna
	Natálya	Natásha
	Ól'ga	Ólya
	Irína	Íra
	Ánna	Ánya
	Svetlána	Svyéta
Men's names	Sergéi	Seryózha
	Alekséi	Alyósha
	Aleksándr	Sásha
	Vladímir	Volódya
	Iván	Ványa

This is by no means a definitive list. A name may have a number of possible short forms, as well as other forms used for expressing affection, etc. (Lyénachka, Natáshenka and many more).

КИСИН
Борис Михайлович
Кандидат технических наук

Москва, 119034
Хилков переулок, 1/2

Тел. 233-46-81
203-05-40

Research Complex "Textile"

BORIS M. KISIN
Cand.Sc.(Technology)

1/2 Hilkov Lane,
Moscow 119034

Tel. 233-46-81
203-05-40

Your turn to speak

5

The last exercise in this unit will give you a chance to practise what you have learned. You will need the following phrases:

меня́ зову́т... [minyá zavút...]
вы ру́сский? [vi rússky?]
да, я ру́сский [da, ya rússky]
э́то мой друг [éta moy druk]
э́то моя́ ма́ма [éta mayá máma]
как вас зову́т? [kak vas zavút?]
о́чень прия́тно [óchin' priyátna]
моя́ фами́лия... [mayá famíliya...]
я бизнесме́н [ya biznismyén]

Now close your book and listen to Andrei's prompts. Remember you can always go back and listen again if it seems difficult the first time.

Answers

Practise what you have learned

Exercise **1**	(i) a (ii) d (iii) c (iv) b
Exercise **2**	(i) c (ii) a (iii) b (iv) d
Exercise **3**	(i) b (ii) a (iii) d (iv) c
Exercise **4**	(i) b (ii) c (iii) e (iv) a

2 TALKING ABOUT YOURSELF AND OTHERS

You will learn

- to talk about members of the family
- to talk about where you live and where you work
- to use numbers up to 20
- one or two crucial phrases for beginners

and you will be given an introduction to Russia and the Russian Federation

Before you begin

As in Unit 1, use the *Study guide* below to check your progress.

Study guide

Dialogues 1, 2: listen without the book
Dialogues 1, 2: listen, read and study one by one
Practise what you have learned
Dialogues 3–5: listen without the book
Dialogues 3–5: listen, read and study one by one
Practise what you have learned
Dialogues 6–8: listen without the book
Dialogues 6–8: listen, read and study one by one
Practise what you have learned
Study the **Key words and phrases**
Read and practise writing the **Alphabet**
Study the **Grammar** section carefully
Read **Did you know?**
Do the exercises in **Your turn to speak**
Listen to all the dialogues once again straight through

Dialogues

1 *Ira asks Anna Ivanovna about her family*

Ira	Скажи́те, у вас есть семья́?	Skazhítye, uvás yest' simyá?
Anna Ivanovna	Да, я за́мужем.	Da, ya zámuzhim.
Ira	А де́ти у вас есть?	A dyéti uvás yest'?
Anna Ivanovna	У меня́ есть до́чка.	Uminyá yest' dóchka.

- **скажи́те (, пожа́луйста)** [skazhítye (, pazhálsta)] tell me (please)
- **у вас есть семья́?** [uvás yest' simyá?] do you have a family? There isn't a common verb 'to have' in Russian. **У вас есть...?** [uvás yest'...?] literally means 'with you is there...?'. The reply will often begin **да, у меня́ есть...** [da, uminyá yest'...] yes, I have...
- **да, я за́мужем** [da, ya zámuzhim] yes, I'm married. This is what a woman would say. A man says **я жена́т** [ya zhinát]. You can say you're *not* married by putting **не** [nye] before the appropriate word: **я неза́мужем** [ya nyezámuzhim] (unmarried woman); **я не жена́т** [ya nye zhinát] (unmarried man). For a man the **не** [nye] is written separately.
- **де́ти у вас есть?** [dyéti uvás yest'?] do you have children? There are no strict rules regarding word order in Russian.
- **у меня́ есть до́чка** [uminyá yest' dóchka] I have a daughter. A more formal word for 'daughter' is **дочь** [doch]. And if Anna Ivanovna had a son she would say:
  у меня́ есть сын [uminyá yest' sin] I have a son

2 *Maria Dmitrievna asks whether Olya has a brother or sister*

Maria Dmitrievna	О́ля, у тебя́ есть брат и́ли сестра́?	Ólya, utibyá yest' brat íli sistrá?
Olya	У меня́ есть брат.	Uminyá yest' brat.
Maria Dmitrievna	А как его́ зову́т?	A kak yivó zavút?
Olya	Ди́ма.	Díma.

и́ли [íli] or

- **у тебя́ есть брат и́ли сестра́?** [utibyá yest' brat íli sistrá?] do you have a brother or sister? **У тебя́ есть...?** [utibyá yest'...?] is used instead of **у вас есть...?** [uvás yest'...?] when asking a child or somebody you know well
- **как его́ зову́т?** [kak yivó zavút?] what is his name? If Olya had a sister, the question would be **как её зову́т?** [kak yiyó zavút?] what is her name?

Practise what you have learned

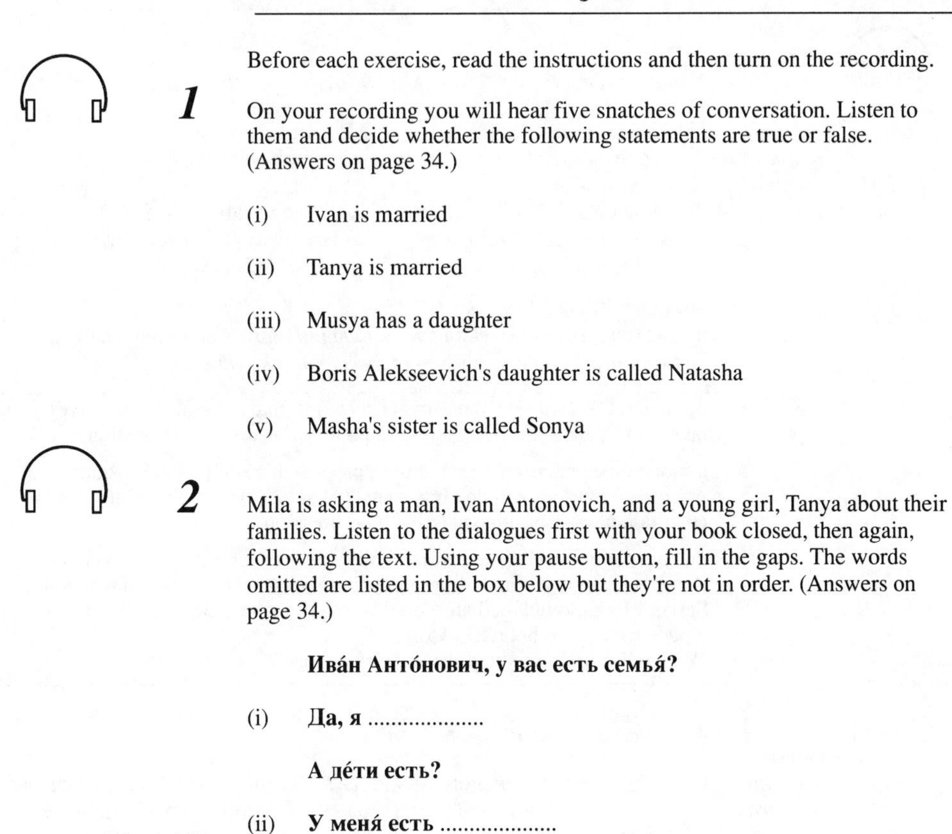

Before each exercise, read the instructions and then turn on the recording.

1

On your recording you will hear five snatches of conversation. Listen to them and decide whether the following statements are true or false. (Answers on page 34.)

(i) Ivan is married

(ii) Tanya is married

(iii) Musya has a daughter

(iv) Boris Alekseevich's daughter is called Natasha

(v) Masha's sister is called Sonya

2

Mila is asking a man, Ivan Antonovich, and a young girl, Tanya about their families. Listen to the dialogues first with your book closed, then again, following the text. Using your pause button, fill in the gaps. The words omitted are listed in the box below but they're not in order. (Answers on page 34.)

Ива́н Анто́нович, у вас есть семья́?

(i) **Да, я** ....

А де́ти есть?

(ii) **У меня́ есть** ....

А как её [yiyó] **зову́т?**

(iii) **Её** [yiyó] .... **О́ля** [Ólya]

She then chats with a young girl, Tanya.

Та́ня, у тебя́ есть брат и́ли [íli] **сестра́?**

(iv) **У меня́** .... **брат.**

(a) **есть** [yest'] (b) **жена́т** [zhinát] (c) **зову́т** [zavút] (d) **до́чь** [dóch]

(The unfamiliar letters in these words are in the *Alphabet* section on page 29.)

Dialogues

3 *Anna Sergeevna asks Sergei Mikhailovich what his profession is*

Anna Sergeevna	Прости́те, а кто вы по специа́льности?	Prastítye, a kto vi paspitsyál'nasti?
Sergei Mikhailovich	Я фило́лог.	Ya filólag.
Anna Sergeevna	А где вы рабо́таете?	A gdye vi rabótaitye?
Sergei Mikhailovich	В изда́тельстве *Сове́тская энциклопе́дия.*	Vizdátil'stvye *Savyétskaya intsiklapédiya.*

фило́лог [filólag] linguist
в изда́тельстве *Сове́тская энциклопе́дия* [vizdátil'stvye *Savyétskaya intsiklapédiya*] for the publishers of *Soviet Encyclopedia*

- **прости́те** [prastítye] excuse me. This word, like **извини́те** [izvinítye], can be used to mean 'sorry' or simply to prepare the way for a question.
- **кто вы по специа́льности?** [kto vi paspitsyál'nasti?] what is your profession? Or, broken down: **кто вы?** [kto vi?] who are you? **по специа́льности** [paspitsyál'nasti] by profession.
- **где вы рабо́таете?** [gdye vi rabótaitye?] where do you work? Verbs in Russian have different endings depending upon *who* is doing the action. If Sergei Mikhailovich had answered with a full sentence, it would have begun: **я рабо́таю** [ya rabótayu] I work.
(You will find more about these verbs on page 119.)

4 *And what is Tamara's profession?*

Lyena	Скажи́те, кто вы по специа́льности?	Skazhítye, kto vi paspitsyál'nasti?
Tamara	Я по специа́льности инжене́р, рабо́таю на заво́де.	Ya paspitsyál'nasti inzhinéer, rabótayu na zavódye.

инжене́р [inzhinéer] engineer (used for both men and women)
на заво́де [na zavódye] in a factory

- **рабо́таю** [rabótayu] I work. **Я** [ya] (I) is often omitted since the ending makes it clear who is doing the action.

5 *Tamara asks Lyena what her husband does*

Tamara	Скажи́те, а кто по специа́льности ваш муж?	Skazhítye, a kto paspitsyál'nasti vash mush?
Lyena	Печа́тник.	Pichátnik.
Tamara	Он рабо́тает в типогра́фии?	On rabótayit ftipagráfiyi?
Lyena	Да.	Da.

печа́тник [pichátnik] printer
в типогра́фии [ftipagráfiyi] at a printing press

- **кто по специа́льности ваш муж?** [kto paspitsyál'nasti vash mush?] what is your husband's profession or job? To find out from a man about his wife's profession, you would ask:
кто по специа́льности ва́ша жена́? [kto paspitsyál'nasti vásha zhiná?].
- **он рабо́тает в типогра́фии?** [on rabótayit ftipagráfiyi?] does he work at a printing press? If we were talking about a woman, the verb would be the same, but the pronoun would change: **она́ рабо́тает** [aná rabótayit] she works.

Practise what you have learned

As before, read the instructions for each particular exercise before you turn on the recording.

3 Ilya asks Darya Ivanovna what she and members of her family do for a living. Listen to the interview and then try matching up the people and their jobs. (Answers on page 34.)

(i)	Darya Ivanovna	(a)	physicist
(ii)	husband	(b)	journalist
(iii)	daughter	(c)	linguist
(iv)	son	(d)	engineer

4 Some people are asked where they work. Listen carefully, then look at the pictures and see if you can name the person in each scene. Their names are given in the box below. (Answers on page 34.)

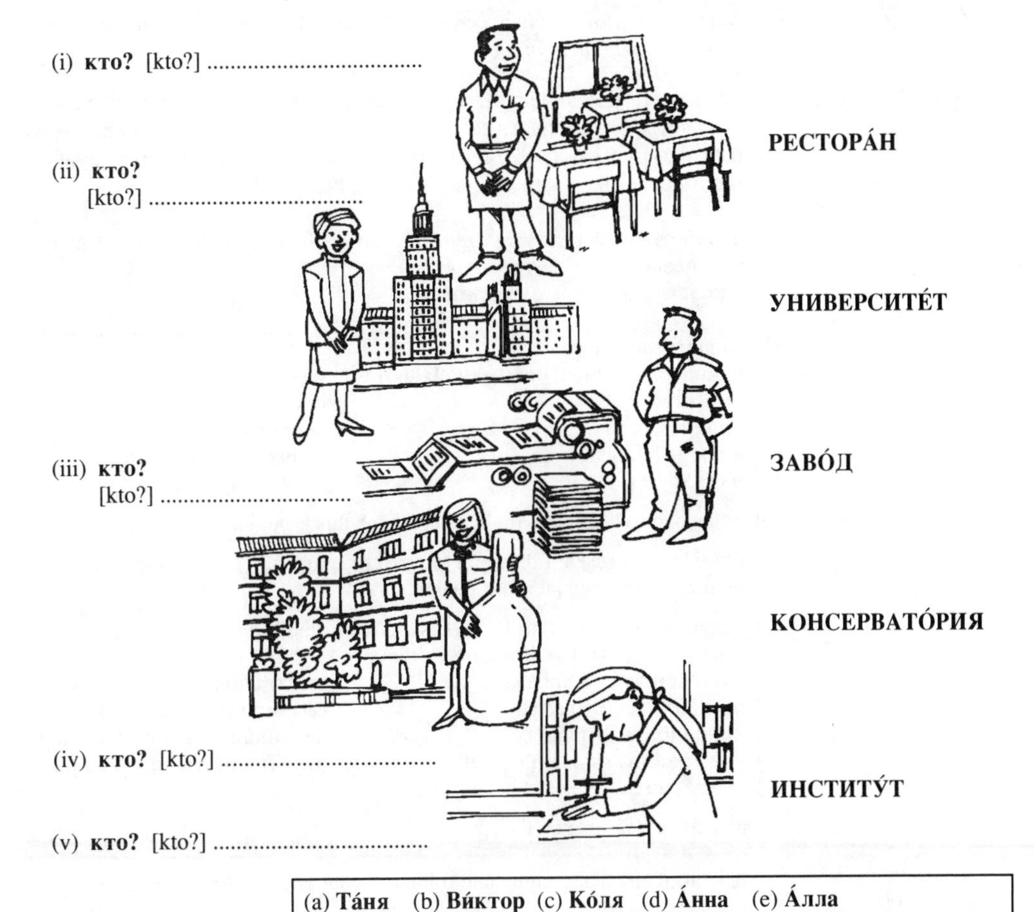

Dialogues

6 *Tanya wants to know where Boris Mikhailovich lives*

Tanya	Извините, Борис Михайлович, а где вы живёте?	Izvinítye, Borís Miháilovich, a gdye vi zhivyótye?
Boris Mikhailovich	На Осто́женке.	Na Astózhinkye.
Tanya	Э́то далеко́ от це́нтра?	Éta dalikó ot tséntra?
Boris Mikhailovich	Недалеко́.	Nidalikó.

на Осто́женке [na Astózhinkye] on Ostozhinka street

где вы живёте? [gdye vi zhivyótye?] where do you live?

я живу́... [ya zhivú...] I live...

э́то далеко́ от це́нтра? [éta dalikó ot tséntra?] is that far from the centre? In Russian one can often form the opposite by prefixing the word with **не-**[nye-], thus Boris Mikhailovich answers **недалеко́** [nidalikó] not far.

7 *Boris Mikhailovich gives Tanya his work and home phone numbers. Can you write them in numerals?*

Boris Mikhailovich	Запиши́те мой телефо́н: два ноль три, четы́ре три, шесть семь. А на рабо́те: три пять три, пять пять, шесть во́семь.	Zapishítye moy tilifón: dva nol' tri, chitýrye tri, shest' syem'. A na rabótye: tri pyat' tri, pyat' pyat', shest' vósim'.

запиши́те мой телефо́н [zapishítye moy tilifón] take down my telephone number
на рабо́те [na rabótye] at work

Numbers up to ten are:

оди́н [adín], **одна́** [adná], **одно́** [adnó]
два [dva]
три [tri]
четы́ре [chitýrye]
пять [pyat']
шесть [shest']
семь [syem']
во́семь [vósim']
де́вять [dyévit']
де́сять [dyésit']

You will also hear **ноль** [nol'] zero, though this is not included when counting.

оди́н [adín] is used if the noun referred to is masculine, **одна́** [adná] if it is feminine and **одно́** [adnó] if neuter.

The numbers from 10 to 19 are easy to learn since you really just add **-надцать** [natsat'] to the numbers above:

оди́ннадцать [adínnatsat']
двена́дцать [dvinátsat']
трина́дцать [trinátsat']
четы́рнадцать [chitýrnatsat']
пятна́дцать [pitnátsat']
шестна́дцать [shisnátsat']
семна́дцать [simnátsat']
восемна́дцать [vosimnátsat']
девятна́дцать [divitnátsat']

and 20 is: **два́дцать** [dvátsat']

Now turn on the recording and follow in your book as Andrei reads the numbers aloud.

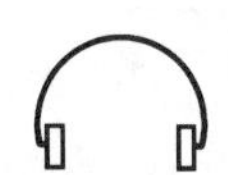

8 *Ira is looking for the nearest underground station*

Ira	Извини́те, пожа́луйста, где здесь ста́нция метро́?	Izvinítye, pazhálsta, gdye zdyes' stántsiya mitró?
Passer-by	Я о́чень пло́хо говорю́ по-ру́сски. Говори́те ме́дленно.	Ya óchin' plókha gavaryú parússki. Gavarítye myédlinna.

здесь [zdyes'] here, in the vicinity
ста́нция метро́ [stántsiya mitró] underground station

> ➧ **я о́чень пло́хо говорю́ по-ру́сски** [ya óchin' plókha gavaryú parússki]
> I speak Russian very badly
>
> Other languages will be formed in the same way:
>
> **я говорю́** [ya gavaryú] {
> **по-англи́йски** [pa-angléeski] I speak English
> **по-францу́зски** [pafrantsúski] I speak French
> **по-неме́цки** [panimyétski] I speak German
>
> You may want to say 'I speak only a little Russian' **я то́лько немно́го говорю́ по-ру́сски** [ya tól'ka nimnóga gavaryú parússki]
>
> ➧ **говори́те ме́дленно** [gavarítye myédlinna] speak slowly

Practise what you have learned

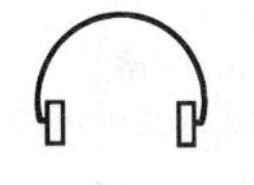

5

Participants in a folk concert in Moscow are asked where they live. Listen to their answers on your recording, then match the names below with the places. (Answers on page 34.)

(i) **Та́ня**; (ii) **Тара́с**; (iii) **Мари́я**; (iv) **Оле́сь**; (v) **Ни́на**
(a) **в Ми́нске**; (b) **в Москве́**; (c) **в Ки́еве**; (d) **в Ве́не**; (e) **в Бо́нне**

6

Masha finds it easiest to add up aloud. Listen to the recording, then fill in the missing numbers. (Answers on page 34.)

(i) **два** [dva] + **оди́н** [adín] = ...
(ii) **семь** [syem'] + ... = **де́вять** [dyévit']
(iii) **оди́н** [adín] + **три** [tri] + **три** [tri] = ...
(iv) .... + **семь** [syem'] = **де́сять** [dyésit']
(v) **де́вять** [dyévit'] + ... = **оди́ннадцать** [adínnatsat']
(vi) **во́семь** [vósim'] + ... = **де́вять** [dyévit']

7

In this exercise, you take the role of a Ukrainian, Oksana. You live in Kiev, and, yes, you do speak Russian, but your English is pretty bad. You will need to use:

я живу́ [ya zhivú]
я говорю́ [ya gavaryú]

Key words and phrases

скажи́те [skazhítye]	tell me
у вас есть...? [uvás yest'...?]	do you have...? (formal or plural)
у тебя́ есть...? [utibyá yest'...?]	do you have...? (to a child or friend)
у меня́ есть... [uminyá yest'...]	I have...
де́ти [dyéti]	children
до́чка / дочь [dóchka / doch]	a daughter
сын [sin]	a son
брат [brat]	a brother
сестра́ [sistrá]	a sister
и́ли [íli]	or
за́мужем [zámuzhim]	married (woman's form)
жена́т [zhinát]	married (man's form)
как его́ зову́т? [kak yivó zavút?]	what is his name?
как её зову́т? [kak yiyó zavút?]	what is her name?
кто вы по специа́льности? [kto vi paspitsyál'nasti'?]	what is your profession?
я / она́ инжене́р [ya / aná inzhinéer]	I am/she is an engineer
я / он фило́лог [ya / on filólag]	I am/he is a linguist
где вы рабо́таете? [gdye vi rabótaitye?]	where do you work?
я рабо́таю [ya rabótayu]	I work
вы рабо́таете [vi rabótaitye]	you work
он/она́ рабо́тает... [on/aná rabótayit...]	he/she works...
на заво́де [na zavódye]	in a factory
в изда́тельстве [vizdátil'stvye]	in a publishing company
где вы живёте? [gdye vi zhivyótye?]	where do you live?
я живу́ [ya zhivú]	I live
далеко́ от це́нтра [dalikó ot tséntra]	far from the centre
где здесь... [gdye zdyes'...]	where around here is there...
ста́нция метро́? [stántsiya mitró?]	an underground (subway) station?
я о́чень пло́хо говорю́ по-ру́сски [ya óchin' plókha gavaryú parússki]	I speak Russian very badly
я то́лько немно́го говорю́... [ya tól'ka nimnóga gavaryú...]	I only speak a little...
вы говори́те по-ру́сски? [vi gavarítye parússki?]	do you speak Russian?
я говорю́... [ya gavaryú...]	I speak...
по-англи́йски [pa-angléeski]	English
по-францу́зски [pafrantsúski]	French
по-неме́цки [panimyétski]	German
говори́те ме́дленно [gavarítye myédlinna]	speak slowly

You'll find the numbers from 1 to 20 in the notes to dialogue 7.

The Russian alphabet

In this unit you will practise reading and writing the letters that you already know and you will learn five new ones. The transliteration should help with pronunciation, but let Andrei guide you.

If you can glance over the alphabet even for just a few minutes every day, you'll find that apparently formidable letters soon become familiar.

The new letters are:

ж	[zh as in *vision*, *pleasure*]
д	[d]
и	[i/ee as in *meet*]
ч	[ch]
ь	['] 'soft sign'

This last letter doesn't have a sound on its own. Instead it makes the consonant *before* it 'soft'. If this means nothing to you, listen to Andrei and try to follow the way he pronounces the following two words:

Гóголь [Gógol'] a famous writer
гол [gol] a goal in sport

Can you recognise the following cities and countries?

КИ́ЕВ	**МАДРИ́Д**	**АМСТЕРДА́М**
МИНСК	**ЕРЕВА́Н**	**ДАМА́СК**
А́ВСТРИЯ	**УКРАЙНА**	**И́НДИЯ**

8

Which word is out of place in each horizontal list? (Answers on page 34.)

ВО́ДКА	**ВИ́СКИ**	**ДА́ТА**	**ВИНО́**
ТЕА́ТР	**КИО́СК**	**КИНОТЕА́ТР**	**ДИСКОТЕ́КА**
ТЕ́ННИС	**ТАКСИ́**	**СТАДИО́Н**	**МАТЧ**

As in Unit 1, try writing out all the words above.

9

A little geography with your Russian! The following lists of cities and countries have been jumbled up. Can you link up each city with its country? Only names with letters you haven't met are transliterated.
(Answers on page 34.)

(i)	**Ки́ев**	(a)	**Испа́ния** [Ispánya]
(ii)	**Москва́**	(b)	**А́встрия**
(iii)	**Ерева́н**	(c)	**Арме́ния**
(iv)	**Минск**	(d)	**Украи́на**
(v)	**Мадри́д**	(e)	**Росси́я**
(vi)	**Ве́на**	(f)	**Белару́сь** [Byelarús']

10

Look at the following pictures and then write out the name of the thing in the space provided. All the words are jumbled in the box below.
(Answers on page 34.)

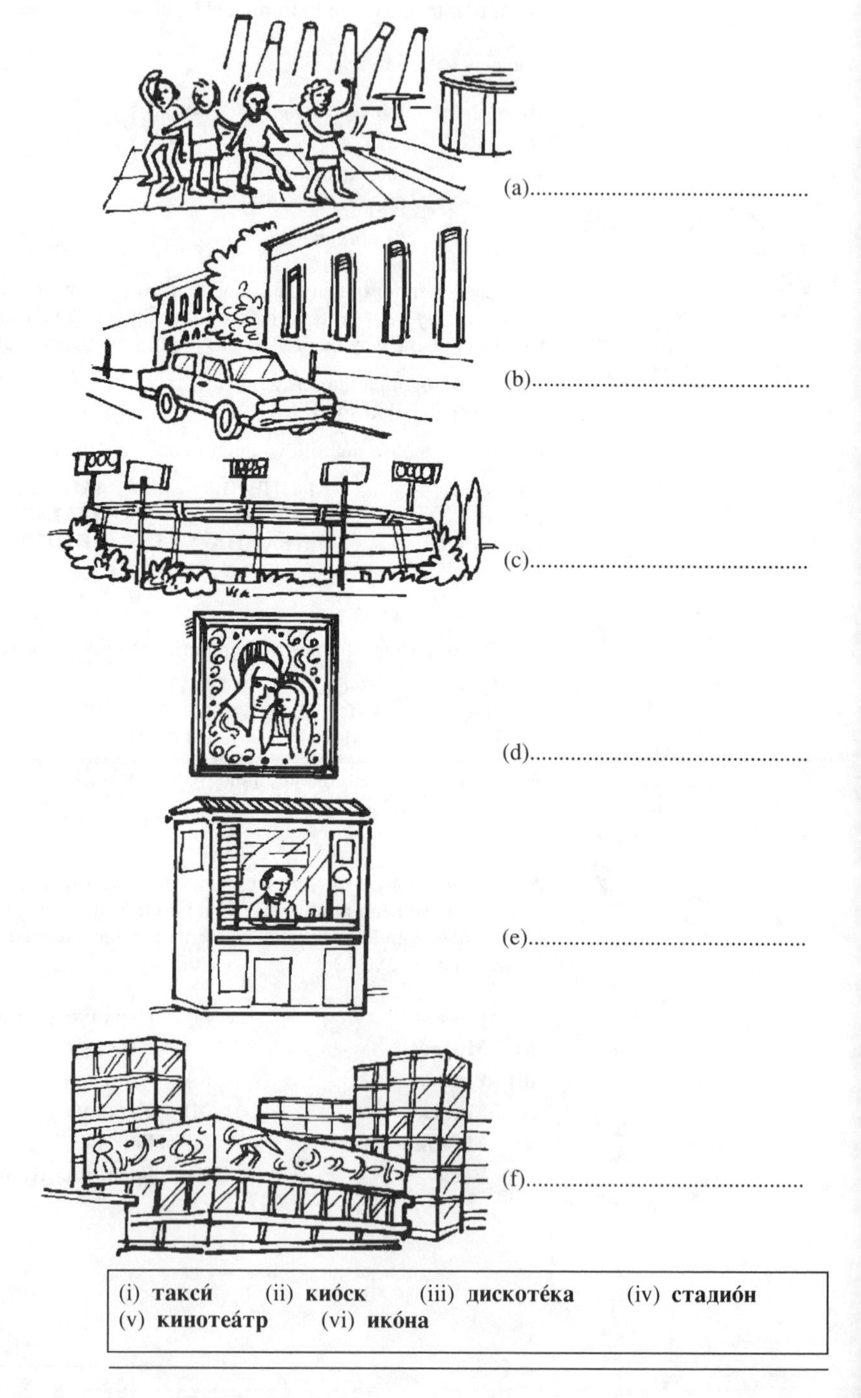

(a)..

(b)..

(c)..

(d)..

(e)..

(f)..

(i) **такси́** (ii) **кио́ск** (iii) **дискоте́ка** (iv) **стадио́н**
(v) **кинотеа́тр** (vi) **ико́на**

Grammar

In Unit 1 you saw how words that *describe* a noun change. This is not all! The noun itself has different endings depending on its role in the sentence, or which preposition it follows. In this unit you will see different endings after **в** [v] and **на** [na] meaning 'in', 'at', 'on'.

Before we look at these endings, a word of advice: you should be *aware* of these endings, but do not let them inhibit you. A wrong ending will rarely prevent you from being understood, and indeed when you listen to people speaking, you may not even be able to hear the ending.

If you ask where something is **где...?** [gdye ....?], the answer is likely to begin with the preposition **в** [v] or **на** [na]. There are rules as to when **в** is used, and when **на**, but there are also a bewildering number of exceptions! Whichever preposition is used, the ending of the noun will change, normally ending in **-е**.

Вот Ки́ев. Я живу́ в Ки́еве. [Vot Kíev. Ya zhivú fKíevye]
Here is Kiev. I live in Kiev.

Вот Москва́. Я живу́ в Москве́. [Vot Maskvá. Ya zhivú vMaskvyé]
Here is Moscow. I live in Moscow.

As you see, **в** before some consonants is pronounced [f]. This is simply because it is impossible to pronounce it as [v]!

11

Here is a list of people along with the cities they live in. Using the first sentence as an example, write down what the other people would say. (Answers on page 34.)

	Та́ня	**Москва́**	**я живу́ в Москве́**
(i)	**Том**	**Манче́стер**	....
(ii)	**Ян**	**Ве́на**	....
(iii)	**Мари́я**	**Мадри́д**	....
(iv)	**Ви́ктор**	**Ерева́н**	....
(v)	**А́нна**	**Минск**	....

12

Can you answer the question next to each picture? The words are listed in the box below, but you'll need to change the endings. (Answers on page 34.)

(i) **где Со́ня?**

она́ в ....

(ii) **где Ива́н?**

он в ....

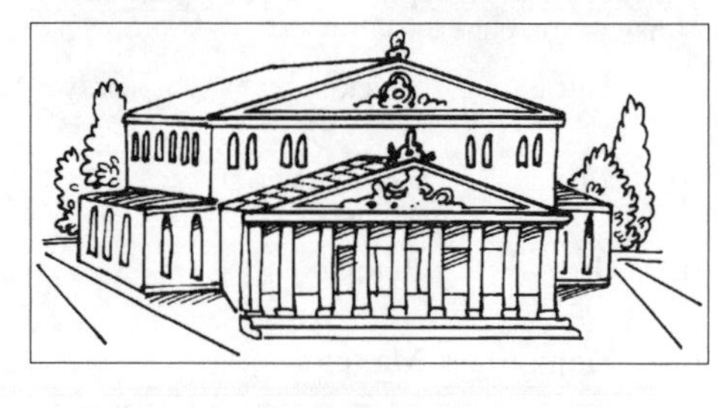

(iii) **где Ри́та?**

она́ в ....

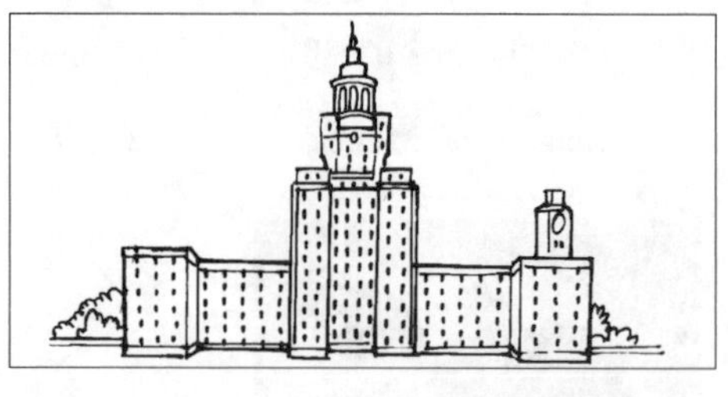

(iv) **где Лари́са?**

она́ в ....

(v) **где Вади́м?**

он на ....

рестора́н	**бар**	**теа́тр**	**университе́т**	**дискоте́ка**

Did you know?

Russia

Since the time of Peter the Great, Russian writers and intellectuals have debated Russia's place in the world: is it part of Europe, part of Asia, or does it have a role peculiarly its own?

We will not attempt to find an answer here, but it is easy to understand how the question might arise. The Russian Federation's huge territory spans two continents, extending from the Black Sea to the Pacific Ocean, and from Murmansk in the far North to Irkutsk near the Chinese border.

Russia's population in 1989 was 145 million. Some 80 per cent are Russians. These, like their neighbours the Ukrainians and Byelorussians, are Eastern Slavs. They trace their common roots to Kievan Rus', which flourished and grew from about AD 900 to AD 1240. Kiev is now the capital of Ukraine, while Russia's capital is Moscow.

There are also a large number of non-Slavic national minorities within the Russian Federation. Some of these have 'autonomous republic' or 'autonomous region' status. During the Soviet period (1917–1991), this autonomy remained largely on paper. With the break-up of the Soviet Union, calls for greater independence have been heard from many ethnic groups.

Russia and the Union of Soviet Socialist Republics (USSR)

There has long been a tendency to treat these two terms as interchangeable. This is quite misleading. Within the Soviet Union the Russian Federal Republic (RSFSR) was the biggest of fifteen republics: the others were Ukraine, Byelarus', Moldova, Georgia, Azerbaijan, Armenia, Lithuania, Latvia, Estonia, Kazakhstan, Turkmenistan, Uzbekistan, Tadzhikistan and Kirgistan. After the failed coup of 1991, the Russian Federal Republic was among the first to declare independence from the Soviet Union and one of the most instrumental in bringing about the latter's demise. The fairly widespread assumption that the Russian Federation is the 'heir apparent' to the Soviet regime has led to resentment in many of the other republics.

Throughout the Soviet period the Russian language was spoken in all the republics. At one stage this was the language for 'getting ahead', and in many republics it was difficult to find a school which taught in the native language. While this has now changed, it is probable that Russian will remain a *lingua franca* in a large number of the republics.

In an attempt to create a new 'Soviet man', the Soviet authorities encouraged people to settle in other republics. Under Stalin vast numbers of people, indeed whole nationalities, were sent into exile or forcibly resettled. As a result, in all the erstwhile republics of the USSR there are a considerable number of Russians and other national minorities. While some have integrated fully, others have not and are increasingly expressing dissatisfaction with their status in the newly independent countries.

Your turn to speak

13

In the first exercise, you will be asking Aleksandr Nikolaevich some questions. You will be using:

у вас есть...? [uvás yest'...?]
как егó зовýт? [kak yivó zavút?]

14

This time you will be playing the role of Anna Sergeevna, a physicist who lives in Moscow and works in an institute. You will need the words:

фи́зик [fízik]
я рабóтаю [ya rabótayu]
institутý

Answers

Practise what you have learned

Exercise **1**	(i) true (ii) false (iii) false (has a son) (iv) true (v) false (Ira)
Exercise **2**	(i) b (ii) d (iii) c (iv) a
Exercise **3**	(i) b (ii) c (iii) d (iv) a
Exercise **4**	(i) c (ii) d (iii) b (iv) a (v) e
Exercise **5**	(i) b (ii) c (iii) e (iv) a (v) d
Exercise **6**	(i) три [tri] (ii) два [dva] (iii) семь [syem'] (iv) три [tri] (v) два [dva] (vi) оди́н [adín]

Alphabet

Exercise **8**	The out of place words are ДÁТА, КИÓСК, ТАКСИ́
Exercise **9**	(i) d (ii) e (iii) c (iv) f (v) a (vi) b
Exercise **10**	(a) iii (b) i (c) iv (d) vi (e) ii (f) v

Grammar

Exercise **11**	(i) в Манчéстере (ii) в Вéне (iii) в Мадри́де (iv) в Ереванé (v) в Ми́нске
Exercise **12**	(i) в ресторáне (ii) в бáре (iii) в теáтре (iv) в университéте (v) на дискотéке

You will learn

- to check in at a hotel
- to ask if there is a room free and how much it will cost
- how to go about changing money
- some useful phrases when seeking information

and you will read about travel to Russia

A hotel lobby

Study guide

Dialogues 1, 2: listen without the book
Dialogues 1, 2: listen, read and study one by one
Practise what you have learned
Dialogue 3: listen without the book
Dialogue 3: listen, read and study one by one
Practise what you have learned
Dialogue 4: listen without the book
Dialogue 4: listen, read and study one by one
Practise what you have learned
Study the **Key words and phrases**
Read and practise writing the **Alphabet**
Study the **Grammar** section carefully
Read **Did you know?**
Do the exercises in **Your turn to speak**
Listen to all the dialogues once again straight through

Dialogues

1 *Tanya is checking in at her hotel*

Tanya	Здра́вствуйте.	Zdrástvuytye.
Receptionist	Здра́вствуйте.	Zdrástvuytye.
Tanya	Для меня́ заброни́рован но́мер.	Dlya minyá zabroníravan nómir.
Receptionist	Ва́ша фами́лия, пожа́луйста.	Vásha famíliya, pazhálsta.
Tanya	Петро́ва. Вот мой па́спорт.	Petróva. Vot moy pásport.
Receptionist	Спаси́бо. Одну́ мину́точку... Ваш но́мер на деся́том этаже́. Вот ва́ша визи́тная ка́рточка.	Spasíba. Adnú minútachku... Vash nómir na disyátam etazhé. Vot vásha vizítnaya kártachka.
Tanya	Спаси́бо.	Spasíba.

одну́ мину́точку [adnú minútachku] just a minute
визи́тная ка́рточка [vizítnaya kártachka] guest's card

для меня́ заброни́рован но́мер [dlya minyá zabroníravan nómir] I have a room booked

вот [vot] here (is) – the word to use when you're handing something over.

на деся́том этаже́ [na disyátam etazhé] on the tenth floor. Other useful floors to know:
на пе́рвом этаже́ [na pyérvam etazhé] on the first floor
на второ́м этаже́ [na ftaróm etazhé] on the second floor
на тре́тьем этаже́ [na tryétyem etazhé] on the third floor
By the way, Russians do not talk about the 'ground floor'. The first floor is the floor at ground level.

спаси́бо [spasíba] thank you

2 *Where can she get the key?*

Tanya	Скажи́те, пожа́луйста, где мо́жно получи́ть ключ?	Skazhítye, pazhálsta, gdye mózhna paluchít' klyuch?
Receptionist	Ключ мо́жно получи́ть у дежу́рной по этажу́.	Klyuch mózhna paluchít' udizhúrny pa-etazhú.
Tanya	А где у вас лифт?	A gdye uvás leeft?
Receptionist	Вот сюда́, пожа́луйста.	Vot syudá, pazhálsta.
Tanya	Спаси́бо.	Spasíba.

у дежу́рной по этажу́ [udizhúrny pa-etazhú] from the woman on duty on your floor
сюда́ [syudá] here, this way

где мо́жно получи́ть ключ? [gdye mózhna paluchít' klyuch?] where can I pick up the key?

где у вас лифт? [gdye uvás leeft?] where is the lift (elevator) here? **У вас** [uvás] is often used in Russian where other languages say 'in *your* hotel, house, country, etc'. It also sounds less abrupt to ask **где у вас...?** [gdye uvás...?] than simply **где...?** [gdye...?]

Practise what you have learned

As before, read the instructions for each exercise before turning on the recording.

1

Three visitors to a hotel write their names on their luggage but forget to write which floor they are on. Listen to the recording and see whether you can fill in the missing numbers. (Answers on page 46.)

2

On your recording you will hear our hotel guests asking where various places are. Write down the correct floor for each. You will find the possible floors listed in the box below. (Answers on page 46.)

Where is your restaurant? (i) **на** [na] ....

Where is the telephone? (ii) **на** [na] ....

Where is the discotheque? (iii) **на** [na] ....

на пéрвом этажé [na pyérvam etazhé]
на вторóм этажé [na ftaróm etazhé]
на трéтьем этажé [na tryétyem etazhé]

Dialogues

3 *The man next to Tanya doesn't have a booking*

Man	Скажи́те, пожа́луйста, у вас есть свобо́дные номера́ на сего́дня?	Skazhítye, pazhálsta, uvás yest' svabódniye namirá na sivódnya?
Receptionist	Вам ну́жен но́мер на одного́?	Vam núzhin nómir na adnavó?
Man	Нет, мне ну́жен но́мер на двои́х.	Nyet, mnye núzhin nómir na dvayíkh.
Receptionist	На ско́лько дней?	Na skól'ka dnyey?
Man	На три дня.	Na tri dnya.
Receptionist	Одну́ мину́точку.... Да, у нас есть номера́.	Adnú minútachku.... Da, unás yest' namirá.
Man	Скажи́те, пожа́луйста, ско́лько сто́ит но́мер в су́тки?	Skazhítye, pazhálsta, skól'ka stóit nómir fsútki?
Receptionist	Но́мер сто́ит сто два́дцать до́лларов.	Nómir stóit sto dvátsat' dóllaraf.

сто два́дцать до́лларов [sto dvátsat' dóllaraf] 120 dollars

- **у вас есть свобо́дные номера́?** [uvás yest' svabódniye namirá?] do you have any vacant rooms?
- **на сего́дня** [na sivódnya] for today. **На** [na] is often used to mean 'for', particularly with bookings. If the man had wanted a room for tomorrow he would have said **на за́втра** [na záftra].
- **вам ну́жен но́мер на одного́?** [vam núzhin nómir na adnavó?] do you need a single room? (lit. a room for one person). The man wants a room **на двои́х** [na dvayíkh] for two. For three would be **на трои́х** [na trayíkh].
- **на ско́лько дней?** [na skól'ka dnyey?] for how many days? In his reply the man says **на три дня** [na tri dnya] for three days, using a quite different ending. Numbers make nouns do some very funny things! You say:
  на оди́н день [na adín dyen'] for one day
  на два (три, четы́ре) дня [na dva (tri, chitýrye) dnya] for two (three, four) days
  на пять (шесть, ...) дней [na pyat' (shest', ...) dnyey] for five (six, ...) days
  If this seems too much to remember, just say **на** [na] with the number, and leave out the noun altogether!
- **у нас есть номера́** [unás yest' namirá] we have rooms. **У нас есть...** [unás yest'...] means '*we* have...'
- **ско́лько сто́ит но́мер?** [skól'ka stóit nómir?] how much does a room cost?
- **в су́тки** [fsútki] per day. **Су́тки** [sútki] is a 24-hour period.

A guest's card for the hotel 'Tourist'

Practise what you have learned

3 A new reception clerk has completely muddled some visitors' registration forms. Here they are in translation. After listening to the dialogues on your recording, see if you can spot and correct the mistakes. (Answers on page 46.)

REGISTRATION FORM

NAME: *POSLOV*

NO. OF GUESTS *3 PEOPLE*

NO. OF NIGHTS *2 NIGHTS*

(i)

REGISTRATION FORM

NAME: *LUZHIN*

NO. OF GUESTS *1 PERSON*

NO. OF NIGHTS *1 NIGHT*

(ii)

REGISTRATION FORM

NAME: *DOBRIN*

NO. OF GUESTS *2 PEOPLE*

NO. OF NIGHTS *7 NIGHTS*

(iii)

REGISTRATION FORM

NAME: *MASLOV*

NO. OF GUESTS *3 PEOPLE*

NO. OF NIGHTS *3 NIGHTS*

(iv)

4 This time you are a tourist seeking a hotel room. Andrei will give you instructions.

Dialogues

4 *Tanya has found the money exchange desk*

Tanya	Здра́вствуйте.	Zdrástvuytye.
Clerk	Здра́вствуйте.	Zdrástvuytye.
Tanya	Мо́жно обменя́ть валю́ту?	Mózhna abminyát' valyútu?
Clerk	Да, пожа́луйста. А что у вас?	Da, pazhálsta. A shtó uvas?
Tanya	Фу́нты.	Fúnty.
Clerk	Ско́лько вы меня́ете?	Skól'ka vi minyáitye?
Tanya	Два́дцать.	Dvátsat'.
Clerk	Да́йте, пожа́луйста, ва́шу деклара́цию и де́ньги.	Dáitye, pazhálsta, váshu diklarátsiyu i dyén'gi.
Tanya	Вот, пожа́луйста.	Vot, pazhálsta.
Clerk	Здесь ва́ша по́дпись, пожа́луйста.	Zdyes' vásha pótpees', pazhálsta.
Tanya	Пожа́луйста.	Pazhálsta.
Clerk	Ва́ши де́ньги, пожа́луйста.	Váshi dyén'gi, pazhálsta.
Tanya	Спаси́бо.	Spasíba.
Clerk	До свида́ния.	Da svidánya.
Tanya	До свида́ния.	Da svidánya.

деклара́ция [diklarátsiya] official declaration of how much currency you bring into the country
де́ньги [dyén'gi] money (a plural noun)

что у вас? [shtó uvas?] what have you got? The answer was **фу́нты** [fúnty] pounds. Most words denoting currencies are more obvious: **до́ллары** [dóllary] dollars, **ма́рки** [márki] marks, etc.

ско́лько вы меня́ете? [skól'ka vi minyáitye?] how much are you changing? Conveniently, Tanya is changing an amount you know:
два́дцать [dvátsat'] 20. She might have asked for:
три́дцать [trítsat'] 30
со́рок [sórak] 40
пятьдеся́т [pit'disyát] 50
You will be pleased to hear that you now know all the numbers to 50, or 59 to be exact. For 21, 22, etc. you simply use the number for 20 and add one, two, three etc., i.e.:
два́дцать оди́н, два́дцать два, два́дцать три [dvátsat' adín, dvátsat' dva, dvátsat' tri]
And 59? No problem – **пятьдеся́т де́вять** [pit'disyát dyévit']

да́йте, пожа́луйста, ... [dáitye, pazhálsta, ...] give me please...

здесь ва́ша по́дпись [zdyes' vásha pótpees'] your signature here

Practise what you have learned

5 On your recording you will hear people exchanging currency at the exchange desk. Can you fill in the spaces on their receipts? (Answers on page 46.)

(i)

CURRENCY EXCHANGE FORM

Currency	*Amount*
________________	________________

(ii)

CURRENCY EXCHANGE FORM

Currency	*Amount*
________________	________________

(iii)

CURRENCY EXCHANGE FORM

Currency	*Amount*
________________	________________

6 You are a tourist with pounds to change. Andrei will tell you what to ask for at the exchange desk.

Key words and phrases

для меня́ заброни́рован но́мер [dlya minyá zabroníravan nómir]	I have a room booked
вот [vot]	here (is)
спаси́бо [spasíba]	thank you
на пе́рвом этаже́ [na pyérvam etazhé]	on the first (ground) floor
на второ́м этаже́ [na ftaróm etazhé]	on the second floor
на тре́тьем этаже́ [na tryétyem etazhé]	on the third floor
на деся́том этаже́ [na disyátam etazhé]	on the tenth floor
где у вас (лифт)? [gdye uvás (leeft)?]	where is your (lift)?
где мо́жно... [gdye mózhna...]	where can one...
получи́ть ключ? [paluchít' klyuch?]	get the key?
обменя́ть валю́ту? [abminyát' valyútu?]	change foreign currency?
у вас есть свобо́дные номера́... [uvás yest' svabódniye namirá?...]	do you have any vacant rooms...
на сего́дня? [na sivódnya?]	for today?
на за́втра? [na záftra?]	for tomorrow?
вам ну́жен но́мер на одного́? [vam núzhin nómir na adnavó?]	do you need a single room?
на двои́х? [na dvayíkh?]	(a room) for two?
на трои́х? [na trayíkh?]	(a room) for three?
мне ну́жен... [mnye núzhin...]	I need...
на ско́лько дней? [na skól'ka dnyey?]	for how many days? (see note on page 38)
ско́лько сто́ит но́мер в су́тки? [skól'ka stóit nómir fsútki?]	how much does a room cost per day?
как он рабо́тает? [kak on rabótayit?]	how (what hours) does it work?
что у вас? [shtó uvas?]	what do you have?
ско́лько вы меня́ете? [skól'ka vi minyáitye?]	how much are you changing?
да́йте, пожа́луйста, ... [dáitye, pazhálsta, ...]	please give me...
ва́шу деклара́цию [váshu diklarátsiyu]	your declaration
де́ньги [dyén'gi]	money

The Russian alphabet

In this unit you will learn five new letters. In total you have now met more than two thirds of the alphabet. Read the letters and the words below, then turn on the recording and listen to how Andrei pronounces them.

The letters are:

б [b]
л [l]
п [p]
э [e like the first *e* in *edifice*]
й called 'short и'. It sounds and behaves just like the *y* in *boy*, *way*, *New York* etc. One sees it very often in names: **Толсто́й** (Tolstóy), **Достое́вский** (Dostoévsky).

7

Who's who and who's in the wrong place? (Answers on page 46.)

(i)	**МА́ЛЕР**	**ЧАЙКО́ВСКИЙ**	**БРАМС**	**ДА́РВИН**
(ii)	**Э́ЛВИС ПРЕ́СЛИ**	**ПОЛ СА́ЙМОН**	**БИ́ТЛЗ**	**БОБ ДИ́ЛАН**
(iii)	**ПЛАТО́Н**	**МАКИАВЕ́ЛЛИ**	**БА́ЙРОН**	**АРИСТО́ТЕЛЬ**
(iv)	**НИКОЛА́Й**	**АЛЕКСА́НДР**	**АЛЬБЕ́РТ**	**ВЛАДИ́МИР**

After you have practised these letters and the words above, see if you can work out the following crossword puzzle. If you have answered each question correctly, the beginning letters of each word read vertically will give you the name of a famous Russian ballerina. (Answers on page 46.)

8

Clues

1 You need this when travelling
2 A place you might try if you have a headache or cold
3 An alcoholic drink and probably your first Russian word
4 Big Ben is in the centre of this famous capital
5 A Scandinavian capital
6 The French are famous drinkers of this alcoholic beverage
7 The name of three Russian Tsars

New word **апте́ка** [aptyéka] chemist

Grammar

The accusative case

Some nouns have different endings in Russian when they become the *direct object* of a verb. Less abstractly, in the sentence 'Ivan reads a book', Ivan is the *subject*, he is *doing* the reading. The book is the *direct object*, it is being read.

It is important to be aware of these endings even if you don't always remember to use them. In a language without set word order they can provide vital clues to help you understand *who* is doing *what!*

In the dialogue, Tanya was asked for her currency declaration:

Дáйте, пожáлуйста, вáшу декларáцию
[Dáitye, pazhálsta, váshu diklarátsiyu]

In the dictionary the word for 'declaration' would be written:
декларáция [diklarátsiya]. This is a feminine noun and it changes when it becomes the object of the verb **дáйте** [dáitye] give (me). Similarly, the word for 'foreign currency' is feminine: **валю́та** [valyúta], but Tanya asked:
мóжно обменя́ть валю́ту? [mózhna abminyát' valyútu?]
May I change some currency?

Fortunately these are the only endings for the moment. Neuter nouns never change in the accusative case, nor do masculine nouns which refer to *things*. If Tanya had been asked for her passport, you would have heard:

Дáйте, пожáлуйста, ваш пáспорт [Dáitye, pazhálsta, vash pásport]

9

Tanya was in the foreign currency shop of the hotel, and saw the following items which she wanted:

шоколáд [shakalát]	chocolate
вóдка [vótka]	vodka
винó [vinó]	wine
конья́к [kanyák]	cognac
газéта [gazyéta]	newspaper
матрёшка [matryóshka]	matryóshka doll

She asked for each of the above, beginning each time with **дáйте, пожáлуйста, ...** [dáitye, pazhálsta,...] give me please... . Can you write in the item with the correct endings? (Answers on page 46.)

дáйте, пожáлуйста, ...
[dáitye, pazhálsta, ...]

(i) ....

(ii) ....

(iii) ....

(iv) ....

(v) ....

(vi) ....

Did you know?

Travel to Russia and the Soviet Union

Up to the late 1980s the majority of foreign visitors came to the USSR on package tours arranged by the State organisation Intourist.

There was relatively little choice since a visa was only issued on proof of accommodation and hotel rooms booked by individuals were classified as first class and priced accordingly.

To the foreign traveller, the advantage of package tours was that they largely eliminated the problems with accommodation, transportation and general service which plague Russian travellers. The chief disadvantage was that most tourists, especially if they knew no Russian, saw little of the country. Indeed Intourist hotels were built to provide anything that a tourist (in their opinion!) might wish for: bars, restaurants, saunas, shops, etc.

At the time of writing, much of the above is still applicable; none the less noticeable changes have taken place. It has become relatively easy to visit friends in Russia. Easy, that is, for those invited – there is considerable bureaucratic red tape at the Russian end! Visitors must live at the address written on their visa, and need to receive an official stamp in their passport.

Intourist is also increasingly losing its monopoly as more enterprises open. Some of these offer package tours, while others offer accommodation in private homes or rented apartments and offices.

HOTEL REGULATIONS

— the guest's card is a pass to the hotel;
— the room key is available at the floor desk and is given by the floor maid in exchange for your guest's card;
— your visitors can receive a temporary pass to the hotel at the pass bureau on your request made througt the floor made and can stay in the hotel from 8 a. m. to 11 p. m.;
— the floor maid must be informed of the date of your departure two days in advance;
— long-distance phone calls must be paid within 24 hours;
— when departing, please, ask the floor maid for a pass to your luggage, leave her the room key and your guest's card.

IT IS STRICTLY FORBIDDEN:

— to use electric heating devices in your room;
— to leave guests in your room when you are absent and to let anybody use your key and your guest's card.

In case you lose your guest's card the hotel bears no responsibility for the safty of your belongings. You are kindly requwsted to observe the hotel regulations and fire safety rules.

A guest's card from Hotel 'Moskva', issued in 1990.
The rules are no longer quite so stringent.

Your turn to speak

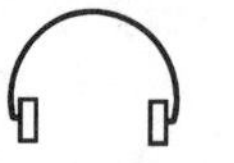

10

You will be playing the role of Misha Ivanov, who is checking in at a hotel, and finding his bearings. As usual, read the following words and phrases and then turn on the recording.

для меня́ заброни́рован но́мер [dlya minyá zabroníravan nómir]
спаси́бо [spasíba]
где у вас...? [gdye uvás...?]

Answers

Practise what you have learned

Exercise **1**	(i) 2 (ii) 1 (iii) 10
Exercise **2**	(i) на тре́тьем этаже́ [na tryétyem etazhé] (ii) на пе́рвом этаже́ [na pyérvam etazhé] (iii) на второ́м этаже́ [na ftaróm etazhé]
Exercise **3**	(i) 4 days (ii) for 2 people (iii) 6 days (iv) 4 days
Exercise **5**	(i) pounds, 35 (ii) dollars, 40 (iii) Deutschmarks, 50

Alphabet

Exercise **7**	(i) Да́рвин (ii) Би́тлз (iii) Ба́йрон (iv) Альбе́рт
Exercise **8**	па́спорт, апте́ка, во́дка, Ло́ндон, О́сло, вино́, Алекса́ндр. The ballerina is **Па́влова**

Grammar

Exercise **9**	(i) шокола́д (ii) во́дку (iii) вино́ (iv) конья́к (v) газе́ту (vi) матрёшку

4 ORDERING DRINKS AND SNACKS

You will learn

- to find out what is available for a meal, or part of a meal
- to make your choice
- to ask advice about cafés and about recommended dishes
- to ask for a seat at a table
- to pay for your meal

and you will be introduced to traditional Russian cuisine

Sweet wrappers

Study guide

- **Dialogues 1, 2:** listen without the book
- **Dialogues 1, 2:** listen, read and study one by one
- Practise what you have learned
- **Dialogues 3, 4:** listen without the book
- **Dialogues 3, 4:** listen, read and study one by one
- Practise what you have learned
- **Dialogues 5–7:** listen without the book
- **Dialogues 5–7:** listen, read and study one by one
- Practise what you have learned
- Study the **Key words and phrases**
- Read and practise writing the **Alphabet**
- Study the **Grammar** section carefully
- Read **Did you know?**
- Do the exercises in **Your turn to speak**
- Listen to all the dialogues once again straight through

Dialogues

1 *Tanya has stayed the night at a friend's*

Tanya	Тама́ра, а что у нас сего́дня на за́втрак?	Tamára, a shto unás sivódnya na záftrak?
Tamara	Ка́ша, бутербро́ды с колбасо́й и́ли с сы́ром.	Kásha, buterbródy skalbasóy íli sýram.
Tanya	Дай мне про́сто хлеб с ма́слом.	Dai mnye prósta khlyep smáslam.
Tamara	Пожа́луйста.	Pazhálsta.
Tanya	Спаси́бо.	Spasíba.

ка́ша [kásha] porridge
про́сто [prósta] simply

- **что у нас сего́дня на за́втрак?** [shto unás sivódnya na záftrak?] what do we have for breakfast today? At appropriate times of the day **на за́втрак** [na záftrak] could be substituted by:
  на обе́д [na abyét] for lunch, the middle meal of the day
  на у́жин [na úzhin] for dinner.
- **бутербро́ды** [buterbródy] sandwiches. One sandwich would be **бутербро́д** [buterbrót]; **с колбасо́й** [skalbasóy] with sausage, salami; **с сы́ром** [sýram] with cheese.
- **дай мне про́сто хлеб с ма́слом** [dai mnye prósta khlyep smáslam] give me just bread and butter. Tanya is speaking to a friend, and therefore she says **дай** [dai] rather than the formal **да́йте** [dáitye].
- **мне** [mnye] means 'to me' and is used after verbs such as **да́йте** [dáitye] i.e. 'give to me'.

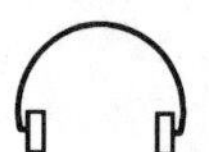

2 *What about coffee?*

Tamara	А ко́фе ты бу́дешь?	A kófye ti búdish?
Tanya	Ой, с удово́льствием.	Oi, sudavól'stvyem.
Tamara	Тебе́ чёрный и́ли с молоко́м?	Tibyé chórny íli smalakóm?
Tanya	С молоко́м, е́сли мо́жно.	Smalakóm, yésli mózhna.
Tamara	Пожа́луйста.	Pazhálsta.
Tanya	Спаси́бо.	Spasíba.

ой [oi] oh
е́сли мо́жно [yésli mózhna] if possible

- **ко́фе ты бу́дешь?** [kófye ti búdish?] will you have coffee? If you were on more formal terms with someone, you would be asked: **ко́фе вы бу́дете?** [kófye vi búditye?]. You are also likely to be offered **чай** [chai] tea, which is always drunk without milk.
- **с удово́льствием** [sudavól'stvyem] with pleasure
- **тебе́** [tibyé] for you. This is the same kind of ending as **мне** [mnye]. It is often used when offering or making a choice. Here the choice is:
  чёрный ко́фе [chórny kófye] black coffee *or*
  ко́фе с молоко́м [kófye smalakóm] coffee with milk.
  Again if you use **вы** [vi] with a person, the appropriate form here would be **вам** [vam] instead of **тебе́** [tibyé].
- **с молоко́м** [smalakóm] with milk. If you drink coffee with sugar, you'll want to know:
  с са́харом [sákharam] with sugar.

Practise what you have learned

1 Ol'ga Ivanovna has a family – Marina, Vasily and their two children Natasha and Ira – staying with her. Listen to their orders for breakfast and then decide whether the following statements are true or false. You'll notice that the children use **дайте** [dáitye] when they speak to Ol'ga Ivanovna, an adult. (Answers on page 58.)

(i) Vasily asks for porridge and black coffee.
(ii) Natasha asks for salami sandwiches.
(iii) Ira wants porridge with sugar.
(iv) Marina wants white coffee and salami sandwiches.

Grocery packaging for sugar lumps (below) and 'Hercules' oatflakes (right)

2 Later on Natasha asks everyone what they would like to drink but becomes hopelessly muddled. Listen to the recording and match the request with the person. (Answers on page 58.)

(i) Mama	(a) tea
(ii) Papa	(b) coffee with milk and sugar
(iii) Ira	(c) coffee with milk
(iv) Ol'ga Ivanovna	(d) black coffee

3 Your name is Nina and you will be finding out from your brother what there is for breakfast. Andrei will prompt you.

Dialogues

3 *Natasha drops into the work canteen for lunch*

Natasha	До́брый день.	Dóbry dyen'.
Serving lady	Здра́вствуйте.	Zdrástvuytye.
Natasha	Что у вас сего́дня на пе́рвое?	Shto uvás sivódnya na pyérvaye?
Serving lady	Есть суп горо́ховый с мя́сом и суп ры́бный с карто́шечкой.	Yest' sup garókhavy smyásam i sup ribny skartóshichkay.
Natasha	Что вы мне порекоменду́ете?	Shto vi mnye parikamendúitye?
Serving lady	Я бы вам порекомендова́ла суп ры́бный, мя́гкий, не́жный, со́чный суп.	Ya bi vam parikamendavála sup ribny, myákhki, nyézhny, sóchny sup.
Natasha	Хорошо́. Спаси́бо.	Kharashó. Spasíba.
Serving lady	Пожа́луйста.	Pazhálsta.

суп горо́ховый с мя́сом [sup garókhavy smyásam] pea soup with meat
суп ры́бный с карто́шечкой [sup ribny skartóshichkay] fish soup with potato

- **что у вас сего́дня на пе́рвое?** [shto uvás sivódnya na pyérvaye?] What is there for the first course today? For other dishes, you would ask:
  что у вас сего́дня... [shto uvás sivódnya...]
  на второ́е? [na ftaróye?] for the second course?
  на тре́тье? [na tryétye?] for the third course?
  на десе́рт? [na disyért?] for dessert?
- **с карто́шечкой** [skartóshichkay] with potatoes. The more common word for potatoes is **карто́шка** [kartóshka] and '*with* potatoes' **с карто́шкой** [skartóshkay].
- **что вы мне порекоменду́ете?** [shto vi mnye parikamendúitye?] what would you recommend?
  я бы вам порекомендова́ла... [ya bi vam parikamendavála...] I would recommend... The lady uses a different form of the verb. Don't worry about learning this – it's the question you will need.
- **суп ры́бный – мя́гкий, не́жный, со́чный суп** [sup ribny – myákhki, nyézhny, sóchny sup] fish soup – delicate, gentle, juicy soup. (These adjectives are *not* the most common words used to describe a soup!) You will find out more about how to use adjectives in Unit 6.

4 *Lyena is next in the queue and asks about the second course*

Lyena	Что у вас на второ́е?	Shto uvás na ftaróye?
Serving lady	На второ́е? Ры́ба отварна́я, беф-стро́ганов, мя́со тушёное, бифште́кс с лу́ком, запека́нка творо́жная со смета́ной.	Na ftaróye? Riba atvarnáya, befstróganof, myása tushónaye, bifshtéks slúkam, zapikánka tvarózhnaya sa smitanay.
Lyena	Да́йте мне, пожа́луйста, бифште́кс.	Dáitye mnye, pazhálsta, bifshtéks.
Serving lady	Бифште́кс с лу́ком. А како́й гарни́р жела́ете?	Bifshtéks slúkam. A kakóy garnéer zhiláyitye?
Lyena	Карто́фельное пюре́.	Kartófil'naye pyuré.
Serving lady	Пожа́луйста.	Pazhálsta.
Lyena	Большо́е спаси́бо.	Bal'shóye spasíba.
Serving lady	Пожа́луйста. Прия́тного аппети́та!	Pazhálsta. Priyátnava appitíta!
Lyena	Спаси́бо.	Spasíba.

ры́ба отварна́я [ríba atvarnáya] poached fish
беф-стро́ганов [befstróganof] beef Stroganoff
мя́со тушёное [myása tushónaye] stewed meat

бифштéкс с лýком [bifshtéks slúkam] beefsteak with onion
запекáнка творóжная со сметáной [zapikánka tvarózhnaya sa smitánay] baked cottage cheese dish with sour cream
картóфельное пюрé [kartófil'naye pyuré] mashed potatoes

- **какóй гарни́р желáете?** [kakóy garnéer zhiláyitye?] what would you like with it?
  желáть [zhilát'] can mean 'to desire' and is not the most common verb in this context. You will more often hear **какóй гарни́р вы *хоти́те*?** [kakóy garnéer vi khatítye?], to which you could reply '**я хочý...**' [ya khachú...] I want...
- **большóе спаси́бо** [bal'shóye spasíba] thank you very much (or, literally, a big thank you)
- **прия́тного аппети́та!** [priyátnava appitíta!] bon appetit! It is quite normal for Russians to say this whenever they see somebody eating.

Practise what you have learned

4 Oleg and Larisa find the following menu in a local cafeteria. See how much you can make out before looking at the transliterated version below.

МЕНЮ́

ПЕ́РВОЕ	**ВТОРО́Е**	**ГАРНИ́Р**
горóховый суп	**беф-строгáнов**	**картóфельное пюрé**
ры́бный суп	**бифштéкс**	**салáт**
борщ	**гуля́ш**	**винегрéт**

MINYÚ

PYÉRVAYE	FTARÓYE	GARNÉER
garókhavy sup	befstróganof	kartófil'naye pyuré
ríbny sup	bifshtéks	salát
borshch	gulyásh	vinigryét

Listen to the recording and mark the correct box. (Answers on page 58.)

(i) The man serving recommends:
- (a) **ры́бный суп** [ríbny sup] ☐
- (b) **горóховый суп** [garókhavy sup] ☐
- (c) **борщ** [borshch] ☐

(ii) For her main course Larisa asks for:
- (a) **гуля́ш** [gulyásh] ☐
- (b) **бифштéкс** [bifshtéks] ☐
- (c) **беф-строгáнов** [befstróganof] ☐

(iii) What does she want with her meal?
- (a) **салáт** [salát] ☐
- (b) **винегрéт** [vinigryét] ☐
- (c) **картóфельное пюрé** [kartófil'naye pyuré] ☐

5 Still using the same menu, this time it's your turn to order. Follow Andrei's instructions.

Dialogues

5 *Lyena is now at the cashier's desk*

Lyena	Ско́лько с меня́?	Skól'ka sminyá?
Cashier	А что у вас?	A shtó uvas?
Lyena	У меня́ бифште́кс с карто́фельным пюре́.	Uminyá bifshtéks skartófil'nym pyuré.
Cashier	Три́дцать во́семь копе́ек.	Trítsat' vósim' kapyéek.
Lyena	Вот, пожа́луйста.	Vot, pazhálsta.
Cashier	Спаси́бо.	Spasíba.
Lyena	Пожа́луйста.	Pazhálsta.

- **ско́лько с меня́?** [skól'ka sminyá?] how much do I owe you? (lit. 'how much from me?'!)
- **у вас** [uvás], **у меня́** [uminyá]: It is difficult for a learner to know when to use **у меня́ есть...** [uminyá yest'...] and when **у меня́** [uminyá] by itself is enough. **Есть** [yest'] is used when out of the blue you inform somebody that you *have* something. It is omitted if you are simply describing *what* you have. If this sounds confusing, simply listen to whether it is used or not, and follow suit!
- **три́дцать во́семь копе́ек** [trítsat' vósim' kapyéek] 38 copecks

A word of warning – from the beginning of 1992 the cost of living in Russia increased dramatically, making the prices quoted here and elsewhere quite outdated.

6 *Lyena has taken her tray and is looking for a seat*

Lyena	Извини́те, пожа́луйста, здесь свобо́дно?	Izvinítye, pazhálsta, zdyes' svabódna?
Other customer	Да, сади́тесь, пожа́луйста.	Da, sadítyes', pazhálsta.
Lyena	Спаси́бо.	Spasíba.

- **сади́тесь** [sadítyes'] take a seat
- **здесь свобо́дно?** [zdyes' svabódna?] is this place free? If it were not, the reply would probably have been **нет, здесь за́нято** [nyet, zdyes' zányata] no, it's taken.

7 *Ira doesn't have much luck finding a place to eat*

Ira	Извини́те, пожа́луйста, где здесь мо́жно бы́стро пообе́дать?	Izvinítye, pazhálsta, gdye zdyes' mózhna bístra paabyédat'?
Passer-by	Здесь пообе́дать? Здесь пообе́дать о́чень тру́дно. Мо́жно то́лько вы́пить ча́шку ко́фе в кафе́ вот ря́дом.	Zdyes' paabyédat'? Zdyes' paabyédat' óchin' trúdna. Mózhna tól'ka výpit' cháshku kófye fkafé vot ryádam.
Ira	Спаси́бо большо́е.	Spasíba bal'shóye.
Passer-by	Пожа́луйста.	Pazhálsta.

то́лько [tól'ka] only

где здесь мо́жно бы́стро пообе́дать? [gdye zdyes' mózhna bístra paabyédat'?] where around here can one get a quick meal? The verb 'to have lunch' is formed from the noun for lunch – **обе́д** [abyét]. If you wanted to find out where you could get breakfast – and not necessarily quickly! – you would leave out **бы́стро** [bístra] (quickly) and ask:
где здесь мо́жно поза́втракать? [gdye zdyes' mózhna pazáftrakat'?]
and dinner:
где здесь мо́жно поу́жинать? [gdye zdyes' mózhna paúzhinat'?].

здесь пообе́дать о́чень тру́дно [zdyes' paabyédat' óchin' trúdna] it is very difficult to get lunch around here

вы́пить ча́шку ко́фе [vypit' cháshku kófye] to have (lit. to drink) a cup of coffee. If Ira had wanted a coffee, she would have asked **где здесь мо́жно вы́пить ча́шку ко́фе?** [gdye zdyes' mózhna výpit' cháshku kófye?]

вот ря́дом [vot ryádam] just here, next door

Пирог открытый с повидлом

Мука — 546, сахар — 38, маргарин столовый — 27, яйца для теста — 27, соль — 5, дрожжи — 16, вода — 230, повидло — 333, яйца для смазки пирога — 27, жир для смазки листа — 3,3.

Выход — 1 кг.

Дрожжевое тесто, приготовленное так же, как для булочки дорожной, раскатать в пласт толщиной 1 см, положить на смазанный жиром лист и выровнять поверхность. Сверху на тесто положить подогретое до 30 °С повидло. Края теста загнуть на 1,5—2 см, а сверху на повидло положить узкие полоски теста в виде решетки и смазать яйцом. Оставить пирог в теплом месте для расстойки 20—30 мин и выпекать при температуре 200 °С.

Recipe for an open jam tart

Now turn over for the exercises based on these dialogues.

Practise what you have learned

6

The price list below is in a sorry state. Listen to the recording and match each dish with its price. (Answers on page 58.)

(i)	**суп горо́ховый с мя́сом** [sup garókhavy smyásam]	(a)	**39 копе́ек**
(ii)	**гуля́ш** [gulyásh]	(b)	**25 копе́ек**
(iii)	**беф-стро́ганов** [befstróganof]	(c)	**37 копе́ек**
(iv)	**бифште́кс с лу́ком** [bifshtéks slúkam]	(d)	**48 копе́ек**
(v)	**борщ** [borshch]	(e)	**45 копе́ек**

7

Ol'ga Ivanovna's guests ask passers-by for advice about where they can 'fortify themselves' during a long day's excursion. Listen to their conversation and fill in the missing words in Vasily's diary. You will find the answers out of order beneath the diary. (Answers on page 58.)

(i) **за́втрак** [záftrak] ....

(ii) **обе́д** [abyét] ....

(iii) **у́жин** [úzhin] ....

(iv) **ко́фе** [kófye] ....

(a) **в рестора́не на Осто́женке** [vrestoránye na Astózhinkye]
(b) **в кафе́ ря́дом** [fkafé ryádam]
(c) **в кафе́ на Арба́те** [fkafé na Arbátye]
(d) **в рестора́не 'Прия́тного аппети́та'** [vrestoránye 'Priyátnava appitíta']

NB Russians will of course *write* rather than *print*, but then they already know the printed alphabet very well! For now, use the printed form when writing.

8

It's time to pay for the meal you ordered in the previous exercises. Don't worry if you've forgotten what you had – Andrei will guide you.

Key words and phrases

что у нас сегóдня на зáвтрак? [shto unás sivódnya na záftrak?]	what do we have for breakfast today?
на обéд? [na abyét?]	for lunch?
на ýжин? [na úzhin?]	for dinner?
что у вас на пéрвое? [shto uvás na pyérvaye?]	what do you have for the first course?
на вторóе? [na ftaróye?]	second course?
на трéтье? [na tryétye?]	third course?
на десéрт? [na disyért?]	dessert?
дай мне... [dai mnye...]	give me... (asking a friend or child)
дáйте мне... [dáitye mnye...]	give me... (formal)
хлеб с мáслом [khlyep smáslam]	bread and butter
бутербрóды с колбасóй [buterbródy skalbasóy]	sandwiches with salami
бутербрóды с сыром [buterbródy sýram]	sandwiches with cheese
чёрный кóфе [chórny kófye]	black coffee
кóфе с молокóм [kófye smalakóm]	coffee with milk
с удовóльствием [sudavól'stvyem]	with pleasure
что вы порекомендýете? [shto vi parikamendúitye?]	what would you recommend?
скóлько с меня́? [skól'ka sminyá?]	how much do I owe you?
здесь свобóдно? [zdyes' svabódna?]	is this place free?
где здесь мóжно (быстро)... [gdye zdyes' mózhna (bístra)...]	where can one (quickly)...
позáвтракать? [pazáftrakat'?]	have breakfast?
пообéдать? [paabyédat'?]	have lunch?
поýжинать? [paúzhinat'?]	have dinner?
вы́пить чáшку кóфе? [výpit' cháshku kófye?]	have a cup of coffee?
прия́тного аппетúта! [priyátnava appitíta!]	bon appetit!

To understand

кóфе ты бýдешь? [kófye ti búdish?]	will you have coffee? (to a friend or child)
кóфе вы бýдете? [kófye vi búditye?]	will you have coffee? (more formal)
какóй гарнúр желáете? / хотúте? [kakóy garnéer zhiláyitye? / khatítye?]	what would you like with it?
я хочý... [ya khachú...]	I would like...
здесь пообéдать óчень трýдно [zdyes' paabyédat' óchin' trúdna]	it's very difficult to get lunch here

The Russian alphabet

The five letters we will look at in this unit are:

ш [sh]
ё [yo]. This vowel is always in stressed position
ф [f]
ы [*y* in *bury* – but this is approximate so listen to the recording]
г [*g* in *good*]

9 Can you match the following capital cities with their country? (Answers on page 58.)

(i)	**СОФИ́Я**	(a)	**НОРВЕ́ГИЯ**
(ii)	**ЛО́НДОН**	(b)	**АФГАНИСТА́Н**
(iii)	**ДУ́БЛИН**	(c)	**ЛА́ТВИЯ**
(iv)	**КАБУ́Л**	(d)	**БОЛГА́РИЯ**
(v)	**МАНИ́ЛА**	(e)	**А́НГЛИЯ**
(vi)	**О́СЛО**	(f)	**ИРЛА́НДИЯ**
(vii)	**РИ́ГА**	(g)	**ФИЛИППИ́НЫ**

10 (a) Which of the following would you be unlikely to *eat*? (Answers on page 58.)

(i)	**РЫ́БНЫЙ СУП**	(ii)	**ШАШЛЫ́К**
(iii)	**БИФШТЕ́КС**	(iv)	**ВАЛЮ́ТА**

(b) And who might feel a little out of place?

(i)	**ШОСТАКО́ВИЧ**	(ii)	**НАПОЛЕО́Н**
(iii)	**ШУ́БЕРТ**	(iv)	**ПРОКО́ФЬЕВ**

11 Here are some signs you might want to look out for:

(i) **БУФЕ́Т**
(ii) **КАФЕ́**
(iii) **РЕСТОРА́Н**
(iv) **ГРИЛЬ-БА́Р**
(v) **СТОЛО́ВАЯ** (cafeteria, canteen)

(a) For which place might you need to make a booking? ....

(b) Where could you go for a snack? ....

(c) Where would you probably find grilled chicken? ....
(Answers on page 58.)

A word of warning: **г** [g] is sometimes pronounced quite differently – as [v]. This happens for example in the word **сего́дня** [sivódnya] today. As a rule it happens with the combinations **-ого** [-ovo] or **-его** [-yevo], but since there are exceptions even to this, be patient with such eccentricity and just try to remember the words in question.

Grammar

'With'

Кóфе чёрный или с молокóм? [kófye chórny íli smalakóm?]
Coffee black or with milk?

C [s] is used before a noun to mean 'with' (in grammatical terms it is a preposition). In addition, however, the ending of the noun changes.

Masculine and *neuter* nouns normally end in **-ом** ([om] but pronounced [am] if not stressed). Hence **бутербрóды** [buterbródy] with **сыр** [syr] becomes **бутербрóды с сы́ром** [buterbródy sýram] 'sandwiches with cheese'. And **кóфе** [kófye] with **молокó** [malakó] becomes **кóфе с молокóм** [kófye smalakóm] 'coffee with milk'.

Feminine nouns normally end in **-ой** ([oy] but pronounced [ay] if not stressed). So **бутербрóды** [buterbródy] with **колбасá** [kalbasá] becomes **бутербрóды с колбасóй** [buterbródy skalbasóy] 'salami sandwiches'.

The **c** [s] is normally pronounced as part of the next word.

12

Four friends are perusing the menu in a canteen. Katya is ravenous, Kolya just a little hungry, Tanya is a vegetarian and Ira only wants something to drink. What might each order?

МЕНЮ́

БУТЕРБРÓДЫ [buterbródy] (sandwiches)	**СМЕТÁНА** [smitána] (sour cream)
БИФШТÉКС [bifshtéks] (beefsteak)	**КОЛБАСÁ** [kalbasá] (salami)
БЕФ-СТРÓГАНОВ [befstróganof] (beef Stroganoff)	**ЛУК** [luk] (onion)
ЗАПЕКÁНКА ТВОРÓЖНАЯ [zapikánka tvarózhnaya] (baked cottage cheese dish)	**РИС** [rees] (rice)
КÓФЕ [kófye] (coffee)	**МОЛОКÓ** [malakó] (milk)
ЧЁРНЫЙ КÓФЕ [chórny kófye] (black coffee)	**CÁXAP** [sákhar] (sugar)
ЧАЙ [chai] (tea)	**ЛИМÓН** [limón] (lemon)

Katya ....

Kolya ....

Tanya ....

Ira ....

Did you know?

Traditional Russian cuisine is very rich. Much of it is fried and may then be served with dollops of sour cream. For breakfast your hotel or some of the cooperative cafés are likely to offer **блины́** [bliný] pancakes or **сы́рники** [sýrniki] cottage cheese patties, possibly **со смета́ной** [so smitánay] with sour cream. If you prefer a lighter breakfast, there will probably be **сыр** [syr] cheese, **колбаса́** [kalbasá] sausage, **я́йца** [yáitsa] eggs, **ка́ша** [kásha] porridge and **хлеб** [khlyep] bread. **Чёрный хлеб** [chórny khlyep] black bread is particularly tasty!

One should not, however, assume that this is how Russians normally eat. The above dishes are time-consuming to make, and more often than not some of the ingredients will be **дефици́тные** [difitsítniye], i.e. unobtainable.

Russians normally eat a large breakfast. What it consists of is to a large extent dependent on the time of the year, and what is available in the shops. Buckwheat, oats and semolina (all called **ка́ша** [kásha]) are common, though quite often breakfast is fried potato or vermicelli, with sausage or whatever meat is around.

Breakfast is normally eaten at home. The number of cafés even in the larger cities is still not high, and not everyone can afford to wait in the long lines which form even around street vendors selling **пирожки́** [pirashkí] filled yeast buns, ice cream and other snacks.

Your turn to speak

13

You will be ordering breakfast in the hotel restaurant. Read the following phrases, then turn on your recording and let Andrei guide you.

здесь свобо́дно? [zdyes' svabódna?]
что у вас сего́дня на за́втрак? [shto uvás sivódnya na záftrak?]
да́йте, пожа́луйста, ... [dáitye, pazhálsta, ...]
с удово́льствием! [sudavól'stvyem!]
ко́фе с молоко́м [kófye smalakóm]

Answers

Practise what you have learned

Exercise **1**	(i) false (white coffee) (ii) false (with cheese) (iii) false (salami sandwiches) (iv) true
Exercise **2**	(i) c (ii) a (iii) b (iv) d
Exercise **4**	(i) b (ii) a (iii) b
Exercise **6**	(i) e (ii) c (iii) d (iv) a (v) b
Exercise **7**	(i) b (ii) a (iii) d (iv) c

Alphabet

Exercise **9**	(i) d (ii) e (iii) f (iv) b (v) g (vi) a (vii) c
Exercise **10**	(a) iv (b) ii
Exercise **11**	(a) iii (b) i, ii, v (c) iv

5 GETTING WHAT YOU WANT IN SHOPS (1)

You will learn

- to ask for stamps, postcards and newspapers
- to enquire how much things cost
- to buy tickets for the opera
- to shop for groceries
- to ask for something cheaper, or in another language,

and you will find out about shopping in Russia

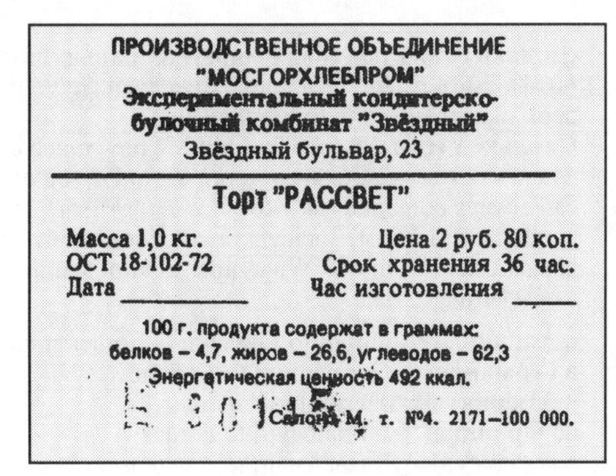

Label from a pre-packed cake box. Details include weight, price, how long it will keep, and date of baking – which hasn't been marked!

Study guide

- **Dialogues 1, 2:** listen without the book
- **Dialogues 1, 2:** listen, read and study one by one
- Practise what you have learned
- **Dialogues 3, 4:** listen without the book
- **Dialogues 3, 4:** listen, read and study one by one
- Practise what you have learned
- **Dialogues 5–8:** listen without the book
- **Dialogues 5–8:** listen, read and study one by one
- Practise what you have learned
- Study the **Key words and phrases**
- Read and practise writing the **Alphabet**
- Study the **Grammar** section carefully
- Read **Did you know?**
- Do the exercises in **Your turn to speak**
- Listen to all the dialogues once again straight through

Dialogues

1 *Lyena asks how much a stamp for a letter to England costs*

Lyena	Скажи́те, ско́лько сто́ит почто́вая ма́рка для авиаконве́рта в А́нглию?	Skazhítye, skól'ka stóit pachtóvaya márka dlya aviakanvyérta vÁngliyu?
Assistant	Пятьдеся́т копе́ек.	Pit'disyát kapyéek.
Lyena	Да́йте, пожа́луйста, три.	Dáitye, pazhálsta, tri.
Assistant	Рубль пятьдеся́т с вас.	Rubl' pit'disyát svas.
Lyena	Спаси́бо.	Spasíba.
Assistant	Пожа́луйста.	Pazhálsta.

ско́лько сто́ит почто́вая ма́рка для авиаконве́рта в А́нглию? [skól'ka stóit pachtóvaya márka dlya aviakanvyérta vÁngliyu?] how much does an airmail stamp to England cost?
Ско́лько сто́ит...? [skól'ka stóit...?] how much does... cost? can be used whenever you want to know a price. And if you don't know the word, you can always point and ask **ско́лько э́то сто́ит?** [skól'ka éta stóit?] how much does that cost? Incidentally the word **почто́вая** [pachtóvaya] postage can be left out. What other kind of stamps would you be buying in a post office?

в А́нглию [vAngliyu] to England. For other countries you would say:
в Герма́нию [vGermániyu] to Germany
в Аме́рику [vAmériku] to America
во Фра́нцию [va Frántsiyu] to France
в Казахста́н [fKazakhstán] to Kazakhstan
You can find out why these endings are used on page 105.

рубль пятьдеся́т [rubl' pit'disyát] one rouble fifty

с вас... [svas...] that will be... (lit. 'from you...'). This could be the answer to the question **ско́лько с меня́?** [skól'ka sminyá?] how much will that be?

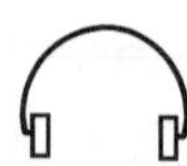

2 *Lyena also needs some postcards*

Lyena	Скажи́те, у вас есть откры́тки с ви́дами Москвы́?	Skazhítye, uvás yest' atkrítki svídami Maskvý?
Assistant	Да, пожа́луйста. Выбира́йте, вот не́сколько ви́дов.	Da, pazhálsta. Vybiráitye, vot nyéskal'ka vídaf.
Lyena	Да́йте, пожа́луйста, вот э́ту с ви́дом Кремля́.	Dáitye, pazhálsta, vot étu svídam Krimlyá.
Assistant	Э́то Спа́сская ба́шня Кремля́. Шесть копе́ек с вас.	Éta Spásskaya báshnya Krimlyá. Shest' kapyéek svas.
Lyena	Пожа́луйста.	Pazhálsta.

выбира́йте [vybiráitye] choose
Спа́сская ба́шня Кремля́ [Spásskaya báshnya Krimlyá] Saviour tower in the Kremlin

откры́тки [atkrítki] postcards. A single postcard would be **откры́тка** [atkrítka].

с ви́дами Москвы́ [svídami Maskvý] with views of Moscow. This ending **-ами** [ami] is used for most nouns in the plural after **с** meaning 'with'.

- **вот нéсколько вúдов** [vot nyéskal'ka vídaf] here are several views
- **э́ту с вúдом Кремля́** [étu svídam Krimlyá] this one with the view of the Kremlin. Even in such telegraphic speech, the word for 'this' **э́ту** [étu] still has to be feminine like the noun it refers to. If Lyena wanted an envelope – **конвéрт** [kanvyért], a masculine noun – she would ask: **дáйте вот э́тот** [dáitye vot état].

Practise what you have learned

1

Listen to the recording and then see if you can work out how much each customer spends in the post office. A little arithmetic is required! (Answers on page 72.)

(i) first customer (stamps to Kiev) ....

(ii) second customer (postcards) ....

(iii) third customer (postcard and stamps) ....

(iv) fourth customer (stamps to Germany) ....

2

On the postcards below, two vital details are missing: the name of the city from which they have been written and the name of the country to which they are being sent. Listen to the transactions in the post office and then fill in the gaps. (Answers on page 72.)

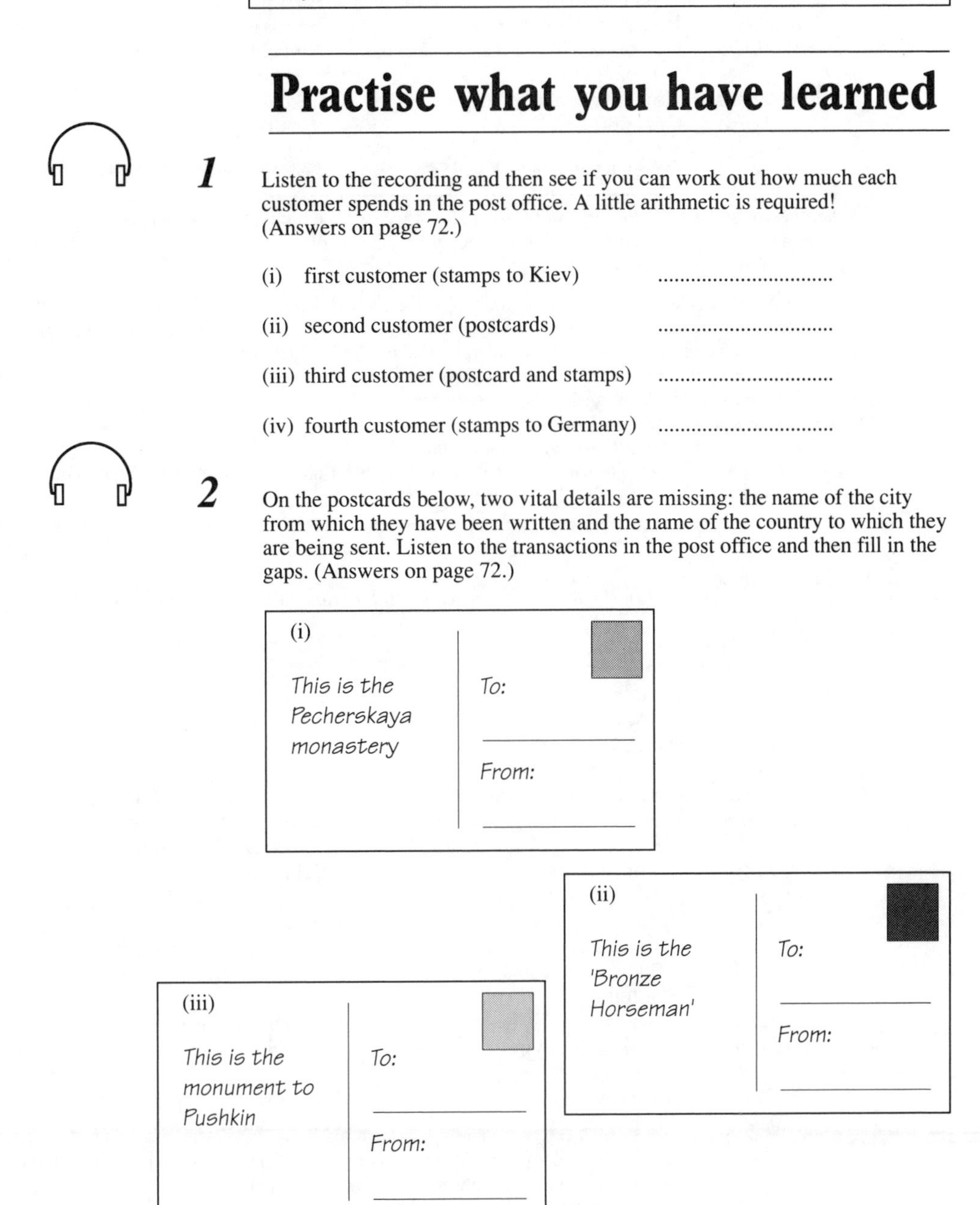

Dialogues

3 *Tanya has dropped into the hotel kiosk for a paper*

Tanya	У вас есть *Моско́вские но́вости*?	Uvás yest' *Maskófskiye nóvosti*?
Assistant	У нас есть *Моско́вские но́вости* на англи́йском языке́.	Unás yest' *Maskófskiye nóvosti* na angléeskam yizikyé.
Tanya	А на ру́сском?	A na rússkam?
Assistant	На ру́сском нет.	Na rússkam nyet.
Tanya	Ну тогда́ да́йте на англи́йском, пожа́луйста.	Nu tagdá dáitye na angléeskam, pazhálsta.
Assistant	Пожа́луйста. Вот газе́та.	Pazhálsta. Vot gazyéta.
Tanya	Спаси́бо.	Spasíba.

тогда́ [tagdá] then, in that case

газе́та [gazyéta] newspaper

Моско́вские но́вости [*Maskófskiye nóvosti*] *Moscow News* is a high-quality weekly newspaper published in several languages. At the time of recording, it was often more difficult to obtain a copy in Russian than in English, French or Greek!

на англи́йском языке́ [na angléeskam yizikyé] in the English language. Tanya wants it in Russian, so asks **на ру́сском нет?** [na rússkam nyet?] you don't have it in Russian? (The word for 'language' is understood.) You could also ask for *Moscow News* in the following languages:
на францу́зском языке́ [na frantsúskam yizikyé] in French
на испа́нском языке́ [na ispánskam yizikyé] in Spanish
на ара́бском языке́ [na arápskam yizikyé] in Arabic
Or if you want any newspaper, in German for example:
У вас есть газе́ты на неме́цком языке́? [uvás yest' gazyéty na nimyétskam yizikyé?] do you have any papers in German? (More about plurals on page 70.)

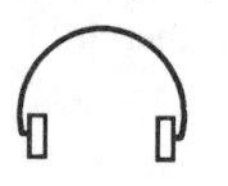

4 *Still in the hotel, Tanya wants to buy tickets to the Bolshoi Theatre*

Tanya	Здра́вствуйте.	Zdrástvuytye.
Assistant	Здра́вствуйте.	Zdrástvuytye.
Tanya	У вас есть биле́ты в Большо́й теа́тр?	Uvás yest' bilyéty vBal'shóy teátr?
Assistant	А что вас интересу́ет?	A shto vas interisúyit?
Tanya	Пожа́луй, о́пера.	Pazháluy, ópera.
Assistant	О́пера... Когда́?	Ópera... Kagdá?
Tanya	Е́сли мо́жно, на за́втра.	Yésli mózhna, na záftra.
Assistant	За́втра идёт о́пера Ри́мского-Ко́рсакова *Снегу́рочка.*	Záftra idyót ópera Rímskava-Kórsakava *Snigúrachka.*
Tanya	О́чень хорошо́.	Óchin' kharashó.
Assistant	А ско́лько вам биле́тов?	A skól'ka vam bilyétaf?
Tanya	Два.	Dva.
Assistant	Сейча́с. Есть два биле́та. Оди́н биле́т сто́ит два́дцать три до́ллара.	Sichás. Yest' dva bilyéta. Adín bilyét stóit dvátsat' tri dóllara.
Tanya	Пожа́луйста... Два.	Pazhálsta... Dva.
Assistant	Сда́чи, пожа́луйста, четы́ре до́ллара.	Sdáchi, pazhálsta, chitýrye dóllara.
Tanya	Спаси́бо.	Spasíba.
Assistant	Пожа́луйста.	Pazhálsta.

что вас интересу́ет? [shto vas interisúyit?] what would you be interested in?
пожа́луй, о́пера [pazháluy, ópera] perhaps opera
о́чень хорошо́ [óchin' kharashó] very good

- **билéты в Большóй теáтр** [bilyéty vBal'shóy teátr] tickets to the Bolshoi Theatre.

  To ask about tickets for the cinema (movies), you would also use **в** [v]:
  билéты в кинó [bilyéty fkinó]
  but if you are talking about the *performance* itself, use **на** [na]:
  билéты на óперу [bilyéty na óperu] tickets for the opera
  билéты на балéт [bilyéty na balyét] tickets for the ballet.

- **когдá?** [kagdá?] when? Tanya wants tickets for tomorrow **на зáвтра** [na záftra]. For today would be **на сегóдня** [na sivódnya].

- **идёт óпера Ри́мского-Кóрсакова *Снегýрочка*** [idyót ópera Rímskava-Kórsakava *Snigúrachka*] Rimsky-Korsakov's opera *The Snow Maiden* is on.
  To find out *what* is on you would ask **что идёт...?** [shto idyót...?].

- **скóлько вам билéтов?** [skól'ka vam bilyétaf?] how many tickets would you like? The answer is **два билéта** [dva bilyéta] two tickets. There is an explanation of numbers and their quirks on page 93.

- **сдáчи четы́ре дóллара** [sdáchi chitýrye dóllara] four dollars change. At the time of recording, tickets to the Bolshoi Theatre were virtually impossible to obtain for roubles.

Practise what you have learned

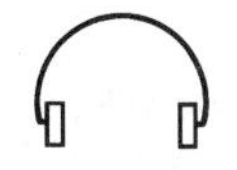

3 On your recording you will hear some hotel guests asking for newspapers and books in various languages. Listen, then decide whether the following statements are true or false. (Answers on page 72.)

(i) *Moscow News* is available in Russian and French
(ii) You can buy *Anna Karenina* in English and Russian
(iii) Chekhov's works are only available in German and French
(iv) Pushkin's works are available in German

4 The lady selling theatre tickets has developed an efficient system for recording tickets. Listen to your recording and fill in the number of tickets under the right day. (Answers on page 72.)

		(a) **сегóдня**	(b) **зáвтра**
(i)	**балéт *Жизéль***	....	....
(ii)	**óпера Вéрди**	....	....
(iii)	**óпера Ри́мского-Кóрсакова**	....	....
(iv)	**балéт *Ромéо и Джульéтта***	....	....

5 You want to buy two tickets to the Bolshoi, preferably to the opera. Read the programme below, then let Andrei guide you.

сегóдня.......... ***Снегýрочка* Ри́мского-Кóрсакова** .... **(óпера)**
***Ромéо и Джульéтта* Прокóфьева** ....**(балéт)**
зáвтра........... ***Бори́с Годунóв* Мýсоргского** .... **(óпера)**

Dialogues

5 *Olya is buying some groceries*

Olya	Молоко́ есть?	Malakó yest'?
Assistant	У́тром бы́ло, уже́ нет.	Útram býla, uzhé nyet.
Olya	А ма́сло?	A másla?
Assistant	Ма́сло есть.	Másla yest'.
Olya	А ско́лько сто́ит ма́сло?	A skól'ka stóit másla?
Assistant	Три пятьдеся́т килогра́мм.	Tri pit'disyát kilagrámm.
Olya	Две́сти грамм, пожа́луйста.	Dvyésti gramm, pazhálsta.
Assistant	Плати́те в ка́ссу се́мьдесят копе́ек.	Platítye fkássu syém'disyat kapyéek.
Olya	Спаси́бо.	Spasíba.
Assistant	Пожа́луйста.	Pazhálsta.

у́тром [útram] in the morning
ма́сло [másla] butter

- **молоко́ есть?** [malakó yest'?] is there any milk? A telegraphic version of **у вас есть молоко́?** [uvás yest' malakó?] do you have milk?
- **у́тром бы́ло, уже́ нет** [útram býla, uzhé nyet] there was this morning, it's already gone
- **три пятьдеся́т килогра́мм** [tri pit'disyát kilagrámm] three roubles fifty a kilogram. The words for roubles and copecks are often left out, especially in shops.
- **две́сти грамм** [dvyésti gramm] 200 grams. One often asks also for half a kilogram – **полкило́** [palkiló].
- **плати́те в ка́ссу** [platítye fkássu] pay at the cash desk. You will find an explanation of the procedure in *Did you know?*
- **се́мьдесят копе́ек** [syém'disyat kapyéek] 70 copecks. The numbers 60, 70 and 80 follow the same pattern as **пятьдеся́т** [pit'disyát] (50). Thus:
  шестьдеся́т [shist'disyát] 60
  се́мьдесят [syém'disyat] 70
  во́семьдесят [vósim'disyat] 80.
  90 and 100 break this pattern:
  девяно́сто [divyanósta] 90
  сто [sto] 100

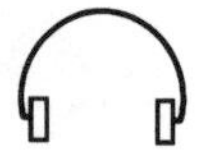

6 *Olya goes to the cashier*

Olya	Се́мьдесят копе́ек, пожа́луйста.	Syém'disyat kapyéek, pazhálsta.
Cashier	Како́й отде́л?	Kakóy atdyél?
Olya	Моло́чный.	Malóchny.
Cashier	Пожа́луйста.	Pazhálsta.
Olya	Спаси́бо.	Spasíba.

- **како́й отде́л?** [kakóy atdyél?] which section? Olya replies **моло́чный** [malóchny] milk or dairy products section. However, always look for a number – more often than not, you'll be able to say **пе́рвый** [pyérvy] first, **второ́й** [ftaróy] second, **тре́тий** [tryétyi] third, etc.

7 *And then back to the counter for her purchase*

Olya	Пожáлуйста, чек.	Pazhálsta, chek.
Assistant	Пожáлуйста, мáсло.	Pazhálsta, másla.
Olya	Спасúбо.	Spasíba.
Assistant	Пожáлуйста.	Pazhálsta.

чек [chek] the receipt you hand over at the counter in order to receive your purchase

> You will have noticed how few words were used in the above dialogues. This is quite normal, and *very* convenient for learners!

8 *Tamara is at the market and wants some tomatoes*

Tamara	Скажúте, пожáлуйста, скóлько стóят помидóры?	Skazhítye, pazhálsta, skól'ka stóyat pamidóry?
Trader	Три рублń.	Tri rublyá.
Tamara	Скажúте, а подешéвле нет?	Skazhítye, a padishévlye nyet?
Trader	Есть по два.	Yest' pa dva.
Tamara	Хорошó. Дáйте мне, пожáлуйста, килогрáмм пó два рублń.	Kharashó. Dáitye mnye, pazhálsta, kilagrámm pó dva rublyá.
Trader	Два рублń.	Dva rublyá.

помидóры [pamidóry] tomatoes. A single tomato is **помидóр** [pamidór]

- **Скóлько стóят помидóры?** [skól'ka stóyat pamidóry?] how much do the tomatoes cost? The ending of the verb **стóят** [stóyat] has changed because it refers to a noun in the plural. It's not a major point since you can scarcely *hear* the difference.
- **три рублń** [tri rublyá] 3 roubles. Numbers make *any* noun change. As well as **три рублń** [tri rublyá], you have seen **три дня** [tri dnya] three days and **три дóллара** [tri dóllara]. You will find more details on page 93.
- **подешéвле нет?** [padishévlye nyet?] are there none a little cheaper?

  Other useful comparative forms:
  побóльше [paból'she] a bit bigger *or* a bit more
  помéньше [pamyén'she] a bit smaller *or* a bit less.
  But when you are buying fruit, vegetables etc., use:
  покрупнée [pakrupnyéye] a bit bigger
  помéльче [pamyél'che] a bit smaller.
- **по два** [pa dva *or* pó dva] for two (roubles)

Now turn over for the exercises based on these dialogues.

Practise what you have learned

6 In the pictures below the names of the items have been omitted. If you listen to your recording, you will discover what they are. (Answers on page 72.)

(a)

20 копе́ек кг.

(b)

3 рубля́ кг.

(c)

3 рубля́ 70 копе́ек кг.

(d)

2 рубля́ 70 копе́ек кг.

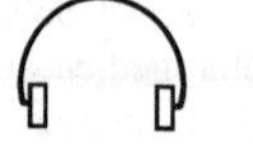

7 The man selling tomatoes in the market was having quite a morning. One after another his customers made extra requests, until he was forced to make a list. But has he taken down all the requests correctly? Listen to your recording and pick out his mistakes. (Answers on page 72.)

(i) 1st man	2 kilograms, smaller size tomatoes
(ii) 1st woman	1 kilogram, cheaper (2.50)
(iii) 2nd man	3 kilograms, larger size
(iv) 2nd woman	2 kilograms at 2 roubles

8 You are buying some vegetables for dinner. And money *is* an object! Andrei will guide you.

Key words and phrases

To use

ско́лько сто́ит... [skól'ka stóit...]	how much is...
ма́рка для авиаконве́рта [márka dlya aviakanvyérta]	a stamp for an airmail envelope
в А́нглию? [vÁngliyu?]	to England?
ма́сло? [másla?]	butter?
молоко́? [malakó?]	milk?
ско́лько сто́ят... [skól'ka stóyat...]	how much are...
помидо́ры? [pamidóry?]	the tomatoes?
откры́тки с ви́дами Москвы́? [atkrítki svídami Maskvý?]	postcards with views of Moscow?
да́йте вот э́ту с ви́дом Кремля́ [dáitye vot étu svídam Krimlyá]	give me this one with the view of the Kremlin
э́тот [état]	this one (referring to a masculine noun)
на ру́сском языке́ [na rússkam yizikyé]	in the Russian language
на англи́йском языке́ [na angléeskam yizikyé]	in the English language
биле́ты в Большо́й теа́тр [bilyéty vBal'shóy teátr]	tickets to the Bolshoi theatre
в кино́ [fkinó]	to the cinema
на о́перу [na óperu]	to the opera
биле́ты на сего́дня [bilyéty na sivódnya]	tickets for today
на за́втра [na záftra]	for tomorrow
подеше́вле нет? [padishévlye nyet?]	you don't have any cheaper?
побо́льше [paból'she]	a bit bigger, a bit more
покрупне́е [pakrupnyéye]	a bit bigger (fruit, etc.)
поме́ньше [pamyén'she]	a bit smaller, a bit less
поме́льче [pamyél'che]	a bit smaller (fruit, etc.)
килогра́мм по два рубля́ [kilagrámm pa dva rublyá]	a kilogram at 2 roubles

To understand

с вас... [svas...]	that will be...
идёт о́пера... [idyót ópera...]	the opera... is on
ско́лько вам биле́тов? [skól'ka vam bilyétaf?]	how many tickets do you need?
оди́н рубль [adín rubl']	one rouble
2, 3, 4 рубля́ [2, 3, 4 rublyá]	2, 3, 4 roubles
5, 6... рубле́й [5, 6... rublyéy]	5, 6... roubles
оди́н до́ллар [adín dóllar]	one dollar
2, 3, 4 до́ллара [2, 3, 4 dóllara]	2, 3, 4 dollars
5, 6... до́лларов [5, 6... dóllaraf]	5, 6... dollars
плати́те в ка́ссу [platítye fkássu]	pay at the cash desk
како́й отде́л? [kakóy atdyél?]	which section?

The Russian alphabet

Congratulations! When you have studied the five letters below, you will have completed your introduction to the Russian alphabet. Do not worry if you still find it difficult – and slow! – to read in Russian. Remember how hard it was at the beginning – you have come a long way since then!

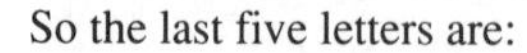

So the last five letters are:

ю	[yu]
ц	[ts]
щ	[shch]
х	[kh this is pronounced ch as in Scottish *loch*]
ъ	'hard sign'. This letter has almost disappeared in modern Russian. Once you have made sure that it *is* a hard sign (i.e. that it has a little squiggle at the top!) we recommend that you ignore it – the effect it has on how a word sounds is very slight.

A few small but crucial words:

ВХОД (entrance) **ВЫ́ХОД** (exit) **ЦЕНТР** **МЕНЮ́**

The following people played a role in Russian history:

ХРУЩЁВ **ТРО́ЦКИЙ** **ЦАРЬ НИКОЛА́Й II** **Е́ЛЬЦИН**

And a role in Russian literature:

А́ННА АХМА́ТОВА **МАРИ́НА ЦВЕТА́ЕВА**

МИХАЙЛ БУЛГА́КОВ

ГОСУДАРСТВЕННЫЕ МУЗЕИ МОСКОВСКОГО КРЕМЛЯ
Серия 07
БИЛЕТ №
147512
НА САМОСТОЯТЕЛЬНЫЙ ОСМОТР МУЗЕЯ ПРИКЛАДНОГО ИСКУССТВА И БЫТА РОССИИ XVII ВЕКА
Цена 50 коп.
КОНТРОЛЬ

Областное управление культуры при Ростоблисполкоме
РОСТОВСКИЙ АКАДЕМИЧЕСКИЙ ТЕАТР ДРАМЫ
Гастроли в помещении областного драматического театра им. А. С. Пушкина
ПАРТЕР
РЯД 7
МЕСТО 14
Серия РО
000032
Цена 3 руб. 50 коп.

Here are some of the posters you might see around theatres and cinemas in Russia. Do you know the works advertised?

	Театр на Таганке сегодня идёт:	
Мусоргский	***БОРИС ГОДУНОВ***	(опера)
	завтра	
Прокофьев	***РОМЕО И ДЖУЛЬЕТТА***	(балет)

	Большой театр сегодня идёт:	
Римский-Корсаков	***СНЕГУРОЧКА***	(опера)
	завтра:	
Чайковский	***ЕВГЕНИЙ ОНЕГИН***	(опера)

	Кинотеатр 'Россия' фильм сегодня:
Андрей Тарковский	***АНДРЕЙ РУБЛЁВ***

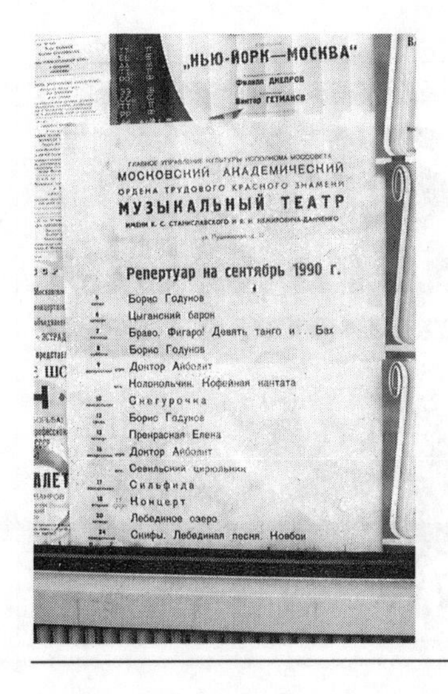

Grammar

Plural of nouns

Most of the nouns you have met so far in the plural have the ending **-ы** (sometimes spelled **-и**). This applies to both masculine and feminine nouns. Thus:

помидóр [pamidór] tomato — **помидóры** [pamidóry] tomatoes
газéта [gazyéta] newspaper — **газéты** [gazyéty] newspapers

Neuter nouns, those nouns which end in **-о** or **-е** in the singular, normally end in **-а** or **-я** in the plural. For example:

письмó [pis'mó] letter — **пи́сьма** [pís'ma] letters
плáтье [plátye] dress — **плáтья** [plátya] dresses

There are of course exceptions to the above, but any irregularities will be noted in a dictionary. We will point out important ones along the way.

9

Complete the sentences below putting the noun in round brackets into the plural. (Answers on page 72.)

(i) **У вас есть .... с колбасóй?** (бутербрóд)

(ii) **Скóлько стóят .... для авиаписьмá в Áнглию?** (мáрка)

(iii) **Что у вас? У меня́ ....** (фунт)

(iv) **У вас есть .... в Большóй теáтр?** (билéт)

(v) **У вас есть .... на немéцком языкé?** (газéта)

(vi) **Скóлько стóят .... ?** (мандари́н)

(vii) **Скóлько стóят .... ?** (плáтье)

Milk and tea packaging

Did you know?

The majority of visitors to the Russian Federation shop exclusively in 'Beryozka' shops, and at kiosks in their hotels. These shops accept only foreign currency, travellers' cheques and credit cards. As you might expect, they stock the souvenirs traditionally popular among tourists: dolls, varnished boxes, vodka, caviare and, inevitably, fur hats. They also, however, have other items – foodstuffs, cosmetics, technical equipment etc. – which are not available for roubles. This strange situation has led, amongst other things, to a flourishing – and nasty – black market in foreign currency.

Such shops are convenient, but since you are learning Russian, it seems safe to assume that you would like to see something of the life led by ordinary people in the Russian Federation, *and*, of course, practise your Russian!

In this unit we have talked only about government-owned shops, leaving markets and the new cooperatives to Unit 6. As you saw when Olya was buying groceries, there are at least two, sometimes three steps to making a purchase in a Russian shop. First you have what you want weighed and priced, then you pay the cashier, then finally you return to the counter with your receipt and take your purchase. Experienced shoppers, if they are sure that the product is available and that it won't have run out before they reach the front of the queue, will generally dispense with the first step.

This rather cumbersome system has not created the chronic problems of shortages and queues, but it certainly increases the already considerable amount of time people spend each day doing shopping.

Your turn to speak

10 In the final exercise on your recording, you will be playing the role of a tourist in Moscow. You will need to use the following words and phrases:

ско́лько сто́ит...? [skól'ka stóit...?]
да́йте, пожа́луйста, ... [dáitye, pazhálsta, ...]
на англи́йском языке́ [na angléeskam yizikyé]
оди́н килогра́мм [adín kilagrámm]
нет подеше́вле? [nyet padishévlye?]
пе́рсики [pyérsiki] peaches
мандари́ны [mandaríny] mandarins
помидо́ры [pamidóry] tomatoes

Answers

Practise what you have learned

Exercise **1**	(i) 30 коп. (ii) 15 коп. (iii) 110 (= 1р. 10 коп.) (iv) 35 коп.
Exercise **2**	(i) England; Kiev (ii) France; St Petersburg (iii) New York; Moscow
Exercise **3**	(i) false (only French) (ii) true (iii) false (English also) (iv) false (only Russian)
Exercise **4**	(i) a, 3 (ii) b, 1 (iii) a, 2 (iv) b, 3
Exercise **6**	(a) хлеб (b) смета́на (c) ма́сло (d) сыр
Exercise **7**	(i) bigger (ii) 2 kg (iii) 1 kg (iv) 1 kg

Grammar

Exercise **9**	(i) бутербро́ды (ii) ма́рки (iii) фу́нты (iv) биле́ты (v) газе́ты (vi) мандари́ны (vii) пла́тья

6 GETTING WHAT YOU WANT IN SHOPS (2)

You will learn

- more about making purchases
- how to select what you want
- to ask for medicine in a chemist (pharmacy)
- a few useful phrases to use in a queue

and more about shops and markets in Russia

Before you begin

From now on the dialogues and notes will be only in the Cyrillic script. You will probably need to go more slowly at first, and do read over the first five units if some of the letters seem unfamiliar. It is well worth the time!

Remember that Russian spelling does not always reflect pronunciation. This won't be a problem if you listen carefully to the dialogues and particularly to Andrei's advice.

Study guide

Dialogues 1, 2: listen without the book
Dialogues 1, 2: listen, read and study one by one
Practise what you have learned
Dialogues 3–5: listen without the book
Dialogues 3–5: listen, read and study one by one
Practise what you have learned
Dialogues 6, 7: listen without the book
Dialogues 6, 7: listen, read and study one by one
Practise what you have learned
Study the **Key words and phrases**
Study the **Grammar** section carefully
Do the exercises in **Read and understand**
Read **Did you know?**
Do the exercises in **Your turn to speak**
Listen to all the dialogues once again straight through

Dialogues

1 *Tamara wants to buy a 'matryoshka' doll, but the price deters her*

Tamara Скажи́те, пожа́луйста, у вас есть матрёшки?
Assistant У нас есть, но они́ о́чень дороги́е.
Tamara А ско́лько сто́ит матрёшка?
Assistant Сто два́дцать рубле́й.
Tamara Ой, э́то о́чень до́рого. А у вас есть что́-нибудь подеше́вле?
Assistant Есть. У нас есть платки́.

они́ they

- **матрёшки** (singular: **матрёшка**) traditional wooden dolls which open up to reveal another doll, and then another...
- **они́ о́чень дороги́е** they're very expensive. You will find an explanation of adjectives and their endings in the grammar section.
- **сто два́дцать** 120. Three-digit numbers are also formed by simply adding the different parts.
- **э́то о́чень до́рого** that is very expensive. If you want to say that it's *not* very expensive, just use **не**:
  э́то не (о́чень) до́рого
- **у вас есть что́-нибудь подеше́вле?** do you have anything cheaper? **Что́-нибудь** means 'anything'. If you wanted something smaller, you would ask for **что́-нибудь поме́ньше**, and something larger, **что́-нибудь побо́льше**.
- **платки́** scarves (singular: **плато́к**). Here are a few other items of clothing you might be interested in:

блу́зка blouse	**ю́бка** skirt	**пла́тье** dress
га́лстук tie	**брю́ки** trousers (pants)	**руба́шка** shirt

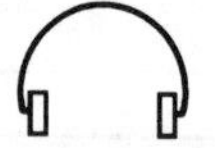

2 *So can she see the headscarves?*

Tamara Платки́? А покажи́те, пожа́луйста.
Assistant А вам како́го цве́та ну́жно?
Tamara Покажи́те, каки́е у вас есть.
Assistant У нас есть си́ние и ро́зовые.
Tamara Хорошо́. Ско́лько сто́ит ро́зовый плато́к?
Assistant Ро́зовый сто́ит два се́мьдесят.
Tamara Два се́мьдесят. Хорошо́, я куплю́ ро́зовый плато́к.
Assistant Тогда́ пройди́те в ка́ссу и заплати́те.
Tamara Хорошо́, спаси́бо.

хорошо́ good, all right
тогда́ пройди́те в ка́ссу и заплати́те then go to the cashier and pay

- **покажи́те, пожа́луйста** show (me) please. This request is especially useful since in most shops in Russia goods are behind the counter.
- **вам како́го цве́та ну́жно?** what colour would you like? (lit. do you need?). Here are the colours mentioned in the dialogue and a few others:

ро́зовый pink	**бе́лый** white
си́ний dark blue	**чёрный** black
кра́сный red	**зелёный** green

Another question you will often be asked is **вам како́го разме́ра ну́жно?** what size do you need? If you're not sure of the precise size, you can approximate with one of the following:
большо́й big **сре́дний** average **ма́ленький** small

Покажи́те, каки́е у вас есть show (me) the ones you've got. Without the first word this could have been a question:
каки́е у вас есть? what ones do you have?

я куплю́... I will buy...

Practise what you have learned

1

Read the following statements about some shoppers' purchases, then listen to your recording and find the one incorrect detail in each. (Answers on page 84.)

(i) Nina doesn't want to pay 35 roubles for a blouse so she decides to buy a scarf for 7 roubles.

(ii) Victor thinks that 6.70 is a reasonable price for a tie and asks to see the blue ones.

(iii) Yura thinks that he can afford 125 roubles for a pair of trousers and asks the shop assistant to show him some black ones.

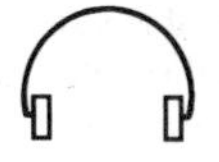

2

You are in Moscow buying a present for a woman friend. Good friend though she is, you can't afford to spend too much. Listen to Andrei's prompts.

A well-known music shop in Moscow

Dialogues

3 *Anna Sergeevna sees a woman selling flowers outside the underground (subway)*

Anna Sergeevna Скажи́те, почём цветы́?
Woman Два се́мьдесят буке́т. Из семи́ ве́точек роз. Ро́зы све́жие, краси́вые, души́стые.
Anna Sergeevna Све́жие?
Woman Души́стые, све́жие.
Anna Sergeevna Пожа́луйста, мне оди́н. Нет, нет, друго́й... вот э́тот, вот э́тот.
Woman Пожа́луйста. Пожа́луйста.
Anna Sergeevna Пожа́луйста.
Woman Так, прошу́ вас.
Anna Sergeevna Э́ти де́ньги ва́ши.
Woman Пожа́луйста.
Anna Sergeevna Спаси́бо.
Woman Пожа́луйста. Счастли́во!

из семи́ ве́точек роз with seven roses
так прошу́ вас something like 'if you please'
счастли́во! a friendly way of saying 'goodbye'

- **почём цветы́?** how much are your flowers? **Почём...?** is a colloquial equivalent of **ско́лько сто́ит...?** Its uses are more limited.
- **два се́мьдесят буке́т** 2.70 a bouquet. Very often flowers and other products are sold by the piece **шту́ка**. A single rose for two roubles seventy would be **два се́мьдесят шту́ка**.
- **ро́зы све́жие, краси́вые, души́стые** fresh, beautiful, fragrant roses – she does want to sell them after all! All the words after **ро́зы** are adjectives in the plural (see the grammar section).
- **пожа́луйста, мне оди́н** one please. The word for a rose – **ро́за** – is feminine. Therefore if Anna Sergeevna had wanted one rose, she would have said **мне одну́**.
- **друго́й, вот э́тот...** the other one, yes that one... This combination of pointing and giving directions is probably as efficient a way as any of indicating what you want! Anna Sergeevna uses **друго́й** 'the other' and **э́тот** 'that one' because she is referring to a masculine noun. If it were one rose or any other feminine noun, she would say: **другу́ю, вот э́ту**.
- **э́ти де́ньги ва́ши** this is your money. The word for 'money' – **де́ньги** – is plural in Russian.

4 *Masha is looking for the end of a long queue*

Masha Прости́те, кто после́дний?
Queuer Наве́рное, я.
Masha Спаси́бо, я за ва́ми.

наве́рное probably, I suppose

- **кто после́дний?** who's last? You always use this masculine form even if there are only women in the queue!
- **я за ва́ми** I'm behind you

5 *Masha doesn't want to lose her place*

Masha Я отойду́ на мину́тку. Вы ска́жете, что я за ва́ми занима́ла?
Queuer Пожа́луйста.
Masha Спаси́бо.

- **я отойду́ на мину́тку** I'm going away for a moment
- **вы ска́жете, что я за ва́ми занима́ла?** Will you say that I'm behind you? There is a whole culture about standing in queues. People establish their position, and go off for a while – often to join another queue!

Practise what you have learned

3

Volodya is looking for flowers to take to a friend. Prices are high so he has to shop around. How much do each vendor's flowers cost? (Answers on page 84.)

(i)

(ii)

(iii)

(i) **цветы́** ....

(ii) **ро́зы** ....

(iii) **цветы́** ....

4

Walking down the Arbat, Volodya and Tanya pass a number of people loudly advertising their wares. Which adjectives refer (according to their sellers!) to each thing? (Answers on page 84.)

(i) **матрёшки**

(ii) **ро́зы**

(iii) **платки́**

(a) **души́стые**	(b) **си́ние**
(c) **ру́сские**	(d) **традицио́нные**
(e) **све́жие**	(f) **недороги́е**

Dialogues

6 *Misha is looking for something to drink*

Misha Скажи́те, у вас есть минера́льная вода́?
Shop Assistant Минера́льной воды́ нет.
Misha А что есть?
Shop Assistant Есть сок.
Misha А ну, бу́дьте любе́зны, тогда́ со́ка.
Shop Assistant Пожа́луйста, в ка́ссу шестьдеся́т пять копе́ек.

сок fruit juice
ну well
бу́дьте любе́зны please, be so kind
тогда́ then

➧ **минера́льная вода́** mineral water. Misha is told that there isn't any: **минера́льной воды́ нет**. **Нет** means 'there isn't/aren't', and the endings of the words have changed. This *always* happens after **нет**. The case is called the genitive. If there were no fruit juice **сок** (a masculine noun) or milk **молоко́** (neuter noun), Misha would be told: **со́ка нет, молока́ нет**. Don't worry at this stage if you can't remember the endings. Do, however, notice those endings you see here, and be prepared for a word sounding rather different from the form you would find in your dictionary.

➧ **со́ка** some juice. Misha has changed the ending here (also genitive) to indicate 'some juice'. He could also have said **сок**.

➧ **в ка́ссу шестьдеся́т копе́ек** 65 kopecks to the cashier (**плати́те** is understood)

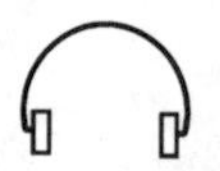

7 *In the chemist (pharmacy)*

Vladimir У вас есть что́-нибудь от на́сморка?
Chemist Менто́ловое ма́сло, четы́ре копе́йки.
Vladimir От головно́й бо́ли?
Chemist То́лько аспири́н, шесть копе́ек.
Vladimir Анальги́на нет?
Chemist Анальги́на пока́ нет.
Vladimir Ско́лько э́то сто́ит всё?
Chemist Де́сять копе́ек. В ка́ссу, пожа́луйста.
Vladimir В ка́ссу. Спаси́бо.
Chemist Пожа́луйста.

менто́ловое ма́сло menthol oil
пока́ нет not at the moment
аспири́н aspirin

➧ **у вас есть что́-нибудь от на́сморка?** do you have anything for a cold? You may also want to know how to ask for the following:
что́-нибудь от головно́й бо́ли for a headache
что́-нибудь от ка́шля for a cough

➧ **четы́ре копе́йки**
шесть копе́ек
Like all nouns **копе́йка** and **рубль** have different endings depending on the number. Use the following table as reference.

(э́то сто́ит)	**одну́ копе́йку**	**оди́н рубль**
	2–4 копе́йки	**2–4 рубля́**
	5, 6... копе́ек	**5, 6... рубле́й**

➧ **анальги́на нет?** is there no analgin (a popular painkiller)? The noun is **анальги́н** when it is not followed by **нет**.

Practise what you have learned

5 On your recording you will accompany Alla on a shopping expedition. It is not especially successful – very few of the items on her list are available. Can you find the ones which are? (Answers on page 84.)

(i) **ма́сло**
(ii) **колбаса́**
(iii) **сыр**
(iv) **минера́льная вода́**
(v) **сок**
(vi) **хлеб**

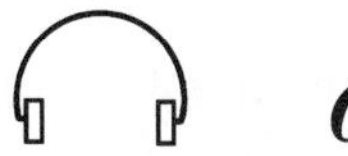

6 Below are pictures of three people all feeling ill, but in different ways. Listen to the recording and see what the chemist is able to offer each of them. (Answers on page 84.)

You will need to know the word **микстýра** 'cough mixture'.

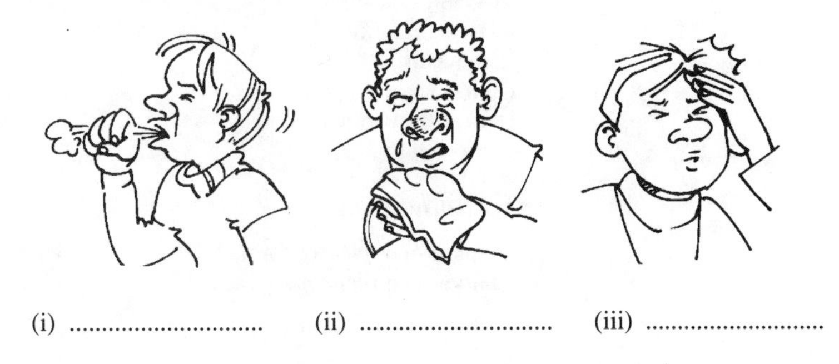

(i) .... (ii) .... (iii) ....

A chemist on Arbat. In this street, popular with tourists, street traders often display their goods on the outside of shop windows.

Key words and phrases

To use

э́то о́чень до́рого	that's very expensive
у вас есть что́-нибудь...	do you have anything...
подеше́вле?	cheaper?
от на́сморка?	for a head cold?
от головно́й бо́ли?	for a headache?
от ка́шля?	for a cough?
купи́ть	to buy
я куплю́ ро́зовый плато́к	I will buy a pink scarf
ро́зовый, -ая, -ое	pink
си́ний, -яя, -ее	dark blue
кра́сный, -ая, -ое	red
бе́лый, -ая, -ое	white
чёрный, -ая, -ое	black
зелёный, -ая, -ое	green
большо́й, -а́я, -о́е	big
сре́дний, -яя, -ее	average, medium
ма́ленький, -ая, -ое	small
покажи́те, каки́е у вас есть	show (me) the ones that you've got
како́й, -а́я, -о́е	which
дорого́й, -а́я, -о́е	expensive
све́жий, -ая, -ее	fresh
краси́вый, -ая, -ое	beautiful
друго́й, -а́я, -о́е	(the) other
кто после́дний?	who's last?
я за ва́ми	I'm behind you
(да́йте) мне оди́н	give me one (masculine noun)
(да́йте) мне одну́	give me one (feminine noun)

To understand

вам како́го цве́та ну́жно?	what colour would you like?
вам како́го разме́ра ну́жно?	what size would you like?

Grammar

An adjective *describes* a person or a thing. In Unit 1 we mentioned that *any* word describing a noun has to 'agree' with it, that is, have the same number and gender. In the dictionary you will find an adjective written thus:

ро́зовый, -ая, -ое pink

This tells you the endings for masculine, feminine and neuter nouns in the singular. So:

ро́зовый плато́к a pink scarf
ро́зовая ю́бка a pink skirt
ро́зовое пла́тье a pink dress

There will sometimes be differences in spelling or pronunciation, but the entry will show you that, for example:

си́ний, -яя, -ее dark blue

If the noun is in the plural, there *is* another ending to learn, but at least only one! Whatever the gender the adjective will end in **-ые** (sometimes spelled **- ие**):

ро́зовые платки́ pink scarves
дороги́е матрёшки expensive matryoshka dolls
си́ние пла́тья dark blue dresses

You may have guessed that if a noun has different endings depending on its *function* in a sentence, so too will adjectives describing it.

You will have most use for the accusative case (the object of a verb). And best of all, normally only the feminine endings change! In the second dialogue you heard Tamara say that she would buy the pink scarf:

Я куплю́ ро́зовый плато́к

Similarly, nothing would have changed if she had wanted a pink dress:

Я куплю́ ро́зовое пла́тье

But for the feminine noun:

Я куплю́ ро́зовую ю́бку

Before you try the next exercise, we would repeat once again that endings are something you may aim to master in the long term but if you don't remember them at present, it *won't* matter!

7

In the following shop dialogues, the endings of the adjectives have been left out. Can you fill them in? (Answers on page 84.)

(i) - **У вас есть ро́зов__ платки́?**
- **Нет, но у нас есть чёрн__ , кра́сн__ и зелён__ платки́.**
- **Хорошо́, я куплю́ зелён__ плато́к.**

(ii) - **А у вас есть чёрн__ ю́бки?**
- **Нет, но у нас есть кори́чнев__ , кра́сн__ и ро́зов__ ю́бки.**
- **Да́йте, пожа́луйста, кра́сн__ ю́бку.**

(iii) - **У вас есть кра́сн__ вино́?**
- **Нет, но у нас есть бе́л__ вино́.**
- **Хорошо́, я куплю́ бе́л__ вино́.**

Read and understand

8

A group of tourists dropped into the 'Beryozka' shop in their hotel. Beside their names you will find written down what they were looking for. Read the advertisement below and then write down which of the tourists were completely satisfied, and which only partially. (Answers on page 84.)

Tom	looking for an English tie, can't spend a lot
Louis	wants an expensive French wine
Lesya	wants a pretty scarf, Ukrainian or Byelorussian
Roy	looking for a typically Russian toy for his child
Ann	wants a black skirt, preferably of Italian make
Hans	wants a bottle of Russian vodka, doesn't want to pay the earth

!! БЕРЁЗКА !!

У нас есть

НЕДОРОГА́Я РУ́ССКАЯ ВО́ДКА
КРАСИ́ВЫЕ УКРАИ́НСКИЕ ПЛАТКИ́
ИТАЛЬЯ́НСКИЕ Ю́БКИ - РО́ЗОВЫЕ, СИ́НИЕ
РУ́ССКИЕ МАТРЁШКИ
НЕДОРОГО́Е ФРАНЦУ́ЗСКОЕ ВИНО́
НЕДОРОГИ́Е НЕМЕ́ЦКИЕ ГА́ЛСТУКИ

(i) *Tom* ....

(ii) *Louis* ....

(iii) *Lesya* ....

(iv) *Roy* ....

(v) *Ann* ....

(vi) *Hans* ....

9

On the left-hand side you will see signs from various shops in Moscow. On your right is a box with items Tamara intends to buy. It would of course be much more efficient to have the items next to the name of the shop... (Answers on page 84.)

(i) АПТЕКА

(ii) ГАСТРОНОМ

(iii) УНИВЕРМАГ

(iv) ПОЧТА

(a) **пла́тья** (b) **ма́рки** (c) **ма́сло**
(d) **менто́ловое ма́сло** (e) **молоко́**
(f) **откры́тки** (g) **анальги́н**
(h) **платки́** (i) **матрёшки**

(i) **апте́ка** (chemist/ pharmacy) ....

(ii) **гастроно́м** (food shop) ....

(iii) **универма́г** (department store) ....

(iv) **по́чта** (post office) ....

Did you know?

One way of avoiding the time-consuming system described in the previous unit is to shop at the market. *If*, that is, you can afford it. Perhaps the reason you seldom stand in a queue at a market is that the prices are very high. Markets have always been expensive. People from collective farms, allowed to grow produce on a small piece of land, would bring it to the city to sell. They brought small amounts and so charged a lot.

At the time of writing, government stores were empty enough to drive many to shop at the market, and prices had reached record levels.

None the less, even if you don't buy anything, markets are a colourful and interesting sight. The availability of fruit and vegetables depends to a large degree on the time of the year, though many come from Georgia and Azerbaijan, where the climate is milder. Meat is generally also on sale, and sometimes even handmade items of clothing.

As in markets the world over, you don't need to accept the first price quoted – you know enough Russian to haggle! You can also normally try the fruit, salted cucumbers etc. before buying them (indeed some try this *instead* of buying!).

As well as market traders, you also find people selling produce – at the same kind of prices – outside underground (subway) stations.

Towards the end of the 1980s there was a noticeable easing in the restrictions on private trading. As a result, many new kiosks have opened, selling handmade items, Western goods and anything which the average person can't find in the shops. Prices, however, are often extrortionate and frequently provoke resentment.

Your turn to speak

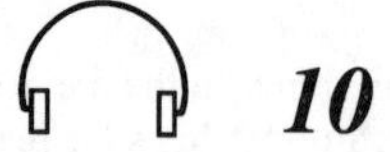

10

In these exercises you will be enquiring about and purchasing things in a chemist (pharmacy). You'll need to use the following phrases:

у вас есть что́-нибудь от на́сморка / от головно́й бо́ли?
у вас нет анальги́на?
я куплю́...

Answers

Practise what you have learned

Exercise **1**	(i) scarf costs 5 roubles (ii) asks to see all that they have (iii) trousers cost 50 roubles
Exercise **3**	(i) 3.50 буке́т (ii) 2 рубля́ шту́ка (iii) 2.70 буке́т
Exercise **4**	(i) c, d (ii) a, e (iii) b, f
Exercise **5**	(i), (vi)
Exercise **6**	(i) cough mixture (ii) menthol oil (iii) aspirin

Grammar

Exercise **7**	(i) ро́зовые; чёрные, кра́сные, зелёные; зелёный (ii) чёрные; кори́чневые, кра́сные, ро́зовые; кра́сную (iii) кра́сное; бе́лое; бе́лое

Read and understand

Exercise **8**	(i) inexpensive, but German ties (ii) French wine, but inexpensive (iii) pretty Ukrainian scarves (iv) Russian matryoshka dolls (v) Italian skirts, but pink or blue (vi) inexpensive Russian vodka
Exercise **9**	(i) d, g (ii) c, e (iii) a, h, i (iv) b, f

You will learn

- to ask what the time is
- to understand the answer!
- to ask when shops, etc. open and close
- to talk about what you do on days of the week and at different times of the year

and a little about what Russians do on their days off

An information bureau

Study guide

- **Dialogues 1–4:** listen without the book
- **Dialogues 1–4:** listen, read and study one by one
- Practise what you have learned
- **Dialogues 5, 6:** listen without the book
- **Dialogues 5, 6:** listen, read and study one by one
- Practise what you have learned
- **Dialogues 7, 8:** listen without the book
- **Dialogues 7, 8:** listen, read and study one by one
- Practise what you have learned
- Study the **Key words and phrases**
- Study the **Grammar** section carefully
- Do the exercises in **Read and understand**
- Read **Did you know?**
- Do the exercises in **Your turn to speak**
- Listen to all the dialogues once again straight through

Dialogues

1 *What is the time?*

Кото́рый час?
Во́семь часо́в.

- **кото́рый час?** what is the time?
- **во́семь часо́в** eight o'clock. **Часо́в** is used with numbers from five onwards. From two to four the ending is different: **два, три, четы́ре** ***часа́***, while one o'clock is simply **час**.

2 *Tanya is asking the time*

Tanya Вы не зна́ете, кото́рый час?
Boris Mikhailovich Без двадцати́ де́вять.
Tanya Прости́те?
Boris Mikhailovich Во́семь со́рок.
Tanya Спаси́бо.

- **вы не зна́ете,...** you don't happen to know...? Just about *any* question in Russian is felt to be more polite when made negative.
If you actually *don't* know, you will answer: **я не зна́ю**.
- **без двадцати́ де́вять** twenty to nine. Literally this is 'without twenty, nine' (more details in the grammar section).
- **прости́те?** sorry? Tanya hasn't understood either! Instead of **прости́те?** she could also ask **повтори́те, пожа́луйста** please repeat that.
- **во́семь со́рок** eight forty. In this simpler 'digital' form of the time, the words for hours and minutes are often omitted. In railway stations, airports etc. '24-hour digital' time is commonly used. You may hear people using '12-hour digital' time. However, in their day-to-day life, Russians still tend to use the first type of answer.

3 *Now Tamara wants to know the time*

Tamara Ско́лько сейча́с вре́мени?
Misha Пять мину́т четвёртого.

- **Ско́лько сейча́с вре́мени?** what is the time? This is another common way of asking the same question.
- **пять мину́т четвёртого** five minutes of the fourth ('hour' understood), i.e. five past three. You will find a list of these ordinal numbers on page 93.

4 *Tanya and Tamara have finished breakfast*

Tanya А ты не зна́ешь, ско́лько сейча́с вре́мени?
Tamara Полови́на девя́того.
Tanya Ой, я уже́ опа́здываю.

ой here an expression of consternation
уже́ already

- **ты не зна́ешь...?** the same question as in the first dialogue, but Tanya is talking here to a close friend.
- **полови́на девя́того** half-past eight
- **я уже́ опа́здываю** I'm already late

Practise what you have learned

1

Before you begin these exercises, read the grammar section on page 93.

On your recording you will hear people asking the time. Listen very carefully then see if you can put the following times in their correct order. (Answers on page 96.)

(i) 9.45 ....

(ii) 4.15 ....

(iii) 2.00 ....

(iv) 4.45 ....

(v) 6.00 ....

(vi) 1.30 ....

2

Your turn to ask the time. Andrei will guide you.

A café's opening hours

Dialogues

5 *Misha asks about the shop's hours*

Misha Скажи́те, пожа́луйста, когда́ открыва́ется ваш магази́н?
Shop Assistant Наш магази́н открыва́ется в во́семь часо́в утра́.
Misha Спаси́бо. А когда́ у вас переры́в?
Shop Assistant Переры́в с ча́су до двух.
Misha Спаси́бо.

магази́н shop
наш (fem. **на́ша**) our

- **когда́ открыва́ется ваш магази́н?** when does your shop open? If you wanted to find out when the shop shuts, you would ask: **когда́ закрыва́ется ваш магази́н?**
- **в во́семь часо́в утра́** at eight o'clock in the morning. When saying 'at' a particular time, **в** is used before the number (this is often scarcely audible). 'At eight o'clock in the *evening*' would be **в во́семь часо́в ве́чера**. And 'at three o'clock in the afternoon' – **в три часа́ дня**.
- **когда́ у вас переры́в?** when is your break (for lunch)?
- **переры́в с ча́су до двух** break is from one to two. Numbers often have different endings after prepositions such as **с** 'from' and **до** 'to'. 'From 2 to 3' is **с двух до трёх**, 'from 4 to 5' **с четырёх до пяти́**, 'from 6 to 7' **с шести́ до семи́**. From then to 12 the numbers end in **-и**.

  Again you may not need to *use* these numbers, but you will want to *recognise* them. Listen carefully as Andrei reads them, since they can sound quite different from the numbers you are used to.

6 *Tanya wants to know why her train hasn't arrived*

Tanya Почему́ нет по́езда из Яросла́вля? Уже́ три часа́.
Clerk По́езд, наве́рно, опа́здывает и ну́жно слу́шать объявле́ния ди́ктора.

по́езд train
наве́рно probably
опа́здывать to be running late

- **почему́ нет по́езда из Яросла́вля?** why isn't the train from Yaroslavl' here? The word for 'train' is **по́езд** (it has become **по́езда** because it is used after **нет**).
- **почему́...?** why...? A reason as such is not given in this case – Tanya *knows* that the train is late! However, the response to **почему́?** will often be **потому́ что...** because...
- **уже́ три часа́** it is already three o'clock
- **ну́жно слу́шать объявле́ния ди́ктора** you need to listen to the announcements

Practise what you have learned

3 The signs below have fallen off their appropriate shops. Read the opening hours below then listen to your recording, and put the signs back in place. (Answers on page 96.)

(i)	(ii)	(iii)
ПОЧТА	УНИВЕРМАГ	МАГАЗИН

(a)	(b)	(c)
9–18 **перерыв 2–3**	**11–20** **перерыв 1–2**	**8–19** **перерыв 1–2**

4 The customers in the following dialogues all express indignation over shop timekeeping – unfairly, as it turns out. By listening to the recording, you should be able to say how long each customer will have to wait. (Answers on page 96.)

(i) 1st man ....

(ii) woman ....

(iii) 2nd man ....

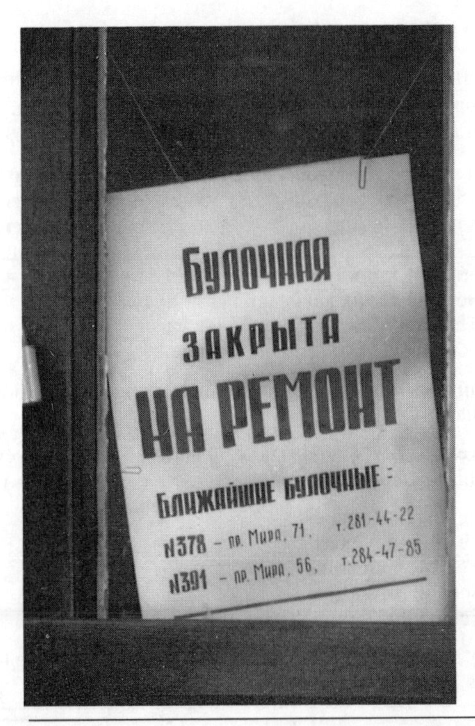

This baker is closed for repairs and gives details of the nearest bakeries

Dialogues

7 *Misha describes a week during term-time*

Misha В понеде́льник я хожу́ в институ́т. Во вто́рник у меня́ свобо́дный день, и я иногда́ хожу́ в библиоте́ку, а иногда́ ничего́ не де́лаю. В сре́ду, в четве́рг и в пя́тницу я опя́ть хожу́ в институ́т. В суббо́ту я занима́юсь спо́ртом. А в воскресе́нье я встреча́юсь с друзья́ми.

иногда́ sometimes
библиоте́ка library
опя́ть again
занима́ться спо́ртом to take part in sport
встреча́ться с друзья́ми to meet with friends

- **в понеде́льник, во вто́рник, в сре́ду, в четве́рг, в пя́тницу, в суббо́ту, в воскресе́нье** on Monday, Tuesday, ...
- **я хожу́ в институ́т** I go to the institute. The verb **ходи́ть (я хожу́, вы хо́дите...)** is used when you say that you go somewhere frequently. It is normally followed by **в** or **на** and a noun in the accusative case. Thus Misha says **я хожу́ в институ́т** but **я хожу́ в библиоте́ку**.
- **свобо́дный день** a free day. Misha means a day 'free' from lectures. A non-working day (for both people and shops, etc.) is **выходно́й день**.
- **я ничего́ не де́лаю** I don't do anything. **Ничего́** means 'nothing'. If it is used with a verb, you need **не** before the latter. Other such phrases:
  я ничего́ не зна́ю I don't know anything
  я ничего́ не хочу́ I don't want anything
  я ничего́ не понима́ю I don't understand anything

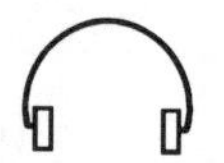

8 *What about the holidays?*

Misha Зи́мние кани́кулы начина́ются в январе́. Ле́тние кани́кулы начина́ются в ию́ле и конча́ются в а́вгусте. Ле́том я люблю́ ходи́ть в похо́ды, а зимо́й я люблю́ ката́ться на лы́жах.

в январе́ in January (see full list of months on page 92)
в ию́ле in July
в а́вгусте in August
ходи́ть в похо́ды to go hiking
ката́ться на лы́жах to ski

- **зи́мние кани́кулы** winter holidays
  ле́тние кани́кулы summer holidays
  The word **кани́кулы** (holidays) usually refers to school and university holidays. Leave for working people is **о́тпуск**.
- **зи́мние кани́кулы начина́ются в январе́** winter holidays begin in January
- **конча́ться** to end. The verb endings **начина́ются** and **конча́ются** are the third person *plural*, used because the noun **кани́кулы** is always plural.
- **ле́том** in summer
  зимо́й in winter
  The two remaining seasons:
  весно́й in spring
  о́сенью in autumn (the fall)
- **я люблю́...** I like... When you are saying 'to like to *do* something', this verb is followed by an infinitive verb.

Practise what you have learned

5 Vera Stepanovna's family always has enormous problems arranging a holiday together. If you listen to the snatches of conversation on your recording and then fill in the missing details below, you will know why.
(Answers on page 96.)

(i) **Ве́ра Степа́новна:** **о́тпуск** begins ...., ends ....

(ii) **Макси́м Петро́вич:** **о́тпуск** begins ...., ends ....

(iii) **Лари́са:** **о́тпуск** begins ...., ends ....

6 In this exercise, you are a student talking about a normal week during term-time.

A newspaper cartoon. The banner says 'I don't understand anything'!

Key words and phrases

кото́рый час? / ско́лько сейча́с вре́мени?	what is the time?
(see *Grammar* for all the times)	
вы не зна́ете, ...?	you don't happen to know...?
я (не) зна́ю	I (don't) know
прости́те?	I beg your pardon?
повтори́те, пожа́луйста	please repeat that
когда́...	when...
открыва́ется магази́н?	does the shop open?
закрыва́ется кио́ск?	does the kiosk close?
у вас переры́в?	is your lunchbreak?
в во́семь часо́в утра́	at 8 a.m.
в два часа́ дня	at 2 p.m.
в шесть часо́в ве́чера	at 6 p.m.
с ча́су до двух	from 1 to 2
с двух до трёх	from 2 to 3
с четырёх до пяти́	from 4 to 5
почему́...?	why...?
потому́ что...	because...
я опа́здываю	I'm running late
по́езд опа́здывает	the train is late
в понеде́льник	on Monday
во вто́рник	on Tuesday
в сре́ду	on Wednesday
в четве́рг	on Thursday
в пя́тницу	on Friday
в суббо́ту	on Saturday
в воскресе́нье	on Sunday
я хожу́ в институ́т	I go to the institute
в библиоте́ку	to the library
свобо́дный день	a free day
выходно́й день	a day off; day when shop etc. is closed
в январе́	in January
в феврале́	in February
в ма́рте	in March
в апре́ле	in April
в ма́е	in May
в ию́не	in June
в ию́ле	in July
в а́вгусте	in August
в сентябре́	in September
в октябре́	in October
в ноябре́	in November
в декабре́	in December
зимо́й	in winter
весно́й	in spring
ле́том	in summer
о́сенью	in autumn (the Fall)

Grammar

Котóрый час? / Скóлько сейчáс врéмени?
What is the time?

On the hour

час	one o'clock	**семь часóв**	seven o'clock
два часá	two o'clock	**вóсемь часóв**	eight o'clock
три часá	three o'clock	**дéвять часóв**	nine o'clock
четы́ре часá	four o'clock	**дéсять часóв**	ten o'clock
пять часóв	five o'clock	**оди́ннадцать часóв**	eleven o'clock
шесть часóв	six o'clock	**двенáдцать часóв**	twelve o'clock

Когдá...? when...?

To say 'at' a particular time, you simply put **в** in front of the number, e.g.:

в два часá at two o'clock

NB Here too endings change after numbers. After two, three and four, the ending is **-а** (genitive singular). From five onwards the ending becomes **-ов** (genitive plural). One o'clock is simply the word for 'hour' – **час**, and it doesn't need an ending. Other masculine nouns have the same endings, take **билéт** ticket and **дóллар** dollar, for example:

оди́н билéт, оди́н дóллар
два (три, четы́ре) билéта, дóллара
пять (шесть, ...) билéтов, дóлларов

One to thirty minutes past the hour

For the first thirty minutes of any hour, Russians talk about so many minutes of the *next* hour. Here are some examples:

пять минýт пéрвого	five past 12
дéсять минýт вторóго	ten past 1
пятнáдцать минýт трéтьего	a quarter past 2
двáдцать минýт четвёртого	twenty past 3
двáдцать пять минýт пя́того	twenty-five past 4
полови́на шестóго	half past 5

The ordinal numbers used in this way are:

пéрвый	first	**седьмóй**	seventh
вторóй	second	**восьмóй**	eighth
трéтий	third	**девя́тый**	ninth
четвёртый	fourth	**деся́тый**	tenth
пя́тый	fifth	**оди́ннадцатый**	eleventh
шестóй	sixth	**двенáдцатый**	twelfth

The most important thing to remember is that Russian always looks *forward* to the next hour. Arriving exactly one hour late could be *very* inconvenient!

After the half-way point

After the half-way point one says that it is so many hours minus the number of minutes, i.e.:

без двадцати́ пяти́ час	twenty-five to 1
без двадцати́ два	twenty to 2
без пятнáдцати три	a quarter to 3
без десяти́ четы́ре	ten to 4
без пяти́ пять	five to 5

The number after **без** 'without' has a new ending – **и**. It is wise to be aware of this since the number can sound quite different.

If this all seems daunting, remember that you won't necessarily ever need to *use* these times, just to understand them if you hear them.

Read and understand

7

Diaries *can* bring order to one's life, but they can also wreak havoc... Read the following notices then explain why Volodya seems to have got *everything* wrong. (Answers on page 96.)

Кафе́
рабо́тает
с 11 до 22
выходно́й день — вто́рник

Музе́й Пу́шкина
вт., ср. откры́т с 10 до 18
чт., пт. откры́т с 10 до 17
сб., вс. откры́т с 14 до 18
выходно́й день — понеде́льник

Гастроно́м
рабо́тает
с 8 до 21
переры́в с ча́су до двух
выходно́й день – воскресе́нье

кинотеа́тр 'Росси́я'
пн. 'Ма́ленькая Ве́ра', нач. в 20.00
вт., ср. 'Покая́ние'
пт., сб. и вс. 'Балла́да о солда́те'
нач. в 19.30

(i)	**в понеде́льник**	**11 часо́в — музе́й Пу́шкина**
(ii)	**во вто́рник**	**12 часо́в — обе́д в кафе́**
(iii)	**в сре́ду**	**20.00 – кино́: 'Ма́ленькая Ве́ра'**
(iv)	**в четве́рг**	**1.30 – купи́ть проду́кты в гастроно́ме**
(v)	**в пя́тницу**	**9 часо́в — музе́й Пу́шкина**
(vi)	**в суббо́ту**	**8 часо́в ве́чера — кино́: 'Балла́да о солда́те'**
(vii)	**в воскресе́нье**	**с 7 до 11 часо́в ве́чера — у́жин в кафе́**

8

The following snatches of conversation have all become jumbled up and make no sense. Using the pictures to guide you, put them in the correct order. (Answers on page 96.)

(i) **Что вы лю́бите де́лать зимо́й?**
(ii) **Магази́н открыва́ется в во́семь часо́в**
(iii) **Ско́лько сейча́с вре́мени?**
(iv) **Я ничего́ не де́лаю**
(v) **Я люблю́ ката́ться на лы́жах**
(vi) **Почему́ нет по́езда? Уже́ де́сять часо́в**
(vii) **Пять мину́т пя́того**
(viii) **Когда́ открыва́ется ваш магази́н?**
(ix) **Что вы де́лаете в суббо́ту?**
(x) **По́езд опа́здывает**

Did you know?

Выходны́е дни (days off)

Shops are open on Saturdays, but for the majority of Russian people the working week ends on Friday. Parents who scarcely see their child or children during the week will spend a lot of time with them on Saturday and Sunday. Despite the fact that both parents normally work, in a two-parent family the father will typically play with the children while the mother cooks, cleans and searches the shops for necessary items.

Since the late 1980s, there has been greater freedom of worship and a marked religious revival, and many will take time to worship in churches, synagogues or mosques. Even in the big centres, people do not very often go to the theatre, cinema or concerts. There are obviously exceptions, but for most people it is difficult to obtain tickets (the very verb used, **доста́ть**, means 'to obtain with difficulty'). Few would eat out in restaurants or cafés except on special occasions, chiefly because such places are scarce. Of late, more have opened, but these are often prohibitively expensive, or require payment in foreign currency. The lack of activities and places for young people to go is particularly sharply felt.

The large cities may often seem transformed at weekends. If at all possible, urban dwellers try to escape the city. Excursions into the forest to pick mushrooms or vitamin-rich berries are favourite occupations. Anyone who can, rents (or buys) a **да́ча**, a small holiday house out of the city. For the average person, this will be no more than a hut, with few conveniences, and it may take a long time to get to it by public transportation. Nevertheless, these dachas are much sought after.

We have talked exclusively about city dwellers. In numerical terms the number of visitors from the countryside and smaller cities more than compensates for those leaving the city at weekends. Although these visitors do sightsee, in general they come to the big cities in order to buy foodstuffs, clothes, and other items not available at home.

A dacha

Your turn to speak

9

You will be a student finding his way around Moscow in the first part of this exercise, then you will have a chance to talk a little more about yourself. The following expressions will come in handy:

когда́ открыва́ется...?
когда́ у вас переры́в?
кани́кулы начина́ются / конча́ются...
я люблю́...
ходи́ть в похо́ды

Answers

Practise what you have learned

Exercise **1**	(iv), (iii), (ii), (vi), (i), (v)
Exercise **3**	(a) ii (b) i (c) iii
Exercise **4**	(i) 1 hour (ii) 1/2 hour (iii) 1 hour
Exercise **5**	(i) January, February (ii) April, May (iii) August, September

Read and understand

Exercise **7**	(i) Mondays closed (ii) Tuesdays café is closed (iii) film only on Monday (iv) lunchbreak 1–2 (v) opens at 10 (vi) begins at 19.30 (vii) closes at 22 hours
Exercise **8**	i, v, viii, ii, iii, vii, ix, iv, vi, x

8

ASKING FOR AND UNDERSTANDING DIRECTIONS

You will learn

- to ask where places are
- and how to get to them
- to understand directions

and there will be some information and advice about public transportation

Before you begin

A word of advice: when a person gives you directions, it is unlikely that you you will understand *every* word. But remember, you don't *need* to! You want the *gist*, the *crucial* words which will tell you *where* to go.

Study guide

- **Dialogues 1, 2:** listen without the book
- **Dialogues 1, 2:** listen, read and study one by one
- Practise what you have learned
- **Dialogues 3, 4:** listen without the book
- **Dialogues 3, 4:** listen, read and study one by one
- Practise what you have learned
- **Dialogues 5–7:** listen without the book
- **Dialogues 5–7:** listen, read and study one by one
- Practise what you have learned
- Study the **Key words and phrases**
- Study the **Grammar** section carefully
- Do the exercises in **Read and understand**
- Read **Did you know?**
- Do the exercises in **Your turn to speak**
- Listen to all the dialogues once again straight through

Dialogues

1 *Lyena is looking for a post office*

Lyena	Вы не ска́жете, где здесь по́чта?
Passer-by	По́чта че́рез доро́гу.
Lyena	Спаси́бо.
Passer-by	Пожа́луйста.

здесь here, in the vicinity **по́чта** post office

- **Вы не ска́жете...?** you couldn't tell me... could you? Like **вы не зна́ете...?**, this is a way of mellowing a request for information.
- **че́рез доро́гу** across the road. Some other common answers to listen for are (the embarrassing) **по́чта ря́дом** 'the post office is next door' and **по́чта за угло́м** 'the post office is around the corner'.

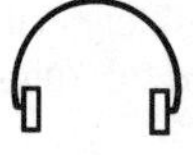

2 *Ira wants to get to the Arbat*

Ira	Де́вушки, извини́те, пожа́луйста, вы не подска́жете, как пройти́ на Арба́т?
Young woman	Пря́мо и че́рез перехо́д.
Ira	А э́то до́лго?
Young woman	Нет, где-то три мину́ты.
Ira	Три мину́ты. А вы не ска́жете, там нахо́дится дом-музе́й Пу́шкина?
Young woman	Да, э́то кварти́ра пят... дом но́мер пятьдеся́т три.
Ira	Пятьдеся́т три, да? Спаси́бо большо́е, извини́те.
Young woman	Не́ за что.

Арба́т a famous street in Moscow
перехо́д subway
там there: the opposite of **здесь**
дом-музе́й Пу́шкина house-museum in which the poet Pushkin lived for a while
кварти́ра apartment
не́ за что don't mention it

- **де́вушки** girls. The age at which this word ceases to be appropriate would be difficult to fix. **Извини́те, пожа́луйста** excuse me please, and a smile work just as well and will *never* offend!
- **вы не подска́жете...?** There's little difference between this question and **вы не ска́жете...?**
- **как пройти́ на Арба́т?** How do I get to Arbát? You can use **как пройти́...?** in asking how to get anywhere on foot.
  Everybody knows what **Арба́т** is, but usually the place you are looking for will be called **у́лица** street, **проспе́кт** avenue or **пло́щадь** square. You might, for example, ask:

как пройти́...	How do I get...
на у́лицу Достое́вского?	to Dostoevsky street?
на проспе́кт Ми́ра?	to 'Peace' avenue?
на пло́щадь Пу́шкина?	to Pushkin square?

  (See also the grammar section on page 105.)
- **пря́мо и че́рез перехо́д** straight ahead and through the subway. Other words you should listen out for are **напра́во** to the right and **нале́во** to the left. A series of instructions may be connected by **пото́м** next.
- **э́то до́лго?** will it take long? A rough translation since Ira's question is telegraphic, omitting all but the key word. The woman replies in similar fashion:
  где-то три мину́ты around three minutes.
- **там нахо́дится дом-музе́й Пу́шкина?** is the Pushkin house-museum there? If the place you are looking for is a fair distance away, you can ask **где нахо́дится...?** where is... located?
- **кварти́ра** apartment. The woman begins to say apartment No. ... then corrects herself. It is in fact **дом пятьдеся́т три** house No. 53.

Practise what you have learned

1

Nina is still finding her way around in a new area. From her house she has been given directions to various places. On your recording you will hear these directions, but *not* the places! Follow the instructions each time, then see if you can complete the questions she asked. (Answers on page 108.)

(i) **Вы не ска́жете, где здесь** ....?

(ii) **Вы не ска́жете, где здесь** ....?

(iii) **Вы не ска́жете, где здесь** ....?

(iv) **Вы не ска́жете, где здесь** ....?

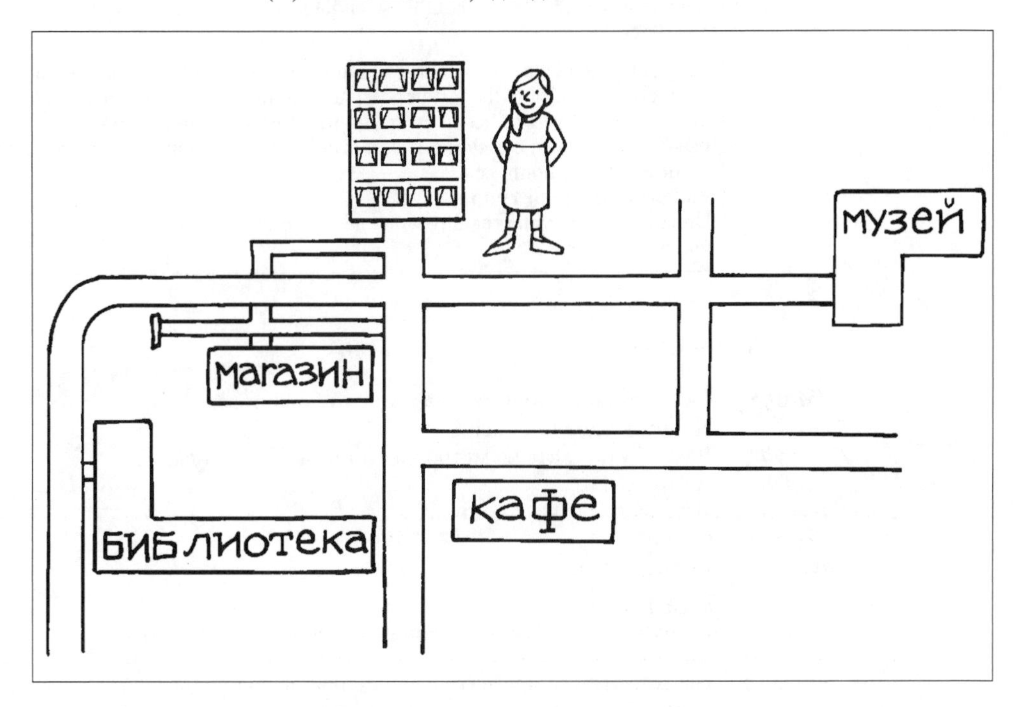

2

A tourist is given some directions and writes them down in translation. Unfortunately there is one mistake in each set of instructions. Listen to your recording, then correct his notes. (Answers on page 108.)

(i) post office – straight ahead, then to the right; across the road from the Bolshoi Theatre
(ii) department store – straight ahead and through the subway; opposite the underground station
(iii) café – through the subway is the Pushkin museum; the café is across the road

Dialogues

3 *Which trolleybuses go to the Pushkin Museum?*

Tanya Тама́ра, ты не зна́ешь, како́й тролле́йбус идёт до музе́я Пу́шкина?
Tamara До музе́я Пу́шкина идёт тролле́йбус второ́й, три́дцать пе́рвый и восемна́дцатый. И ещё идёт авто́бус восьмо́й и пятьдеся́т пя́тый.

како́й тролле́йбус идёт до музе́я Пу́шкина? which trolleybus goes to the Pushkin museum? You can find out about buses or trams by substituting for **тролле́йбус** the words **авто́бус** bus or **трамва́й** tram.
If you wanted to know about trolleybuses to Red Square or Dostoevsky street, you would ask:
како́й тролле́йбус идёт до Кра́сной пло́щади? / до у́лицы Достое́вского? (More about these endings in the grammar section on page 105.)

Tanya can't remember this deluge of numbers either! You met the ordinal numbers up to 12th in the last unit. Up to 20th they are also regular and easy to learn: **трина́дцать** becomes **трина́дцатый, четы́рнадцать – четы́рнадцатый**, etc. From 21st, it is only the last number which changes according to the noun, i.e.:
два́дцать пе́рвый тролле́йбус
Don't forget that you probably won't need to *use* these numbers, just to *understand* them

4 *Masha wants to get to Pushkin Square*

Masha Скажи́те, пожа́луйста, а как мне отсю́да прое́хать на Пу́шкинскую пло́щадь?
Passer-by Вам ну́жно е́хать на метро́ до ста́нции 'Пу́шкинская'.
Masha А э́то до́лго?
Passer-by Нет, всего́ четы́ре остано́вки.
Masha Спаси́бо.
Passer-by Пожа́луйста.

отсю́да from here
Пу́шкинская пло́щадь / пло́щадь Пу́шкина Pushkin square

как мне отсю́да прое́хать на Пу́шкинскую пло́щадь? how do I get to Pushkin Square from here? Since she knows that it is a long way, Masha has used the verb **прое́хать** to get somewhere by vehicle.

как мне пройти́...? / как мне прое́хать...? are set questions when asking for directions. The pronoun **мне** is often omitted.

Вам ну́жно е́хать на метро́ you need to go by underground
Е́хать is the most common verb for 'to go by vehicle'. 'I go by underground' is **я е́ду на метро́**. You may also be told:

вам ну́жно е́хать на авто́бусе	You need to go by bus
вам ну́жно е́хать на тролле́йбусе	You need to go by trolleybus
вам ну́жно е́хать на трамва́е	You need to go by tram
вам ну́жно е́хать на по́езде	You need to go by train

до ста́нции 'Пу́шкинская' to 'Pushkinskaya' station

всего́ четы́ре остано́вки only four stops

Practise what you have learned

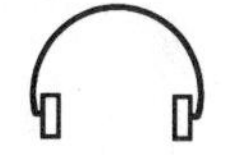

3

Below are pictures of signs you will see on a city street. Look at the numbers of the bus, trolleybus or tram routes which go from each stop and then listen to the dialogues on your recording. Can you tell which stop you need to wait at to get to each place? (Answers on page 108.)

(a)

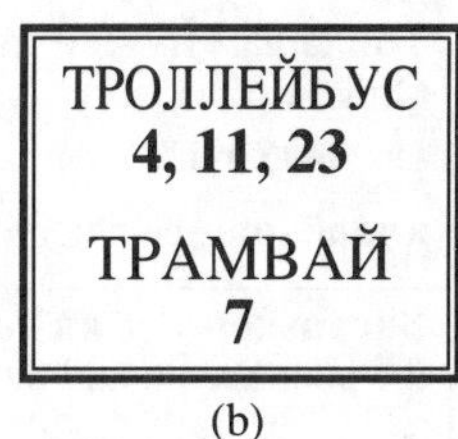

(b)

(c)

(i) **Кра́сная пло́щадь** ....

(ii) **Арба́т** ....

(iii) **Пу́шкинская пло́щадь** ....

4

On your recording you will hear a sightseer asking how to get to various famous places. He understood *at the time*, but later it was just a jumble of words. Listen, and see if you can find the necessary stations on the underground map below. (Answers on page 108.)

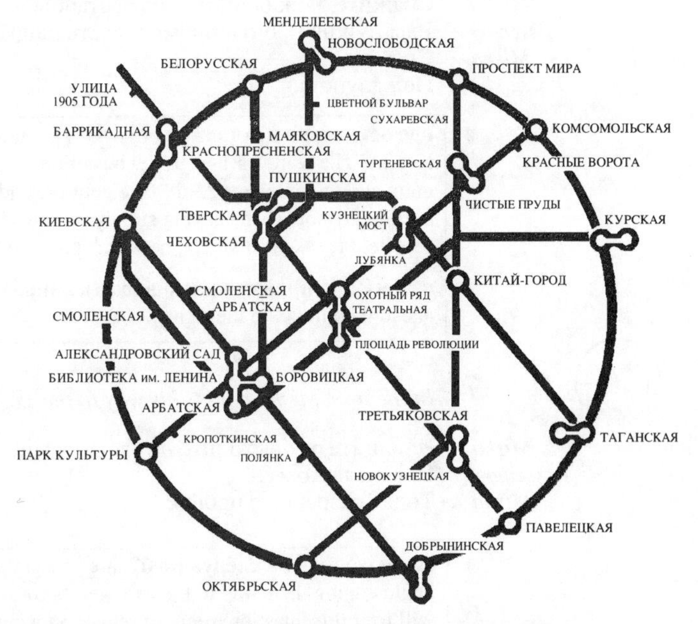

(i) **Кремль** (ii) **музе́й Пу́шкина** (iii) **Большо́й теа́тр**

This was the most up-to-date map available in early 1993, however many stations have new names and more are likely to be renamed (see *Did you know?* on page 177).

Dialogues

5 *Misha is looking for Vagan'kov cemetery*

Misha Скажи́те, как мне прое́хать на Вага́ньковское кла́дбище?
Passer-by Вы хоти́те прие́хать к моги́ле Высо́цкого?
Misha Да.
Passer-by Тогда́ вам ну́жен два́дцать тре́тий трамва́й.
Misha Спаси́бо.
Passer-by Пожа́луйста.

кла́дбище cemetery **тогда́** then

- **Вага́ньковское кла́дбище** Vagan'kov cemetery. An old cemetery where the poet Esenin and the singer/bard Vysotsky are buried.
- **Вы хоти́те прие́хать к моги́ле Высо́цкого?** do you want to go to Vysotsky's grave? Since Vysotsky's death in 1980, this cemetery has been a place of pilgrimage for lovers of his songs and verse.
- **вам ну́жен два́дцать тре́тий трамва́й** you need a No. 23 tram. If the thing needed is a feminine noun, you will hear: **вам нужна́**, and if it is neuter: **вам ну́жно**, e.g.:
  вам нужна́ втора́я остано́вка you need the second stop
  вам ну́жно такси́? do you need a taxi?

6 *Where does he catch a No. 23?*

Misha Скажи́те, пожа́луйста, а где остано́вка два́дцать тре́тьего трамва́я?
Passer-by Вам ну́жно пройти́ пря́мо и е́хать напра́во.
Misha Спаси́бо.
Passer-by Пожа́луйста.

- **где остано́вка два́дцать тре́тьего трамва́я?** where is the stop for the No. 23? The word for bus, trolleybus or tram stop is **остано́вка**, and both the noun and the number ('23rd') take genitive endings after it. In fact, there was nothing to stop Misha asking simply: **а где остано́вка?** Since he had just been told to take the No. 23, he wasn't going to be asking about any other stop!
- **вам ну́жно пройти́ пря́мо и е́хать напра́во** you need to go straight ahead then travel to the right

7 *In the tram Misha battles his way to the exit*

Misha Извини́те, вы выхо́дите на сле́дующей?
Passenger Нет, не выхожу́.
Misha Тогда́ разреши́те пройти́.

- **вы выхо́дите на сле́дующей?** are you getting out at the next stop? People begin edging their way to the exit well before a train or bus stops and you will hear this question often. In reply you would say: **да, я выхожу́** or **нет, я не выхожу́**.
- **разреши́те пройти́** allow me to pass. If you can't remember this, **мо́жно?** may I? will achieve the same result.

Practise what you have learned

5 On your recording you will hear people asking for directions. Listen several times then tick the correct answer. (Answers on page 108.)

You will need the word **телеце́нтр** 'television centre'.

(i) The man needs to travel
  (a) by tram to the television centre
  (b) by trolleybus to the television centre

(ii) The woman asks about
  (a) the stop for a No. 22 bus
  (b) the stop for a No. 25 trolleybus
  (c) the stop for a No. 25 bus

(iii) The man is told that
  (a) the No. 9 trolleybus stop is across the road
  (b) the No. 10 bus is straight ahead

6 You are a tourist trying to get out of a bus.

Key words and phrases

To use

вы не ска́жете, ...?	could you possibly tell me...?
скажи́те, пожа́луйста, ...	tell me please...
извини́те, пожа́луйста, ...	excuse me please...
где здесь...?	where in the vicinity is...?
где нахо́дится...?	where is... located?
как пройти́...	how do I get (by foot)...
как прое́хать...	how do I get (by vehicle)...
на Арба́т?	to the Arbat?
на у́лицу Достое́вского?	to Dostoevsky street?
на Пу́шкинскую пло́щадь?	to Pushkin square?
э́то до́лго?	will that take long?
како́й авто́бус идёт до...	which bus goes to...
музе́я Пу́шкина?	Pushkin museum?
Кра́сной пло́щади?	Red Square?
у́лицы Достое́вского?	Dostoevsky street?
вы выхо́дите на сле́дующей?	are you getting off at the next (stop)?
я (не) выхожу́	I'm (not) getting off
разреши́те пройти́	allow me to pass

To understand

вам ну́жно пройти́...	you need to go (by foot)...
вам ну́жно е́хать...	you need to go (by vehicle)...
пря́мо	straight ahead
напра́во	to the right
нале́во	to the left
че́рез доро́гу	across the road
че́рез перехо́д	through the subway
здесь	here
там	there
е́хать на метро́ до ста́нции	to go by underground to the station
на авто́бусе	by bus
на тролле́йбусе	by trolleybus
на трамва́е	by tram
на по́езде	by train
вам ну́жен тре́тий трамва́й	you need a No. 3 tram
вам нужна́ втора́я остано́вка	you need the second stop

Ordinal numbers

(1st – 12th are in Unit 7 on page 93.)

трина́дцатый, -ая, -ое	thirteenth
четы́рнадцатый, -ая, -ое	fourteenth
пятна́дцатый, -ая, -ое	fifteenth
шестна́дцатый, -ая, -ое	sixteenth
семна́дцатый, -ая, -ое	seventeenth
восемна́дцатый, -ая, -ое	eighteenth
девятна́дцатый, -ая, -ое	nineteenth
двадца́тый, -ая, -ое	twentieth
два́дцать пе́рвый, -ая, -ое	twenty-first

Grammar

Prepositions

Words such as *to*, *through* and *from* are called prepositions. As you would expect, they are particularly useful when asking for directions! You met quite a few in this unit: **в / на** to, **чéрез** through and **до** up to. Easy enough to learn, but unfortunately there are other changes. Each of these prepositions is said to 'take' a particular case, that is, it makes endings change in a particular way. Two cases are common when you are talking about going to places – the *accusative* case, used after **в**, **на** and **чéрез**, and the *genitive* case used after **до**. In Unit 3, you saw that a feminine noun has a new ending if it is the object of the sentence (this is its *accusative* ending). It ends in exactly the same way after the preposition **в** or **на** meaning 'to, into' and after **чéрез** meaning 'across'. For example, the word for street is **ýлица**: to ask how to get *to* Dostoevsky street, you would say:

Как пройти́ на ýлицу Достоéвского?

Masculine and neuter nouns do not have different endings for the accusative.

One warning: **в** and **на** can mean 'to, into' if they come after a verb implying motion. However, they can also mean 'in, on', in which case the endings are different, i.e. **Кремль в Москвé** 'the Kremlin is *in* Moscow' (see the grammar section on page 31). Certain other prepositions, like **до**, take the *genitive* case. Look at the following examples:

какóй автóбус идёт до Арбáта?
какóй автóбус идёт до ýлицы Достоéвского?

A masculine (or neuter) noun will simply add **-а** (sometimes spelled **-я**). A feminine noun will end in **-ы** (sometimes spelled **-и**) after these prepositions.

7 A tourist visiting Byelarus', Ukraine and Russia is asked by a Byelorussian border official which places he plans to see. He produces the following list of cities:

(i) **Минск**	(iii) **Ки́ев**	(v) **Москвá**
(ii) **Одéсса**	(iv) **Полтáва**	(vi) **Петербýрг**

Here is a script of what he *could* have said, but you will need to add the cities with the correct endings. (When talking about movement to a *city*, the preposition **в** is always used.) (Answers on page 108.)

(i) **Я éду** ...., **потóм** (ii) ...., **потóм** (iii) ...., **потóм** (iv) ...., **потóм** (v) ...., **потóм** (vi) ....

8 You have arrived in a new city and want to find the following places:

(i) **пóчта**	(iii) **теáтр**	(v) **ресторáн**
(ii) **магази́н**	(iv) **аптéка**	

You will be travelling by bus, so you will need to ask:
какóй автóбус идёт...

(i) **до** ....?	(iv) **до** ....?
(ii) **до** ....?	(v) **до** ....?
(iii) **до** ....?	(Answers on page 108.)

Read and understand

9

Members of a tourist group in Moscow spurned the services of their guide, asking only for a map of the metro and instructions about how to find some famous places. They managed admirably! Follow their instructions and the map, and mark out the route they would have planned in order to take in all the places.

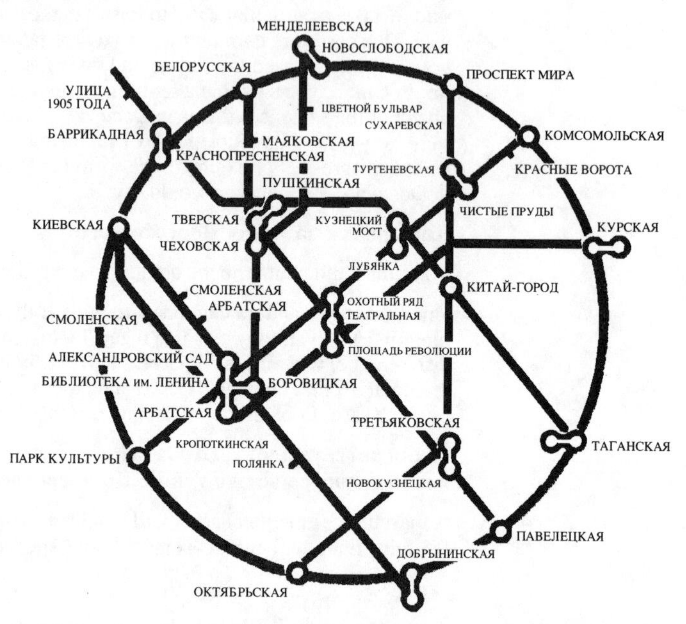

(i) **Большóй теáтр — на метрó до стáнции 'Театрáльная'**
(ii) **Кремль и Крáсная плóщадь — на метрó до стáнции 'Китáй-гóрод'**
(iii) **Третьякóвская галерéя — на метрó до стáнции 'Новокузнéцкая'**
(iv) **Дани́лов монасты́рь — на метрó до стáнции 'Тýльская'**
(v) **Арбáт — на метрó до стáнции 'Арбáтская' и́ли 'Смолéнская'**
(vi) **Музéй Л.Н. Толстóго — на метрó до стáнции 'Кропóткинская'**
(vii) **Кинотеáтр 'Росси́я' — на метрó до стáнции 'Пýшкинская'**

10

Below are two types of tickets commonly used by Muscovites. On what forms of transportation can they use each ticket?
(Answers on page 108.)

(i)

(ii)

....

Did you know?

Getting around in the city

For many years visitors to the Soviet Union were quietly discouraged from travelling around the city by themselves. Tourists were transported from one worthwhile 'sight' to another by coach, and rarely met Soviet people.

Fortunately the atmosphere has changed, and since public transport within cities is good, if crowded, we would recommend that you make your own way about. Especially now that you have learned to ask directions!

Some of the large cities have good underground systems, as well as trolleybuses, trams and buses. In the main cities you will also find **маршру́тные такси́**, minibuses carrying about 10 passengers which follow a fixed route (normally indicated on the side window). You can ask the driver to stop anywhere along the route (just give the name of the place with **пожа́луйста**). Finding a taxi has become quite a problem unless you're outside a hotel, where there are always those wanting to earn some foreign currency. You probably won't need your Russian though – they seem to be able to negotiate their deals in any language!

Tickets

There are special barriers on the underground which only let you through after you have put in your money. However, to use trolleybuses, trams or buses, you need **тало́ны** or, more colloquially, **тало́нчики**. These small tickets are available in booklets of 10, either in special kiosks on the street, or from the driver at a stop. If you are near the little machine, you can clip the ticket yourself. However, if you are wedged in among other commuters, hand it to somebody and say **передáйте, пожа́луйста** (pass it along please). The ticket will soon come back clipped! Those who use public transportation a great deal buy the more economical and convenient **еди́ный**, a travel pass valid for one month.

By the way, despite inevitable tension and friction caused by overcrowding, it is unusual for children or elderly people to have to stand in public transportation.

Moscow

Your turn to speak

11

You have just arrived in Moscow. You need to find out where the chemist (pharmacy) is, how to get to Pushkin square, which trolleybuses go to Arbat and where the trolleybus stop is. You will be using the following phrases:

извини́те, пожа́луйста, ...
скажи́те, пожа́луйста, ...
где здесь...?
как прое́хать в/на...?
како́й тролле́йбус идёт до...?
а где остано́вка?

Answers

Practise what you have learned

Exercise **1**	(i) кафе́ (ii) магази́н (iii) музе́й (iv) библиоте́ка
Exercise **2**	(i) straight ahead, then left (ii) store is *next* to underground station (iii) Pushkin museum is around the corner
Exercise **3**	(i) c (ii) a (iii) b
Exercise **4**	(i) Китай-город (ii) Кропоткинская (iii) Театральная
Exercise **5**	(i) b (ii) c (iii) a

Grammar

Exercise **7**	(i) в Минск (ii) в Оде́ссу (iii) в Ки́ев (iv) в Полта́ву (v) в Москву́ (vi) в Петербу́рг
Exercise **8**	(i) до по́чты (ii) до магази́на (iii) до теа́тра (iv) до апте́ки (v) до рестора́на

Read and understand

Exercise **10**	(i) all types of city transportation (ii) all types except underground

9

MAKING TRAVEL ARRANGEMENTS

You will learn

- to ask how to get to places outside the city
- to buy train and plane tickets
- to ask for information about departure times, where to go, etc.
- to hire a car

and you will read about travel within the Russian Federation

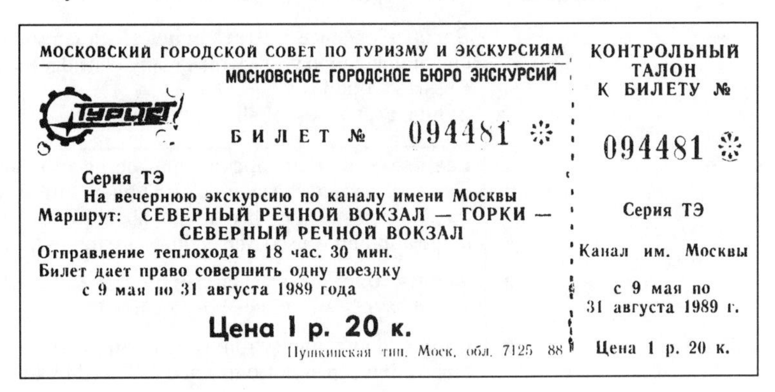

МОСКОВСКИЙ ГОРОДСКОЙ СОВЕТ ПО ТУРИЗМУ И ЭКСКУРСИЯМ
МОСКОВСКОЕ ГОРОДСКОЕ БЮРО ЭКСКУРСИЙ
Турист
БИЛЕТ № 094481
Серия ТЭ
На вечернюю экскурсию по каналу имени Москвы
Маршрут: СЕВЕРНЫЙ РЕЧНОЙ ВОКЗАЛ — ГОРКИ — СЕВЕРНЫЙ РЕЧНОЙ ВОКЗАЛ
Отправление теплохода в 18 час. 30 мин.
Билет дает право совершить одну поездку
с 9 мая по 31 августа 1989 года
Цена 1 р. 20 к.
Пушкинская тип. Моск. обл. 7125 88

КОНТРОЛЬНЫЙ ТАЛОН К БИЛЕТУ №
094481
Серия ТЭ
Канал им. Москвы
с 9 мая по 31 августа 1989 г.
Цена 1 р. 20 к.

Study guide

- **Dialogue 1:** listen without the book
- **Dialogue 1:** listen, read and study
- Practise what you have learned
- **Dialogues 2, 3:** listen without the book
- **Dialogues 2, 3:** listen, read and study one by one
- Practise what you have learned
- **Dialogues 4, 5:** listen without the book
- **Dialogues 4, 5:** listen, read and study one by one
- Practise what you have learned
- **Dialogues 6, 7:** listen without the book
- **Dialogues 6, 7:** listen, read and study one by one
- Practise what you have learned
- Study the **Key words and phrases**
- Study the **Grammar** section carefully
- Do the exercises in **Read and understand**
- Read **Did you know?**
- Do the exercises in **Your turn to speak**
- Listen to all the dialogues once again straight through

Dialogues

1 *Tamara wants to know how to get to Zagorsk*

Tamara Извини́те, вы не ска́жете, как дое́хать до Заго́рска?
Passer-by Лу́чше всего́ на электри́чке.
Tamara Прости́те, а с како́го вокза́ла?
Passer-by С Яросла́вского.
Tamara Большо́е спаси́бо.
Passer-by Пожа́луйста.

Заго́рск or, since 1991, **Се́ргиев Поса́д**, a small city outside Moscow, containing a monastery which many consider the spiritual centre of the Russian Orthodox Church
лу́чше всего́ best of all

- **как дое́хать до Заго́рска?** how do I get to Zagorsk? Yes, the verb *has* changed! **Как дое́хать до...?** isn't much different from **как прое́хать в/на...?**, but it's better when talking about places further away. Since the preposition **до** is used, the endings are those discussed on page 105.
- **на электри́чке** on a suburban train. If Zagorsk were further away, she would have heard **на по́езде** on a train.
- **С како́го вокза́ла?** from which station? A railway station is **вокза́л**. The preposition **с** means 'from' when followed by this genitive ending.

с Яросла́вского from Yaroslavsky station; the word for station has been left out since it is understood.

A station

Practise what you have learned

1 Below is a diagram showing five of Moscow's railway stations and the directions in which they face. Underneath is a jumbled list of cities which one can reach from these stations. After reading it, listen carefully to the dialogues and fill in the city which each arrow is pointing towards. (Answers on page 122.)

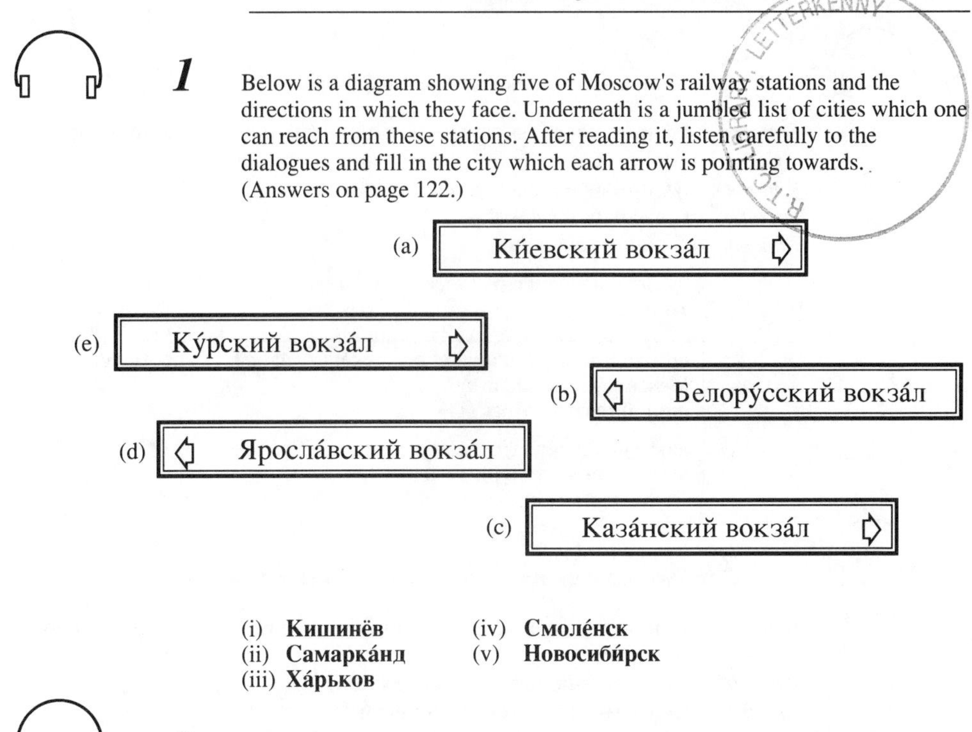

(i) **Кишинёв**
(ii) **Самарка́нд**
(iii) **Ха́рьков**
(iv) **Смоле́нск**
(v) **Новосиби́рск**

2 You will be trying to get to one of the above places. Listen to Andrei's prompts.

A departure and arrivals board

Dialogues

2 *At the station Tamara buys a ticket to Zagorsk*

Tamara Бу́дьте любе́зны, да́йте, пожа́луйста, оди́н биле́т до Заго́рска.
Clerk Вам туда́ и обра́тно и́ли то́лько в оди́н коне́ц?
Tamara Бу́дьте любе́зны, туда́ и обра́тно.
Clerk С вас рубль де́сять.
Tamara Большо́е спаси́бо.

бу́дьте любе́зны please, be so kind
то́лько only

- **оди́н биле́т до Заго́рска** one ticket to Zagorsk. If you wanted a ticket to Moscow you would ask for:
оди́н биле́т до Москвы́
- **вам туда́ и обра́тно?** do you want a return ticket?
в оди́н коне́ц a single ticket

3 *She asks a young woman when the next train will be*

Tamara Извини́те, вы не ска́жете, когда́ ближа́йшая электри́чка до Заго́рска?
Woman Че́рез пятна́дцать мину́т, в 17.30.
Tamara Скажи́те, а с како́й платфо́рмы?
Woman То́чно не по́мню, ка́жется со второ́й. Посмотри́те на табло́.
Tamara Большо́е спаси́бо.
Woman Пожа́луйста.

- **когда́ ближа́йшая электри́чка до Заго́рска?** when is the next train to Zagorsk? A more common way of saying 'the next train' is **сле́дующая электри́чка**.
Электри́чка is a feminine noun. A long-distance train is **по́езд**. Since this noun is masculine, the question would become:
когда́ ближа́йший (or **сле́дующий**) **по́езд до Ки́ева?** when is the next train to Kiev?
Some other useful questions:
Когда́ пе́рвая электри́чка до Заго́рска? when is the *first* train to Zagorsk?
Когда́ после́дняя электри́чка до Москвы́? when is the last train to Moscow?
- **че́рез пятна́дцать мину́т** in 15 minutes. Not too long to wait – she might have been told **че́рез полчаса́** in half an hour, or **че́рез час** in an hour.
- **с како́й платфо́рмы?** from which platform? The word **платфо́рма** is feminine.
- **со второ́й** from the second (this *is* the same preposition 'from' – it is simply impossible to pronounce without the **o**!)
- **то́чно не по́мню** I don't remember exactly
ка́жется I think, it seems (to me)
Beware of such words – if you hear too many in one response, you may want to ask someone else!
- **посмотри́те на табло́** look at the board. In a smaller station, you might be told: **посмотри́те на расписа́ние** look at the timetable.

Practise what you have learned

3 Three friends went on daytrips out of Moscow. Well, they were *supposed* to be daytrips... However, only one bought a return ticket, and the others were stranded. Listen to your recording, then write down what each asked for. (Answers on page 122.)

(i) **Да́йте, пожа́луйста, оди́н биле́т** ....
Вам туда́ и обра́тно и́ли то́лько в оди́н коне́ц? ....

(ii) **Да́йте, пожа́луйста, оди́н биле́т** ....
Вам туда́ и обра́тно и́ли то́лько в оди́н коне́ц? ....

(iii) **Да́йте, пожа́луйста, оди́н биле́т** ....
Вам туда́ и обра́тно и́ли то́лько в оди́н коне́ц? ....

4 Below are signs above platforms in a Moscow railway station. Only the destination is shown. If you listen carefully to the following snatches of conversation, you should be able to add the time of departure and the platform. (Answers on page 122.)

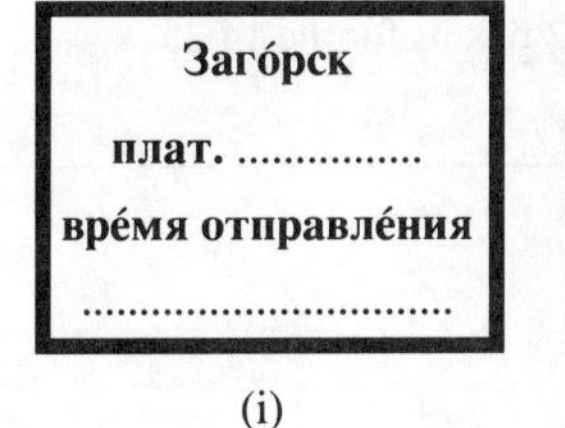
Заго́рск
плат. ....
вре́мя отправле́ния
....

(i)

Клин
плат. ....
вре́мя отправле́ния
....

(ii)

Я́сная Поля́на
плат. ....
вре́мя отправле́ния
....

(iii)

5 You are a tourist wanting to go to Vladimir. As usual, Andrei will guide you.

Dialogues

4 *Ira is at the Aeroflot desk of her hotel booking a flight*

Ira Здрáвствуйте.
Clerk Дóбрый день.
Ira У вас есть билéты до Петербýрга на зáвтра?
Clerk А скóлько вам мест нýжно?
Ira Два.
Clerk Сейчáс посмотрю́... На зáвтра, к сожалéнию, мест нет.

к сожалéнию [ksazhalyényu] unfortunately

- **скóлько вам мест нýжно?** how many seats do you need?
- **сейчáс посмотрю́** I'll just have a look
- **мест нет** there aren't any seats. **Мест** is the genitive plural of **мéсто**, a neuter noun.

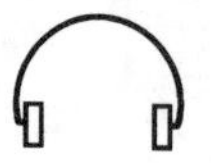

5 *Maybe there are seats for the day after tomorrow?*

Ira А на послезáвтра?
Clerk Оди́н момéнт... На послезáвтра, пожáлуйста, на рéйсы в 7.35, в 14.25, в 18.35 местá есть.
Ira Дáйте, пожáлуйста, два билéта на 14.25.
Clerk Пожáлуйста, кáсса ря́дом, уплати́те, пожáлуйста, за билéт.
Ira Спаси́бо.
Clerk Всегó наилýчшего. Счастли́вого полёта!

оди́н момéнт one moment
кáсса ря́дом the cashier is at the next desk
уплати́те, пожáлуйста, за билéт pay (there) please for the ticket
всегó наилýчшего all the best
счастли́вого полёта! have a good flight!

- **а на послезáвтра?** what about the day after tomorrow? If Ira needed to travel on a specific day of the week she would ask for **билéт на понедéльник, на втóрник, на срéду** etc.
- **на рéйсы в 7.35, в 14.25, в 18.35 местá есть** there are seats on flights at 7.35, at 14.25 and at 18.35
- **два билéта на 14.25** 2 tickets for the 14.25
- **самолёт** aeroplane

Practise what you have learned

6 The Aeroflot assistant has a list of flights still available, with a note of how many tickets are available on each. Listen to your recording. Cross out any flights on your list which are now fully booked. Readjust the number of seats available after all three customers have been served. (Answers on page 122.)

(i)	**на сего́дня**	(12.25)	**(оди́н биле́т)**
(ii)	**на за́втра**	(14.25)	**(два биле́та)**
(iii)	**на послеза́втра**	(18.35)	**(четы́ре биле́та)**

7 You will be buying tickets for flights to Moscow. Listen to Andrei for full details

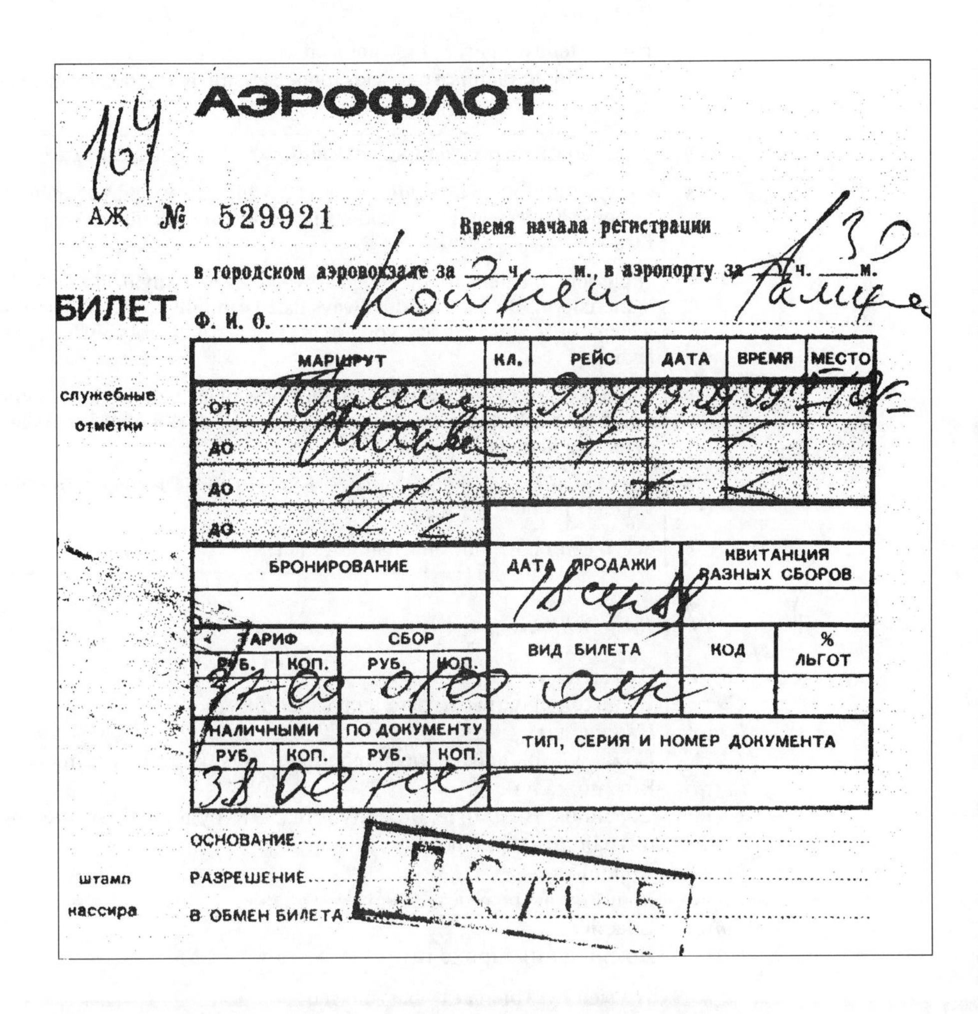

АЭРОФЛОТ

АЖ № 529921

Время начала регистрации

в городском аэровокзале за ___ ч. ___ м., в аэропорту за ___ ч. ___ м.

БИЛЕТ

Ф. И. О. ....

служебные отметки

МАРШРУТ	КЛ.	РЕЙС	ДАТА	ВРЕМЯ	МЕСТО
от					
до					
до					
до					

БРОНИРОВАНИЕ	ДАТА ПРОДАЖИ	КВИТАНЦИЯ РАЗНЫХ СБОРОВ

ТАРИФ		СБОР		ВИД БИЛЕТА	КОД	% ЛЬГОТ
РУБ.	КОП.	РУБ.	КОП.			

НАЛИЧНЫМИ		ПО ДОКУМЕНТУ		ТИП, СЕРИЯ И НОМЕР ДОКУМЕНТА
РУБ.	КОП.	РУБ.	КОП.	

ОСНОВАНИЕ ....

штамп кассира

РАЗРЕШЕНИЕ ....

В ОБМЕН БИЛЕТА ....

Dialogues

6 *At her hotel Tanya asks about hiring a car*

Tanya Здра́вствуйте.
Clerk Здра́вствуйте.
Tanya У вас мо́жно взять напрока́т маши́ну?
Clerk Пожа́луйста. Каку́ю маши́ну вы предпочита́ете?
Tanya Сре́днюю.
Clerk Я рекоменду́ю вам Ни́сан Блубе́рд.
Tanya Хорошо́. А ско́лько э́то бу́дет сто́ить в день?
Clerk Э́то сто́ит 40 до́лларов без страхо́вки.
Tanya А всего́ ско́лько?
Clerk Всего́ э́то бу́дет сто́ить 40 до́лларов плюс 3 до́ллара страхо́вка плюс бензи́н.

я рекоменду́ю вам... I recommend...
плюс три до́ллара страхо́вка плюс бензи́н plus 3 dollars insurance, plus petrol

- **у вас мо́жно взять напрока́т маши́ну?** can I hire a car here?
- **каку́ю маши́ну вы предпочита́ете?** which car would you prefer? In her response Tanya could have said **я предпочита́ю** I prefer, or simply **я хочу́** I want.
- **сре́днюю** medium sized. A big car would be **большу́ю** and a small one **ма́ленькую**. By the way, do always listen carefully to the ending of **како́й?** which? since any adjective you use in response will probably have the same ending.
- **Ско́лько э́то бу́дет сто́ить в день?** how much will that cost per day? She might have asked how much it will cost per week **ско́лько э́то бу́дет сто́ить в неде́лю?**
- **без страхо́вки** without insurance. **Без** 'without' is another preposition which is followed by the genitive case.
- **всего́ ско́лько?** how much all together?

7 *Tanya will take it*

Tanya Э́то меня́ устра́ивает.
Clerk На како́й срок вы хоти́те взять маши́ну?
Tanya На неде́лю.
Clerk Пожа́луйста, да́йте мне свою́ креди́тную ка́рточку и права́.
Tanya Вот, пожа́луйста.
Clerk Спаси́бо... Возьми́те, пожа́луйста... Э́то бу́дет сто́ить вам три́ста пятна́дцать до́лларов.
Tanya Хорошо́.
Clerk Маши́ну вы возьмёте в на́шем гараже́.
Tanya Спаси́бо.
Clerk До свида́ния, приходи́те ещё.

э́то меня́ устра́ивает that suits me
права́ driver's licence (plural in Russian)
в на́шем гараже́ in our garage
приходи́те ещё come again

- **на какóй срок?** for what period of time?

  на недéлю for a week. Or you might want it for two weeks **на две недéли**.

- **дáйте мне своıó кредúтную кáрточку и правá** give me your credit card and driving licence

  своıó/вáшу – both forms are possible here. There is more about **свой, своя́, своё** on page 138.

- **возьмúте, пожáлуйста** take (it) please. The two other forms of the verb **взять** 'to take' you will need are:
  я возьмý I will take
  вы возьмёте you will take

- **трúста** three hundred. Four hundred is **четы́реста** and five hundred **пятьсóт**.

Practise what you have learned

8 In the dialogue below Oleg is looking for a small car. Certain key words have been left out and are jumbled up in the box below. Listen to your recording, then fill in the gaps. (Answers on page 122.)

Oleg **Скóлько бýдет стóить мáленькая машúна в** ....(i) **?**

Clerk **50 дóлларов** ....(ii) **страхóвки**

Oleg **А** ....(iii) **скóлько?**

Clerk **Всегó э́то бýдет стóить 50 дóлларов плюс** ....(iv) **дóллара страхóвка** ....(v) **бензúн.**

Oleg **Э́то меня́ устрáивает.**

Clerk ....(vi) **какóй срок вы хотúте взять машúну?**

Oleg **На** ....(vii)

Clerk **Пожáлуйста, дáйте мне вáшу кредúтную кáрточку и** ....(viii)

Oleg **Вот, пожáлуйста.**

правá	**без**	**на**	**всегó**	**недéлю**	**три**	**день**	**плюс**

9 You are a visitor to Moscow on a fairly limited budget. You will be practising asking for different sizes of car, saying how long you need the car for and asking the crucial question about cost.

Key words and phrases

To use

как доéхать до Загóрска?	how do I get to Zagorsk?
с какóго вокзáла?	from which station?
одúн билéт	one ticket
два (три, четы́ре) билéта	two (three, four) tickets
до Петербýрга	to St. Petersburg
до Москвы́	to Moscow
тудá и обрáтно	there and back
в одúн конéц	one way
когдá слéдующая электрúчка до...?	when is the next suburban train to...?
когдá слéдующий пóезд до...?	when is the next train to...?
с какóй платфóрмы?	from which platform?
у вас есть билéты...	do you have tickets...
на сегóдня?	for today?
на зáвтра?	for tomorrow?
на послезáвтра?	for the day after tomorrow?
на рейс в 14.25?	for the flight at 14.25?
у вас мóжно взять напрокáт...	do you have for hire...
машúну?	a car?
мáленькую машúну?	a small car?
срéднюю машúну?	a medium car?
большýю машúну?	a big car?
скóлько э́то бýдет стóить ...	how much will that cost...
в день?	per day?
в недéлю?	per week?
всегó скóлько?	how much all together?
взять (я возьмý, вы возьмёте)	to take (I will take, you will take)
я хочý взять /я возьмý машúну...	I want to take / I will take the car...
на недéлю	for a week
на две недéли	for two weeks

To understand

на электрúчке	by suburban train
на пóезде	by train
чéрез пятнáдцать минýт	in fifteen minutes
посмотрúте на таблó	look at the board
скóлько вам мест нýжно?	how many seats do you need?
на зáвтра мест нет	there are no seats tomorrow
на зáвтра местá есть	there are seats tomorrow
на какóй срок вы хотúте взять машúну?	for how long would you like the car?
без страхóвки	without insurance
плюс бензúн	plus petrol

Grammar

Verbs

Russian verbs have six different endings depending on *who* is performing the action. There are patterns which you can follow in order to work out the ending for a verb you have never seen before. The first type of verb 'conjugates' (changes its endings) like the verb **знать** (to know):

я зна́ю	I know
ты зна́ешь	you know (sing. to a child or a friend)
он/она́ зна́ет	he/she knows
мы зна́ем	we know
вы зна́ете	you know (pl. or more formal)
они́ зна́ют	they know

The verbs **за́втракать** (to have breakfast), **обе́дать** (to have lunch), **у́жинать** (to have dinner) conjugate in this way, as does the important verb **понима́ть** (to understand).

There are also many verbs whose infinitives end in **-еть** or **-ить**. Most of these will conjugate like **говори́ть** (to speak):

я говорю́	I speak
ты говори́шь	you speak (sing. to a child or a friend)
он/она́ говори́т	he/she speaks
мы говори́м	we speak
вы говори́те	you speak (pl. or more formal)
они́ говоря́т	they speak

Here are three important verbs that follow the same pattern:
смотре́ть (to look, watch)
сто́ить (to cost)
по́мнить (to remember)

A word of warning: You can't be sure that a verb will follow the above patterns. There are quite a lot of irregular verbs which unfortunately just have to be learned.

10

Write in the correct forms of the verbs in brackets. (Answers on page 122.)

(i) **Что вы ....? — Я .... журна́л. (чита́ть** – to read)

(ii) **Ско́лько .... э́та ма́рка для авиаконве́рта в А́нглию? (сто́ить)**

(iii) **Они́ .... до́ма, а .... в рестора́не. (за́втракать, обе́дать)**

(iv) **Вы .... по-ру́сски? — Да, я .... немно́го. (говори́ть)**

(v) **Мы не ...., где э́то кафе́. (знать)**

(vi) **Она́ хорошо́ .... по-францу́зски. (понима́ть)**

(vii) **Ве́чером мы .... му́зыку. (слу́шать** – to listen to)

(viii) **Ты .... по-неме́цки? — Нет, но я .... по-неме́цки. (говори́ть, чита́ть)**

(ix) **Он не ...., где нахо́дится музе́й. (по́мнить)**

(x) **Помидо́ры .... 4 рубля́ килогра́мм. (сто́ить)**

New words:
до́ма at home
ве́чером in the evening

Read and understand

11

Nina has come to the Russian Federation determined to see places with which her favourite writers were connected. So she tells the Intourist guide, whose itinerary goes nowhere *near* those places! Undeterred, Nina finds the necessary timetables and proves to her guide that her plans are quite feasible. What will her revised programme look like?

INTOURIST PROGRAMME

Гóрод	**прибы́тие**	**отправлéние**
Санкт-Петербýрг	**1/7**	**2/7 (ýтром)**
Нóвгород	**2/7**	**5/7 (вéчером)**
Санкт-Петербýрг	**6/7 (ýтром)**	**7/7**
Ростóв Вели́кий	**7/7**	**9/7**
Москвá	**9/7 (вéчером)**	**12/7**
Новосиби́рск	**13/7 (ýтром)**	**14/7**
Иркýтск	**15/7 (ýтром)**	**18/7**
Москвá	**19/7**	**20/7**

New words:

прибы́тие arrival
отправлéние departure
ýтром in the morning

Here are the various possibilities Nina noted from the timetables, *before* she'd seen the Intourist programme.

Автóбус: Нóвгород – Михáйловское

	тудá	обрáтно
2/7	9 ч. утрá	11 ч. вéчера
4/7	8 ч. утрá	10 ч. вéчера
5/7	9 ч. утрá	11 ч. вéчера

Электри́чка: Санкт-Петербýрг – Цáрское Селó

1/7	9 ч. вéчера	2/7	10 ч. утрá
6/7	11 ч. утрá	7/7	9 ч. вéчера
9/7	10 ч. утрá	9/7	7 ч. вéчера

Автóбус: Москвá – Я́сная Поля́на

9/7	7 ч. утрá	9/7	9 ч. вéчера
11/7	7 ч. утрá	11/7	9 ч. вéчера
11/7	5 ч. вéчера	12/7	9 ч. вéчера

Михáйловское – the estate of the great Russian poet Alexander Sergeevich Pushkin.
Цáрское Селó – home of the famous Lycée at which Pushkin and some other poets of the time studied.
Я́сная Поля́на – estate of Leo Tolstoy.

Did you know?

How Russian people travel

The number of private car owners in the Russian Federation is relatively low. Many Russian-made cars such as Lada are easier and much cheaper to buy abroad than in their country of origin! It should not, however, be assumed that the roads are correspondingly safer. They are not! The number of accidents per year is quite disproportionate to the number of cars on the road.

Most people use trains and aeroplanes when travelling long distances. A train journey over one or two days can be a very enjoyable way of meeting Russian people in a relaxed environment. Travellers generally change into comfortable casual clothing and bring bagloads of provisions, as well as cards or chess to while away the time.

Particularly over the summer months it can be quite difficult to obtain tickets. This is nothing, however, in comparison with the problems involved in getting aeroplane tickets. Branches of Aeroflot frequently have queues overflowing into the street, while even a ticket in hand by no means guarantees that you will fly on the day and time designated.

Russian people have necessarily become hardened to such difficulties, and are seldom deterred from travelling.

Travel abroad

Until recently this was merely a dream for all but a privileged few. People quite simply did not have international passports. To obtain one required a 'good' reason for travelling and political 'reliability'. There would also be a stream of bureaucratic demands. The authorities could – and did – refuse people without providing any reason.

The end of the 1980s saw an increase in the number of people granted visas, and a new law which came into effect in January 1993 affirms the right of all citizens to an international passport.

Sheremetyevo 2, Moscow's international airport

Your turn to speak

12

Below is a map of the Russian Federation. We have marked certain famous places, though you may of course be interested in visiting others. The itinerary this time is in your hands! *Before* turning on the recording, work out where you wish to go, then try organising your trip. You will need to ask how to get to places, buy tickets, find out about the next train, flight etc. You may also want to hire a car. And of course you will have to convince Intourist that you know what you are doing!

Here are some useful phrases:

как доéхать до...? how does one get to...?
у вас есть билéты до...? do you have tickets to...?
на зáвтра? / на послезáвтра? for tomorrow? / for the day after tomorrow?
оди́н билéт до..., пожáлуйста one ticket to..., please
тудá и обрáтно there and back
у вас мóжно взять напрокáт маши́ну? can I hire a car here?
я хочý мáленькую маши́ну I want a small car
я хочý доéхать до... I'd like to get to...
нáдо купи́ть... / взять напрокáт... I have to buy... / hire...

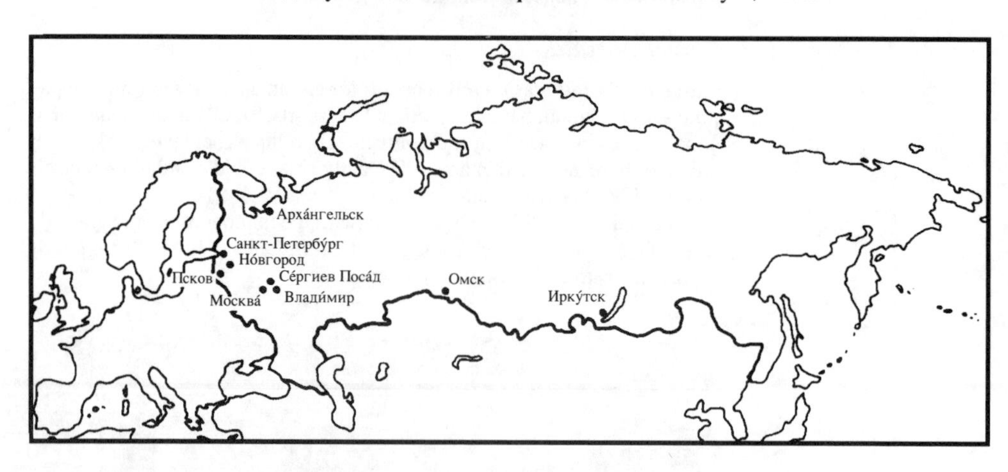

Answers

Practise what you have learned

Exercise **1**	(i) a (ii) c (iii) e (iv) b (v) d
Exercise **3**	(i) до Загóрска, в оди́н конéц (ii) до Влади́мира, в оди́н конéц (iii) до Загóрска, тудá и обрáтно
Exercise **4**	(i) 3; 6.30 (ii) 2; 7 часóв (iii) 5; 10.15
Exercise **6**	(i) мест нет (ii) мест нет (iii) 1 билéт
Exercise **8**	(i) день (ii) без (iii) всегó (iv) три (v) плюс (vi) на (vii) недéлю (viii) правá

Grammar

Exercise **10**	(i) читáете; читáю (ii) стóит (iii) зáвтракают, обéдают (iv) говори́те; говорю́ (v) знáем (vi) понимáет (vii) слýшаем (viii) говори́шь; читáю (ix) пóмнит (x) стóят

10

ORDERING A MEAL

You will learn

- to make a booking in a restaurant
- to order a meal for one and for a group
- to ask for vegetarian dishes
- to find out about drinks
- to ask for the bill

and you will read about how Russians entertain

Before you begin

You will find it useful to look over Unit 4 in conjunction with this unit.

Study guide

Dialogues 1, 2: listen without the book
Dialogues 1, 2: listen, read and study one by one
Practise what you have learned
Dialogues 3, 4: listen without the book
Dialogues 3, 4: listen, read and study one by one
Practise what you have learned
Dialogues 5–7: listen without the book
Dialogues 5–7: listen, read and study one by one
Practise what you have learned
Study the **Key words and phrases**
Study the **Grammar** section carefully
Do the exercises in **Read and understand**
Read **Did you know?**
Do the exercises in **Your turn to speak**
Listen to all the dialogues once again straight through

Dialogues

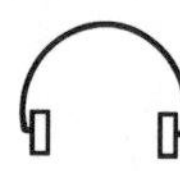

1 *Tanya has dropped in at a cooperative café for lunch*

Tanya Здра́вствуйте.
Waiter До́брый день.
Tanya Да́йте, пожа́луйста, меню́.
Waiter Прошу́ ознако́миться.
Tanya Здесь так мно́го блюд. А что вы порекоменду́ете?
Waiter На холо́дное я вам порекоменду́ю ло́био. Э́то блю́до грузи́нской ку́хни, о́чень вку́сное.
Tanya А на горя́чее?
Waiter А на горя́чее – я так ду́маю, что ки́евскую котле́ту.
Tanya Спаси́бо.

меню́ menu
прошу́ ознако́миться please look at it
ло́био a Georgian vegetable dish with green beans and walnuts
вку́сный, -ая, -ое tasty

- **здесь так мно́го блюд** there are so many dishes here. **Мно́го** 'much/many' is always followed by a noun in the genitive case. **Блюд** is the genitive plural of **блю́до**.
- **что вы порекоменду́ете?** what would you recommend?

  я порекоменду́ю I would recommend
- **на холо́дное** for the cold dish, hors d'oeuvres
  на горя́чее for the hot dish
  Instead of **на холо́дное** you will often hear **на заку́ску**, while **на горя́чее** is another way of saying **на второ́е** for the second course. On this occasion no first course of soup was offered.
- **блю́до грузи́нской ку́хни** a Georgian dish. You might also be offered:
  блю́до ру́сской ку́хни a Russian dish
  блю́до украи́нской ку́хни a Ukrainian dish
- **я так ду́маю, что ки́евскую котле́ту** I would think Kiev cutlet. Although the meaning is clear, this sentence does not bear grammatical scrutiny!

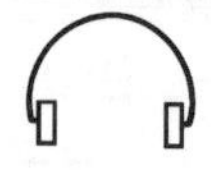

2 *Tanya has finished her meal*

Tanya Спаси́бо за сове́т. Всё бы́ло о́чень вку́сно.
Waiter А что вам принести́ на десе́рт?
Tanya Спаси́бо, я уже́ сыта́. Е́сли мо́жно, ча́шечку ко́фе.
Waiter Бу́дет испо́лнено.

бу́дет испо́лнено it will be done

- **спаси́бо за сове́т** thank you for the advice. 'For' in this sense is **за**. 'Thank you for everything' would be **спаси́бо за всё**.
- **всё бы́ло о́чень вку́сно** it was all very tasty. If you are still eating, you can use the present tense: **всё о́чень вку́сно** it's all very tasty.
- **что вам принести́ на десе́рт?** what can I bring you for dessert? That day the café offered **моро́женое** ice cream, **компо́т** fruit compote, **ро́мовая ба́ба** rum baba and **блины́** pancakes.
- **я уже́ сыта́** I'm already full. A man would say: **я уже́ сыт**.
- **е́сли мо́жно, ча́шечку ко́фе** if possible a cup of coffee. Once again the verb has been left out. She might have said **принеси́те** bring me.
  Ча́шечку is a common diminutive form. You could also ask for **ча́шку ко́фе**.

Practise what you have learned

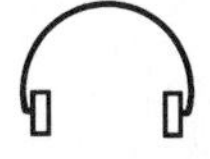

1

The café in the dialogues offers dishes of many nationalities. In the menu, the dishes and their origins are mixed up. If you listen to the following snatches of conversation, you will be able to match them correctly. (Answers on page 134.)

МЕНЮ́

(i) **котле́ты полта́вские**	(a) блю́до грузи́нской ку́хни
(ii) **беф-стро́ганов**	(b) блю́до украи́нской ку́хни
(iii) **хачапу́ри** (cheese dish)	(c) блю́до ру́сской ку́хни

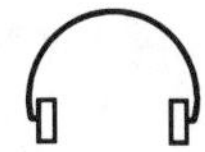

2

Read the following dialogue and see if you can work out which words are missing before listening to your recording. (Answers on page 134.)

Lyena **Спаси́бо** (i) .... **сове́т. Всё бы́ло о́чень** (ii) ....

Waiter **А что вам принести́** (iii) .... **десе́рт?**

Lyena **Спаси́бо, я уже́** (iv) .... **Е́сли мо́жно,** (v) .... **ко́фе.**

Waiter **Пожа́луйста.**

3

Your name is Lara, and you are looking for a lightish meal. Andrei will prompt you.

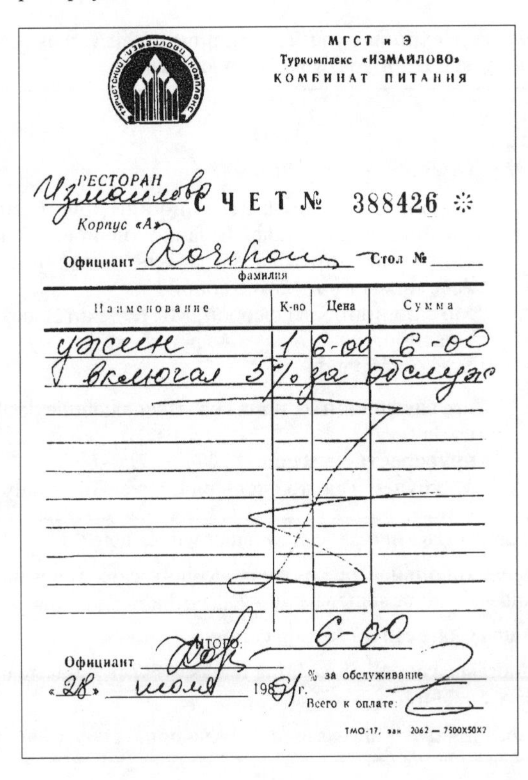

МГСТ и Э
Туркомплекс «ИЗМАЙЛОВО»
КОМБИНАТ ПИТАНИЯ

РЕСТОРАН Измайлово СЧЕТ № 388426
Корпус «А»
Официант ____________ Стол № ____
фамилия

Наименование	К-во	Цена	Сумма
ужин	1	6-00	6-00
включая 5% за обслуж.			

Итого: 6-00
Официант ____________
«28» июля 198_ г.
% за обслуживание
Всего к оплате:

ТМО-17. зак 2062 — 7500Х50Х2

Dialogues

3 *Pavel wants to book a table for this evening*

Pavel Дóбрый вéчер.
Waiter Дóбрый вéчер.
Pavel Вы знáете, у моéй жены́ сегóдня день рождéния.
Waiter Я вас поздравля́ю.
Pavel Могу́ я заказáть сегóдня стóлик?
Waiter Безуслóвно. На котóрый час?
Pavel Часóв на семь, на пять человéк.
Waiter Девятнáдцать ноль ноль, пять персóн. В восемнáдцать три́дцать мы вас ждём.

безуслóвно of course, without a doubt

- **у моéй жены́ сегóдня день рождéния** it's my wife's birthday today. If it was *your* birthday, you would say **у меня́ сегóдня день рождéния**.
- **я вас поздравля́ю** congratulations. More commonly addressed to the person whose birthday it is, but then this waiter has a style of his own...
- **могу́ я заказáть сегóдня стóлик?** may I order a table today? It is more correct to say 'for today' – **на сегóдня**. **Могу́ я...?** can I...? is another way of asking **мóжно...?**
- **на котóрый час?** for what time? Pavel uses **на** in his answer: **часóв на семь** for about seven. You put the noun *before* the number in Russian to indicate *approximation*.
- **на пять человéк** for five people. If there were 2, 3 or 4 he would have said: **на 2, 3, 4 человéка**.
- **Девятнáдцать ноль ноль, пять персóн** 19.00, 5 persons. speak!
- **мы вас ждём** we're expecting you. The infinitive of this verb is **ждать** to expect, to wait for – 'I am expecting/waiting for you' would be **я вас жду**.

4 *Does the café sell alcohol?*

Pavel А мóжно у вас заказáть винó и́ли други́е спиртны́е напи́тки?
Waiter Вы знáете, у нас кафé безалкогóльное. Но приобрести́ и заказáть спиртны́е напи́тки у нас мóжно за валю́ту.
Pavel А éсли мы принесём с собóй?
Waiter Мóжно принести́ с собóй. Мы бу́дем тóлько óчень рáды. Ждём вас.
Pavel Спаси́бо.
Waiter Всегó дóброго.

други́е спиртны́е напи́тки other alcoholic drinks
но but
приобрести́ to acquire
Мы бу́дем тóлько óчень рáды we will be only too pleased

- **мóжно у вас заказáть винó...?** can we order wine... here?
- **у нас кафé безалкогóльное** ours is a non-alcoholic café. The waiter's interpretation of 'non-alcoholic' would seem to be somewhat loose!
- **мóжно за валю́ту** one can for foreign currency
- **éсли мы принесём с собóй?** if we bring it ourselves? If you were by yourself, you would ask: **éсли я принесу́ с собóй?**
- After **мóжно** the infinitive is always used: **мóжно принести́ с собóй** you can bring it with you.

Practise what you have learned

4 Listen to the snatches of conversation on your recording, then fill in the missing spaces in the waiter's list of bookings for the evening.
(Answers on page 134.)

	на котóрый час?	на скóлько человéк?
(i)	**6 часóв**	....
(ii)	....	**на два человéка**
(iii)	**6.30**	....
(iv)	....	**на одногó человéка**

5 Shura rings the café to book a table. Listen to the conversation, then decide which of the statements in your book are true, which false.
(Answers on page 134.)

(i) It is her husband's birthday today.
(ii) She wants a table for 7 people.
(iii) They will come at about 8 o'clock.
(iv) They can get wine but not other alcoholic drinks.

6 You are taking some Russian friends out to dinner. You'll need to book in advance. Listen for Andrei's prompts.

Dialogues

5 *Pavel and his friends are ready to order*

Waiter Добрый вечер. Я вас слушаю.
Pavel Пожалуйста, примите у нас заказ.
Waiter Я вас слушаю.
Pavel Мы решили взять 4 салата из холодных закусок, и из горячих закусок, пожалуйста, свинину по-гречески, свинину натуральную и одну, две свинины на косточке.
Waiter Хорошо.

свинина по-гречески Greek-style pork
свинина натуральная grilled pork
свинина на косточке pork on the bone

- **примите у нас заказ** take our order
- **я вас слушаю** lit. 'I am listening to you.' This is business-like but perfectly polite.
- **мы решили взять...** we have decided to take... If a man was ordering for himself only, he would say: **я решил взять....** A woman would say: **я решила взять...**
- **четыре салата из холодных закусок** four salads from the cold hors-d'oeuvres. Pavel makes a mistake in his next request – he says **из горячих закусок** 'from the hot hors-d'oeuvres', whereas in fact it is **из горячих блюд** 'from the hot *dishes*'. The preposition **из** (from) is also followed by genitive endings.

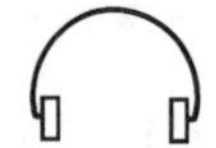

6 *Are there any vegetarian dishes?*

Pavel Вы знаете, вот среди нас есть один вегетарианец. Вы могли бы ему что-нибудь предложить?
Waiter Да, я могу предложить омлет с грибами, с сыром, он без мяса.
Pavel Хорошо, пожалуйста.

омлет с грибами, с сыром an omelette with mushrooms and cheese

- **среди нас есть...** in our group (lit. among us) there is...
- **вегетарианец** (m.) a vegetarian. A vegetarian woman is **вегетарианка**.
- **вы могли бы...?** would you be able to...? This is a very polite formula when making a request. It is commonly used in the negative: **вы не могли бы...?** you couldn't... could you?
- **ему что-нибудь предложить** to suggest something for him. You will find more about **ему** in the grammar section on page 131.
- **он без мяса** it (i.e. the omelette) is without meat. A vegetarian might also want to check that it has no fish: **без рыбы**, and a vegan that it has no dairy products: **без молочных продуктов**.

7 *They have finished the meal and are ready to pay*

Pavel Пожалуйста, принесите нам счёт.
Waiter Прошу вас, счёт готов.
Pavel Спасибо, сдачи не надо. Всё было очень вкусно. Благодарю вас.
Waiter Всего доброго.
Pavel До свидания.

прошу́ вас please
счёт гото́в the bill is ready
благодарю́ вас another way of saying 'thank you'
всего́ до́брого all the best

- **пожа́луйста, принеси́те нам счёт** please bring us our bill
- **сда́чи не на́до** keep the change (lit. no need for change)

Practise what you have learned

Read the menu below before beginning the exercises.

МЕНЮ́

ХОЛО́ДНЫЕ ЗАКУ́СКИ

(i) **сала́т 'Ле́тний'** ....
(ii) **сала́т из помидо́ров** (tomato salad) ....
(iii) **ло́био** ....
(iv) **кра́сная икра́** (red caviare) ....

ГОРЯ́ЧИЕ БЛЮ́ДА

(v) **грибы́ в смета́не** (mushrooms cooked in sour cream) ....
(vi) **свини́на натура́льная** ....
(vii) **свини́на по-гре́чески** ....
(viii) **бифште́кс натура́льный** (grilled beefsteak) ....
(ix) **пиро́г с ры́бой** (fish pie) ....
(x) **омле́т с гриба́ми и сыро́м** ....
(mushroom and cheese omelette)

7 Natasha is ordering for a group of eight people. Listen to the dialogue on your recording, then mark on the menu above how many portions they would like of each dish. (Answers on page 134.)

8 The waiter has never had a group like this before – vegetarians, a vegan, someone on a diet... Listen to your recording and write down how he caters for each person's needs. (Answers on page 134.)

New word: **ма́сло** butter, oil

(i) **что́-нибудь без мя́са** ....
(ii) **что́-нибудь без мя́са и без ры́бы** ....
(iii) **что́-нибудь без мя́са, ры́бы и моло́чных проду́ктов** ....
(iv) **что́-нибудь без ма́сла** ....

9 You will be ordering a meal for yourself and a friend.

Key words and phrases

To use

что вы порекоменду́ете...	what do you recommend...
на холо́дное?	for the cold dish?
на горя́чее?	for the hot dish?
вы могли́ бы что́-нибудь предложи́ть?	would you be able to suggest anything?
мо́жно (/ могу́ я) заказа́ть...	can I order...
сто́лик...	a table...
часо́в на семь?	for about 7 o'clock?
на пять челове́к?	for 5 people?
на 2, 3, 4 челове́ка?	for 2, 3, 4 people?
спиртны́е напи́тки?	alcoholic beverages?
ждать (я жду, мы ждём)	to wait (for), to expect (I am waiting, we are waiting)
принести́ (я принесу́, мы принесём)	to bring (I will bring, we will bring)
принеси́те, пожа́луйста, ...	bring me please...
счёт	the bill
меню́	the menu
прими́те у нас зака́з	take our order
мы реши́ли взять...	we have decided to have...
спаси́бо за сове́т	thank you for the advice
спаси́бо за всё	thank you for everything
всё бы́ло о́чень вку́сно	everything was very tasty
я уже́ сыта́ (f.) / **сыт** (m.)	I'm already full
сда́чи не на́до	keep the change

To understand

я порекоменду́ю...	I would recommend...
блю́до грузи́нской ку́хни	a Georgian dish
блю́до ру́сской ку́хни	a Russian dish
что вам принести́ на десе́рт?	what can I bring you for dessert?
на кото́рый час?	for what time?
у нас кафе́ безалкого́льное	our café is non-alcoholic
мо́жно за валю́ту	one can for foreign currency

Grammar

Pronouns

Pronouns are used instead of nouns when it's clear who is referred to, e.g.: *Tanya reads Pushkin.* ***She*** *reads Dostoevsky too.* Just as a noun can have many endings depending on its function in the sentence, so too can the pronoun.

The *dative* case is used to refer to the indirect object of a sentence, e.g. *give the book* ***to me***. Pronouns with dative endings are particularly useful when you are shopping or ordering meals, being used after verbs such as **дать** 'to give' (**да́йте мне...** give me...), **принести́** 'to bring' and **предложи́ть** 'to offer, suggest'. They are also used after **на́до** and **ну́жно**, both of which mean 'necessary', e.g. **мне на́до рабо́тать** 'I have to work', **вам ну́жен второ́й тролле́йбус** 'you need a No. 2 trolleybus'. Here are all the dative pronoun endings:

мне	to me
тебе́	to you (sing.)
ему́	to him
ей	to her
нам	to us
вам	to you (pl. or formal)
им	to them

Here is an example of how they work:

я хочу́ пообе́дать. Что вы мне порекоменду́ете?
ты хо́чешь пообе́дать? А что тебе́ принести́?
она́ хо́чет пообе́дать. Что вы ей порекоменду́ете?
мы хоти́м пообе́дать. Что вы нам порекоменду́ете?
вы хоти́те пообе́дать. Что вам принести́?
они́ хотя́т пообе́дать. Что вы им порекоменду́ете?

10

Fill in the missing pronouns in the following sentences. (Answers on page 134.)

(i) **Мы не зна́ем, что заказа́ть. Что вы .... порекоменду́ете?**

(ii) **Вы хоти́те прое́хать на Арба́т? .... ну́жен второ́й тролле́йбус.**

(iii) **Моя́ до́чка вегетариа́нка. Вы могли́ бы .... что́-нибудь предложи́ть?**

(iv) **Он не мо́жет обе́дать в рестора́не, ... на́до рабо́тать.**

(v) **Здесь так мно́го блюд. Что вы .... порекоменду́ете? Я .... порекоменду́ю ло́био.**

(vi) **Мы не хоти́м десе́рт. Принеси́те .... счёт, пожа́луйста.**

(vii) **Мой муж на дие́те. Вы не могли́ бы .... что́-нибудь предложи́ть?**

(viii) **Э́то на́ши де́ти. Да́йте .... что́-нибудь вку́сное на обе́д.**

Read and understand

11

Two cooperative cafés have opened in the centre of Moscow. Both hang the day's menu in the window. Read the menus, then decide which café would best suit each of the visitors to Moscow described below. (Answers on page 134.)

(a)

КООПЕРАТИ́ВНОЕ КАФЕ́ 'ТЕРЕМО́К'

Холо́дные блю́да

Ло́био
Блины́ с икро́й
Сала́т без ма́сла

Пе́рвые блю́да

Суп горо́ховый с мя́сом
Украи́нский борщ
Бульо́н

Вторы́е (горя́чие) блю́да

Грибы́ в смета́не
Свини́на натура́льная
Беф-стро́ганов
Бифште́кс натура́льный

Десе́рт

Моро́женое
Ро́мовая ба́ба
Фру́кты

(b)

КООПЕРАТИ́ВНОЕ КАФЕ́ 'МОСКВА́'

Холо́дные блю́да

Сала́т 'Ле́тний'
Сала́т 'Арба́т'
Икра́ кра́сная

Пе́рвые блю́да

Уха́ (ры́бный суп)
Бульо́н
Суп по-вегетариа́нски

Вторы́е (горя́чие) блю́да

Голубцы́
Грибы́ в смета́не
Пиро́г с ры́бой
Омле́т с гриба́ми

Десе́рт

Блины́ с варе́ньем
Моро́женое
Компо́т

New words:
голубцы́ stuffed cabbage
варе́нье jam

(i) Maria would like to try as many national dishes as possible.
(ii) Stefan is a vegetarian (he eats no meat or fish).
(iii) David is on a strict slimming diet.
(iv) Nina prefers fish to meat. She also has a very sweet tooth.

Did you know?

Westerners invited to Russians' homes, or to a restaurant with them, often leave convinced that their friends are well off, and that no problems exist. They don't of course see the queues their friends have waited in, the hours spent obtaining and preparing special dishes, coffee, drinks and sweets.

But then their friends don't *want* them to. Russians do not stop at half-measures when entertaining guests, or celebrating special occasions such as birthdays, namedays (the day of the saint after whom a person is named), New Year.

If you go to somebody's home, *everything* they have is likely to be put on the table at one time, and you will be repeatedly urged to keep eating. (There is a fable by the famous writer Krylov on this very theme – the guest finally rushes out of the house unable to take another mouthful!)

Vodka and other alcoholic drinks will be served just as liberally – *if* they are available. In the mid 1980s, when severe restrictions were put on the sale of alcohol, many people felt resentful that perfectly innocent socialising had been curtailed: how could they invite guests without a single bottle of alcohol to place on the table?

We mentioned in Unit 4 that the majority of Russians do not frequently dine in restaurants. However, they may invite friends for an evening in a restaurant in order to celebrate a special occasion. There they will show the same generosity as in their homes. Incidentally, it would not occur to a waiter to ask diners if they are paying together or separately – it could even be taken as an insult!

ИСПО[illegible] КОМИТЕТ
Дзержи[illegible] Совета
народн[illegible] депутатов
г. [illegible]

КООП[illegible]РАТИВ
„ЗАЙД[illegible]О[illegible]РОБУЙ“

№

На №

Салат 3 × 3,40 = 10,20
Лобио 1 = 3,70
Овощи 1 = 4,50
Свинина 1 = 14,45
Хлеб 12 = 0,24

90-44

Your turn to speak

12

You are staying with some friends in Moscow and would like to take them out for a meal. Study the following menu and expressions. When you have chosen, try ordering the meal, making any necessary requests for vegetarian food, etc. And, of course, you will need to pay! Then turn on your recording to hear what Nadya orders.

прими́те у нас зака́з take our order
на холо́дное for the cold course
на горя́чее for the hot course
на десе́рт for dessert
мы реши́ли взять... we have decided to take...
принеси́те, пожа́луйста, ... bring us please...
всё бы́ло о́чень вку́сно it was all very tasty
сда́чи не на́до keep the change

МЕНЮ́

Холо́дные блю́да	**Горя́чие (вторы́е) блю́да**	**Десе́рт**
ло́био	свини́на на ко́сточке	моро́женое
сала́т	свини́на натура́льная	фру́кты
икра́	омле́т с сы́ром	блины́
	пиро́г с ры́бой	

Answers

Practise what you have learned

Exercise **1** (i) b (ii) c (iii) a

Exercise **2** (i) за (ii) вку́сно (iii) на (iv) сыта́ (v) ча́шечку

Exercise **4** (i) 6 челове́к (ii) 7 часо́в (iii) 3 челове́ка (iv) 8 часо́в

Exercise **5** (i) false (ii) true (iii) false (iv) false

Exercise **7** (i) 2 (ii) 3 (iii) 2 (iv) 1 (v) 0 (vi) 1 (vii) 2 (viii) 2 (ix) 1 (x) 2

Exercise **8** (i) пиро́г с ры́бой (ii) омле́т с сы́ром (iii) ло́био (iv) бифште́кс натура́льный

Grammar

Exercise **10** (i) нам (ii) вам (iii) ей (iv) ему́ (v) мне/нам; вам (vi) нам (vii) ему́ (viii) им

Read and understand

Exercise **11** (i) a (ii) b (iii) a (iv) b

11 EXPRESSING LIKES AND DISLIKES

You will learn

- to talk about what you enjoy doing
- to express preferences
- to talk about places, seasons and foods which you like or dislike

and you will find out about some Russian cities

A Sunday stroll in a Moscow boulevard

Study guide

Dialogues 1, 2: listen without the book
Dialogues 1, 2: listen, read and study one by one
Practise what you have learned
Dialogues 3, 4: listen without the book
Dialogues 3, 4: listen, read and study one by one
Practise what you have learned
Dialogues 5–7: listen without the book
Dialogues 5–7: listen, read and study one by one
Practise what you have learned
Study the **Key words and phrases**
Study the **Grammar** section carefully
Do the exercises in **Read and understand**
Read **Did you know?**
Do the exercises in **Your turn to speak**
Listen to all the dialogues once again straight through

Dialogues

1 *Maria Dmitrievna is chatting with Lyena*

Maria Dmitrievna Ле́на, а ты лю́бишь шко́лу?
Lyena Вы зна́ете, не о́чень.
Maria Dmitrievna А что ты лю́бишь де́лать?
Lyena Я о́чень люблю́ чита́ть, ходи́ть в кино́, игра́ть в те́ннис.

- **ты лю́бишь шко́лу?** do you like school? The **вы** form of this verb is **вы лю́бите**, and the response may well include **я люблю́** 'I like'. The verb **люби́ть** can mean 'to like' *and* 'to love', so do be careful!
- **не о́чень** not much. If she felt more negative she would simply say **я не люблю́**, and if more positive, **я о́чень люблю́** I like... very much.
- **что ты лю́бишь де́лать?** what do you like to do? **Люби́ть** can be followed either by a noun (in the accusative case), or by a verb, *always* in the infinitive (the form shown in a dictionary).
- **ходи́ть в кино́** to go to the cinema. Some other places: **ходи́ть в теа́тр** to go to the theatre, **ходи́ть в рестора́н** to go to a restaurant, **ходи́ть на дискоте́ку** to go to a discotheque. Remember that '*I* go' is **я хожу́**.
- **игра́ть в те́ннис** to play tennis. It's easy to talk about sports in Russian, since the vast majority of words are international, e.g. **игра́ть в футбо́л, в воллейбо́л, в бадминто́н**.

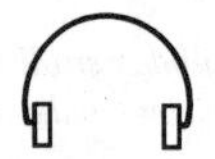

2 *Which subjects does Olya like?*

Maria Dmitrievna О́ля, а каки́е шко́льные предме́ты ты лю́бишь?
Olya Я люблю́ литерату́ру и исто́рию.
Maria Dmitrievna А како́й иностра́нный язы́к ты изуча́ешь?
Olya Англи́йский язы́к.
Maria Dmitrievna А ты уже́ хорошо́ зна́ешь англи́йский?
Olya Уме́ю чита́ть, но ху́же говорю́.

литерату́ра literature
исто́рия history
уже́ already

- **каки́е шко́льные предме́ты ты лю́бишь?** which school subjects do you like?
- **како́й иностра́нный язы́к ты изуча́ешь?** which foreign language do you study? In schools of the Russian Federation only one foreign language is normally studied. Olya has left out the verb in her reply. She might have said: **я изуча́ю англи́йский язы́к**. Other languages commonly studied are **неме́цкий язы́к** German and **францу́зский язы́к** French.
- **уме́ю чита́ть** I can read. **Уме́ть** really means 'to know how to', i.e. 'to have learned'.
- **но ху́же говорю** but I speak it worse. A common complaint! If she didn't speak at all, she would say: **я не уме́ю говори́ть по-англи́йски**. **Ху́же** 'worse' is the comparative form of **пло́хо** 'badly'. She *could* have been less negative, and just said she reads *better* – **я лу́чше чита́ю**.

Practise what you have learned

1

Sasha asks three of his neighbours whether they like their school or work, and what activities they enjoy. You will find their responses jumbled up below. Listen to the recording and unravel who likes (or doesn't like) what. (Answers on page 146.)

(i) **О́ля** (ii) **Ни́на** (iii) **А́нна Все́володовна**

(a) **Я не о́чень люблю́ свою́ рабо́ту.**
(b) **Я не люблю́ шко́лу.**
(c) **Я не о́чень люблю́ свой институ́т.**
(d) **Я люблю́ игра́ть в баскетбо́л и ходи́ть на дискоте́ку. Я не люблю́ чита́ть.**
(e) **Я люблю́ ходи́ть в теа́тр и в кино́. Я не люблю́ спорт.**
(f) **Я люблю́ ходи́ть в теа́тр и чита́ть.**

2

You will be playing the role of Seryozha, a less than communicative university student.

Dialogues

3 *What is Natasha's favourite time of the year?*

Mila Какóе врéмя гóда вы бóльше лю́бите?
Natasha Ну, веснý и́ли лéто, пожáлуй, бóльше лéто.
Mila А почемý и́менно лéто?
Natasha Ну, я не óчень люблю́ свою́ рабóту, а лéтом у меня́ óтпуск, возмóжность отдохнýть на мóре.
Mila Ну, отдохнýть мóжно ведь хорошó и зимóй, катáться на лы́жах, на конькáх, прóсто погуля́ть в зи́мнем лесý.
Natasha Да, но я люблю́ загорáть и плáвать, а лéтом — э́то лýчшее врéмя гóда.

ну well
пожáлуй probably
и́менно specifically
ведь after all
прóсто simply
катáться на лы́жах to ski
катáться на конькáх to ice skate
погуля́ть в зи́мнем лесý to walk in the winter forest
загорáть to sunbathe
плáвать to swim

какóе врéмя гóда вы бóльше лю́бите? what time of the year do you prefer? **Бóльше** means 'more', so **люби́ть бóльше** is 'to like more, to prefer'.

веснý и́ли лéто, пожáлуй, бóльше лéто spring or summer, probably summer more. She might also have preferred **óсень** autumn (the Fall) or **зи́му** winter. All these nouns are in the accusative case after **люби́ть**.

почемý и́менно лéто? why specifically summer?

я не óчень люблю́ свою́ рабóту I don't like my work very much. The pronoun **свой, своя́, своё** can mean 'my own', 'your own', 'his own' etc., depending on who is the subject of the sentence. It has the same endings as **мой, моя́, моё** 'my'.

лéтом у меня́ óтпуск I have my holidays in summer

возмóжность отдохнýть на мóре the possibility of having a holiday (lit. to rest) by the sea

отдохнýть мóжно ведь хорошó и зимóй one can have a good holiday in winter too

э́то лýчшее врéмя гóда it's the best time of the year. The word for 'best' here is an adjective. If you were referring to a masculine noun, you would say: **лýчший**, and if to a feminine noun: **лýчшая**.

4 *How about a cup of coffee?*

Mila Сдéлать вам чáшечку кóфе?
Natasha Я бóльше люблю́ чай.
Mila Но чай у нас тóлько азербайджáнский.
Natasha О нет, я бóльше люблю́ цейлóнский. Тогдá, пожáлуйста, чáшечку кóфе, но брази́льского!

чай tea
тогдá then

сде́лать вам ча́шечку ко́фе? shall I make you a cup of coffee? **Сде́лать** is used rather than **де́лать** to talk about making something *on a specific occasion*. Prefixes are added to many verbs in Russian for this purpose, e.g.:
пить to drink
вы́пить ча́шку ко́фе to drink a cup of coffee
обе́дать to have lunch
где здесь мо́жно бы́стро пообе́дать? where can one get a quick lunch here?
(More about these prefixed verbs on page 189.)

чай у нас то́лько азербайджа́нский we only have Azerbaijani tea. Another type of tea commonly available is **грузи́нский чай** Georgian tea. All the people we spoke to preferred **цейло́нский чай** Sri Lankan tea or **инди́йский чай** Indian tea.

ча́шечку ко́фе, но брази́льского! a cup of coffee, but Brazilian! To ask for a cup of tea, you would say: **ча́шечку ча́я**. If you share Natasha's taste in tea, you can ask: **е́сли мо́жно, цейло́нского** if possible Sri Lankan. You may be in luck!

Practise what you have learned

3

'О вку́сах не спо́рят' (to each his own). Some people are asked which season they like. Listen to their response, and write in the season each picks and why. (Answers on page 146.)

(i) **Ко́ля** ....

(ii) **А́нна** ....

(iii) **Та́ня** ....

New words: **собира́ть грибы́** to collect mushrooms

4

Read the statement below, then listen to your recording and determine what is incorrect in each one. (Answers on page 146.)

(i) Anna would like some grape juice.
(ii) Tanya prefers coffee, but asks for Indian tea.
(iii) Sergei prefers Georgian wine, so asks for vodka.

Dialogues

5 *Is Larisa Alekseevna a Muscovite?*

Boris Mikhailovich Лари́са Алексе́евна, вы москви́чка?
Larisa Alekseevna Да, я родила́сь в Москве́ и всю жизнь живу́ здесь.
Boris Mikhailovich Вы лю́бите Москву́?
Larisa Alekseevna Я люблю́ Москву́, но о́чень люблю́ ста́рую Москву́, там, где я родила́сь.

ста́рый, -ая, -ое old

- **москви́чка** a Muscovite woman. A Muscovite man is **москви́ч**.
- **я родила́сь в Москве́** I was born in Moscow. A man would say: **я роди́лся**.
- **и всю жизнь живу́ здесь** and have lived here all my life. It is the present tense in Russian because she is still living in Moscow now.
- **там, где я родила́сь** where I was born

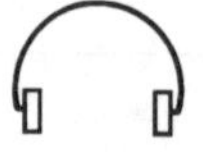

6 *What does Boris Mikhailovich think of Moscow?*

Larisa Alekseevna Бори́с Миха́йлович, вы лю́бите го́род Москву́?
Boris Mikhailovich Я не люблю́ Москву́.
Larisa Alekseevna Почему́?
Boris Mikhailovich Москва́ о́чень большо́й го́род. О́чень мно́го люде́й, мно́го тра́нспорта, нечи́стый во́здух.
Larisa Alekseevna А вы лю́бите Арба́т?
Boris Mikhailovich Арба́т я люблю́. Но я бо́льше люблю́ ма́ленькие города́.
Larisa Alekseevna А каки́е города́ вы лю́бите?
Boris Mikhailovich Я люблю́ ста́рые города́: Росто́в Вели́кий, Но́вгород, Ива́ново и други́е.

- **мно́го люде́й** many people. The word for 'people' is **лю́ди**. We noted in Unit 10 that nouns always go into the genitive case after **мно́го**.
- **мно́го тра́нспорта** much traffic
- **нечи́стый во́здух** polluted air. By removing **не-** you have **чи́стый во́здух** fresh air.
- **го́род** a city; **города́** cities. There are some masculine nouns whose plural ends in **-á**.

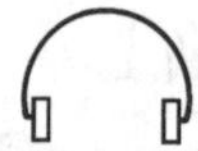

7 *Why does Boris Mikhailovich like Rostov Veliky?*

Larisa Alekseevna А за что вы лю́бите Росто́в Вели́кий?
Boris Mikhailovich В Росто́ве Вели́ком мно́го вся́ких ста́рых па́мятников, церкве́й.
Larisa Alekseevna А вы слу́шали когда́-нибудь росто́вские колокола́?
Boris Mikhailovich Да. Там есть де́йствующие це́ркви, и я слу́шал их звон.
Larisa Alekseevna А вы бы́ли там в монастыре́?
Boris Mikhailovich Да, был, и неоднокра́тно.

па́мятник monument
когда́-нибудь ever
(росто́вские) колокола́ (Rostov) church bells
их their
звон chimes
монасты́рь monastery
неоднокра́тно several times

- **за что вы лю́бите...?** why do you like...? (lit. for what do you like...?)
- **мно́го вся́ких ста́рых па́мятников, церкве́й** many of all kinds of old monuments, churches. All these words have genitive plural endings after **мно́го**. The word for 'church' in the nominative case (the one you'll find in the dictionary) is **це́рковь**.
- **вы слу́шали...?** have you heard...? Boris Mikhailovich replies **я слу́шал** I have heard. A woman would say: **я слу́шала**.
- **де́йствующие це́ркви** active churches, that is, churches used for worship. During the Soviet period, many churches were turned into museums, warehouses or just boarded up.
- **вы бы́ли там...?** were you there...? In the past tense the verb 'to be' *is* needed (otherwise you can't tell that it's in the past!). A man would reply: **я был** 'I was', a woman: **я была́**.

Practise what you have learned

5 A random survey on the Arbat produces some interesting results. Listen to the following replies, then write down where each person lives. (Answers on page 146.)

(i) ....

(ii) ....

(iii) ....

(iv) ....

A scene from St. Petersburg (left), and The Sokolniki Cathedral in Moscow (right)

6 Some people are asked what kind of cities they like. The answers are given below but the city and the reason for liking it have become separated. Listen to your recording and put things right. (Answers on page 146.)

(i)	**Я люблю́ Москву́**	(a)	**Э́то го́род Пу́шкина, Достое́вского**
(ii)	**Я люблю́ Но́вгород**	(b)	**Там мно́го ста́рых па́мятников и церкве́й**
(iii)	**Я люблю́ Петербу́рг**	(c)	**Там мно́го теа́тров**

Key words and phrases

To use

люби́ть (я люблю́, ты лю́бишь, вы лю́бите)	to like, love
свою́ рабо́ту	one's work
чита́ть	to read
ходи́ть в кино́	to go to the cinema
игра́ть в те́ннис	to play tennis
свой, своя́, своё	(my, your, his, her, their) own
изуча́ть (я изуча́ю)...	to study...
ру́сский / англи́йский язы́к	the Russian/English language
уме́ть (я уме́ю)	to be able to, to know how to
пло́хо	badly
ху́же	worse
хорошо́	well
лу́чше	better
вре́мя го́да	time of the year
весна́	spring
ле́то	summer
о́сень	autumn (the Fall)
зима́	winter
о́тпуск	leave, holidays
отдохну́ть (на мо́ре)	to rest (by the sea)
загора́ть	to sunbathe
пла́вать	to swim
ката́ться на лы́жах	to ski
ката́ться на конька́х	to ice skate
москви́ч (m.), **москви́чка** (f.)	Muscovite
я роди́лся (m.), **я родила́сь** (f.)	I was born
я всю жизнь живу́ здесь	I have lived here all my life
ста́рый, -ая, -ое	old
но́вый, -ая, -ое	new
го́род (pl. **города́**)	city
лю́ди (мно́го люде́й)	people (many people)
быть (он был, она́ была́)	to be (he was, she was)

To understand

что ты лю́бишь / вы лю́бите де́лать?	what do you like to do?
како́й иностра́нный язы́к вы изуча́ете?	which foreign language do you study?
како́е вре́мя го́да вы бо́льше лю́бите?	which season do you most like?
за что вы лю́бите...?	why do you like...?
сде́лать вам ча́шечку ко́фе?/ча́я?	can I make you a cup of coffee/tea?

Grammar

The past tense

The past tense is very easy in Russian if you know the infinitive of the verb ('to...'). All you do is remove the last two letters **-ть** from the infinitive and add the following endings:

masculine	**-л**
feminine	**-ла**
neuter	**-ло**
plural	**-ли**

So the verb **быть** (to be) in the past becomes:

он (я, ты)	**был**
она́ (я, ты)	**была́**
оно́	**бы́ло**
они́ (вы, мы)	**бы́ли**

As you see, the only distinctions made in the past tense are between singular and plural, and between masculine, feminine and neuter. The verb ending after **вы** is *always* plural, even if only one person is addressed.

Here are past forms of some of the other verbs you met in this unit. Is it a man or a woman speaking?

Ле́том я был в Я́лте. Там я пла́вал, загора́л, чита́л. Зимо́й я был в Но́вгороде. Там я ката́лся на лы́жах, ходи́л в це́рковь, слу́шал колокола́.

7 Write out how a woman would describe the same activities. (Answers on page 146.)

(i) **Ле́том я** ....

....

(ii) How would she describe the activities if she and her family all participated?

Ле́том мы ....

....

8 Here are some not terribly useful facts about famous people. You'll need to fill in the verbs though! (Answers on page 146.)

(i) **Эйнште́йн** .... **фи́зику** (изуча́ть)

(ii) **Пу́шкни** .... **поэ́т** (быть)

(iii) **А́нна Ахма́това** .... **в Ленингра́де** (жить)

(iv) **Лев Я́шин** .... **в футбо́л** (игра́ть)

(v) **Роме́о** .... **Джулье́тту, и Джулье́тта** .... **Роме́о** (люби́ть)

(vi) **Рахма́нинов** .... **колокола́** (слу́шать)

Read and understand

9 A school in Moscow is looking for penpals for its students. It has received several replies from abroad, and is trying to match people up. Read the following letters and see if you can make matches. (Answers on page 146.)

New words:

слу́шать...	to listen to...
поп-му́зыку	pop music
класси́ческую му́зыку	classical music
джаз	jazz
спортсме́н	sportsman
спортсме́нка	sportswoman
матема́тика	mathematics
футбо́льный матч	football match
поп-конце́рт	pop concert

(i) **Меня́ зову́т Ната́ша, я москви́чка. Я изуча́ю англи́йский язы́к, но пло́хо говорю́ по-англи́йски. Я не о́чень люблю́ шко́лу. Я бо́льше люблю́ игра́ть в те́ннис, ходи́ть в кино́, слу́шать поп-му́зыку.**

(ii) **Меня́ зову́т Са́ша, я москви́ч. Я изуча́ю неме́цкий язы́к и о́чень люблю́ говори́ть по-неме́цки. Я не о́чень люблю́ шко́лу, но люблю́ изуча́ть иностра́нные языки́. Я люблю́ класси́ческую му́зыку.**

(iii) **Меня́ зову́т О́ля, я москви́чка. Я изуча́ю англи́йский язы́к, но я бо́льше люблю́ матема́тику. Я о́чень люблю́ чита́ть.**

(iv) **Меня́ зову́т Ми́ша. Я москви́ч и спортсме́н. Я игра́ю в футбо́л, в те́ннис и люблю́ пла́вать. В шко́ле я изуча́ю францу́зский язы́к, но я не люблю́ иностра́нные языки́. Я чита́ю по-францу́зски пло́хо, и ху́же говорю́!**

(a) **Меня́ зову́т Ян, я не́мец. Я изуча́ю ру́сский язы́к в шко́ле и хочу́ изуча́ть англи́йский язы́к. Я о́чень люблю́ му́зыку — джаз и класси́ческую му́зыку.**

(b) **Меня́ зову́т Мари́, я францу́женка. Я изуча́ю ру́сский язы́к в шко́ле. Я не люблю́ шко́лу, и не о́чень хочу́ изуча́ть иностра́нный язы́к! Я о́чень люблю́ игра́ть в те́ннис и ходи́ть на футбо́льные ма́тчи.**

(c) **Меня́ зову́т Пи́тер, я англича́нин. Я изуча́ю ру́сский язы́к, чита́ю хорошо́, но ху́же говорю́. Я люблю́ шко́лу, люблю́ чита́ть, изуча́ть матема́тику и ру́сский язы́к. Я не люблю́ спорт.**

(d) **Меня́ зову́т Ли́з, я америка́нка. Я изуча́ю ру́сский язы́к в шко́ле. Я не люблю́ шко́лу. Я люблю́ ходи́ть на поп-конце́рты и в кино́. Я о́чень люблю́ спорт.**

Did you know?

Many old Russian cities are renowned for their beauty and are often visited by both Russian and foreign tourists.

Novgorod, one of the oldest cities (dating back to the 9th century), was an important trading centre in Kievan Rus'. From the 12th to the 15th centuries, Novgorod was a federal republic ruled by a **ве́че**, or city assembly. With the rise to power of Moscow, Novgorod lost its political influence.

To the north-east of Moscow is Vladimir, powerful in the 12th century under Prince Andrei Bogolyubsky, who worked to unite North-western Rus' against the hegemony of Kievan Rus'.

Also in the north-east are Rostov, one of only two cities given the title **Вели́кий** (great) – the other being Novgorod – and Suzdal', which now exists as **го́род-музе́й**, a museum city.

In each of these cities, the focus of attention falls upon churches, cathedrals and monasteries. The Russian Orthodox Church took on the traditions, church architecture and art of Byzantine Christianity. The most famous painter of icons was Andrei Rublyov, who lived in the 15th century. However, Novgorod, Pskov, Vladimir and other cities all had famous schools of icon-painting. Icons, like all the rich and beautiful exteriors and interiors of churches, were an integral part of Christian worship of God.

Unfortunately, over a period of many years after the 1917 revolution, thousands of churches and monasteries were destroyed, or closed, stripped of all ornament and used as warehouses etc. There was less destruction in the old historical cities, but the stress was firmly on the architectural value of these churches. Many were made into museums, or opened for tourists only. Despite the apparent abundance of churches, it was often difficult for believers to find a *functioning* ***(де́йствующая)*** church.

In 1988, celebrations held to mark the thousand-year anniversary of Prince Vladimir's conversion to Orthodox Christianity heralded greater freedom of worship. Many old churches and monasteries were allowed to reopen, while others are being rebuilt, often with considerable help from believers both within Russia and abroad.

Your turn to speak

10

This time you will be talking about yourself, your hobbies, likes and dislikes – *and without prompts!* Use the phrases below if appropriate. When you have had a go, turn on the recording and listen to what Nikolai Arkadyevich has to say about his favourite cities, activities etc.

я роди́лся/родила́сь в...	I was born in...
я всю жизнь живу́ в...	I have lived all my life in...
я бо́льше люблю́...	I prefer...
ходи́ть в/на...	to go to...
изуча́ть ру́сский язы́к	to study Russian
я (не) люблю́ свою́ рабо́ту	I (don't) like my work
у меня́ о́тпуск	I have my holiday

Answers

Practise what you have learned

Exercise **1**	(i) b, e (ii) c, d (iii) a, f
Exercise **3**	(i) spring; has his holidays then (ii) autumn; likes to gather mushrooms (iii) summer; likes to swim and sunbathe
Exercise **4**	(i) wants lemonade rather than grape juice (ii) prefers Indian tea (iii) prefers Armenian wine
Exercise **5**	(i) Manchester (ii) Moscow (iii) Paris (iv) Rostov
Exercise **6**	(i) c (ii) b (iii) a

Grammar

Exercise **7**	(i) Ле́том я была́ в Я́лте. Там я пла́вала, загора́ла, чита́ла. Зимо́й я была́ в Но́вгороде. Там я ката́лась на лы́жах, ходи́ла в це́рковь, слу́шала колокола́. (ii) Ле́том мы бы́ли в Я́лте. Там мы пла́вали, загора́ли, чита́ли. Зимо́й мы бы́ли в Но́вгороде. Там мы ката́лись на лы́жах, ходи́ли в це́рковь, слу́шали колокола́.
Exercise **8**	(i) изуча́л (ii) был (iii) жила́ (iv) игра́л (v) люби́л; люби́ла (vi) слу́шал

Read and understand

Exercise **9**	(i) d (ii) a (iii) c (iv) b

12

TALKING ABOUT YOUR TOWN AND THE WEATHER

You will learn

- to talk about what there is to see and do in cities
- to discuss the weather
- to talk about your holidays
- how to express feelings and opinions in Russian

and you will find out about Moscow and St Petersburg

Study guide

- **Dialogues 1, 2:** listen without the book
- **Dialogues 1, 2:** listen, read and study one by one
- Practise what you have learned
- **Dialogue 3:** listen without the book
- **Dialogue 3:** listen, read and study
- Practise what you have learned
- **Dialogues 4, 5:** listen without the book
- **Dialogues 4, 5:** listen, read and study one by one
- Practise what you have learned
- **Dialogue 6:** listen without the book
- **Dialogue 6:** listen, read and study
- Practise what you have learned
- Study the **Key words and phrases**
- Study the **Grammar** section carefully
- Do the exercises in **Read and understand**
- Read **Did you know?**
- Do the exercises in **Your turn to speak**
- Listen to all the dialogues once again straight through

Dialogues

1 *Ira knows Moscow very well*

Ira Я москви́чка, прожила́ в э́том го́роде всю жизнь, и, как у вся́кого москвича́, у меня́ есть свои́ люби́мые места́. Обы́чно я пока́зываю э́ти дороги́е мне места́ мои́м друзья́м и гостя́м. Во-пе́рвых, э́то парк, кото́рый нахо́дится недалеко́ от моего́ до́ма. Э́тот парк и зда́ние в э́том па́рке постро́или изве́стные ру́сские зо́дчие Баже́нов и Казако́в.

обы́чно usually
во-пе́рвых firstly

- **прожила́ в э́том го́роде всю жизнь** I have lived my whole life in this city. Ira could also have used the verb in the present tense **я живу́...**
- **как у вся́кого москвича́** as has every Muscovite. **У** is used to say that somebody *has* something, whether followed by a pronoun (**у меня́ есть...**) or by a noun (**у вся́кого москвича́**). Any word following **у** takes a genitive ending.
- **у меня́ есть свои́ люби́мые места́** I have my own favourite places
- **я пока́зываю э́ти дороги́е мне места́ мои́м друзья́м и гостя́м** I show these favourite (lit. dear to me) places to my friends and guests. There is more about dative endings of nouns in the grammar section.
- **друзья́м** to my friends. The plural of **друг** friend is irregular.
- **парк, кото́рый нахо́дится недалеко́ от моего́ до́ма** a park which isn't far from my home
- **кото́рый** which. This word changes as an adjective. Other examples:
  галере́я, кото́рая нахо́дится в це́нтре a gallery which is located in the centre
  кафе́, кото́рое нахо́дится ря́дом a café which is next door
- **постро́или изве́стные ру́сские зо́дчие Баже́нов и Казако́в** were built by the famous Russian architects Bazhenov and Kazakov

2 *What else does Ira like to do?*

Ira О́чень люблю́ вы́ставки жи́вописи, карти́нные галере́и, где о́чень ча́сто быва́ю со свои́ми друзья́ми. И, коне́чно, я люблю́ гуля́ть по тем места́м, кото́рые опи́саны в на́ших кни́гах, наприме́р, в кни́гах Булга́кова, Пу́шкина и други́х.

вы́ставка жи́вописи exhibition of paintings
карти́нные галере́и picture galleries
наприме́р for example
ча́сто often
коне́чно [kanyéshna] of course

- **о́чень ча́сто быва́ю** I am very often (there). The verb **быва́ть** also means 'to be', but is used to talk about *frequently* or *habitually* being (i.e. going) somewhere.
- **со свои́ми друзья́ми** with my friends
- **гуля́ть по тем места́м, кото́рые опи́саны в на́ших кни́гах** to wander about those places which are described in our books
- **в кни́гах Булга́кова, Пу́шкина...** in the books of Bulgakov, Pushkin... 'Of' is expressed in Russian by the genitive case. There are some Russian names which look like adjectives, e.g. **Достое́вский, Толсто́й**. The genitive is accordingly like the adjective (**в кни́гах**) **Достое́вского, Толсто́го.**
- **и други́х** and of others

Practise what you have learned

1 Three Muscovites all show friends their city. But their interests are so different that you might think it is three cities rather than one. Read the postcards below, and then listen and match the postcard writer with his or her friend. (Answers on page 162.)

(a)

Мы бы́ли на стадио́не, где игра́ет 'Дина́мо'. Мы бы́ли и на Кра́сной пло́щади и в Кремле́.

(b)

Мне о́чень хорошо́ здесь! Ко́ля пока́зывает мне вы́ставки, галере́и. Я был в музе́е Пу́шкина и в Теа́тре на Тага́нке.

(c)

Как хорошо́ здесь! Ди́ма пока́зывает мне места́, кото́рые опи́саны в кни́гах Булга́кова, Пу́шкина. Мы бы́ли в до́ме-музе́е Пу́шкина и в до́ме Толсто́го.

(i) ....

(ii) ....

(iii) ....

Dialogues

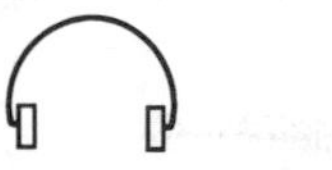

3 *A coach excursion is offered*

Tour guide Уважáемые гóсти. Приглашáем на экскýрсию пó Москвé, обзóрную экскýрсию по гóроду. Крáсную плóщадь, Кремль, центрáльные ýлицы, плóщади, проспéкты, бульвáры, Лéнинские гóры. По сáмым пáмятным местáм столи́цы. Древнéйшие храмы, старéйшие теáтры, прави́тельственные здáния. По сáмым пáмятным местáм Москвы́ на экскýрсию по гóроду, приглашáем.

уважáемые гóсти respected guests
обзóрная экскýрсия a panoramic tour
Крáсная плóщадь Red Square (the woman uses the accusative because they will be *going* there)
Кремль Kremlin
центрáльные ýлицы central streets
плóщади, проспéкты, бульвáры squares, avenues, boulevards
Лéнинские гóры Lenin hills (These hills are now called by their original name: **Воробьёвы гóры**.)
прави́тельственный government (adj.)
здáния (sing. **здáние**) buildings

- **приглашáем на экскýрсию** we invite you on an excursion. If she personally was making the invitation, she would say **я приглашáю**. Any word following **приглашáть в/на** will have an accusative ending.
- **по Москвé, ... по гóроду** around Moscow, ... around the city. Here the preposition **по** means 'around', and it is followed by *dative* endings (see the grammar section).
- **по сáмым пáмятным местáм столи́цы** around the most noteworthy places in the capital. To say something is the *most* (interesting, beautiful, etc.), **сáмый** is used before the adjective. It's easy to use since it changes in exactly the same way as the adjective, e.g.:
  сáмый извéстный пáмятник the most famous monument
  сáмая краси́вая цéрковь the most beautiful church
  сáмое большóе здáние the biggest building
- **древнéйшие храмы, старéйшие теáтры** the most ancient churches, the oldest theatres. Another less common way of forming the superlative ('the most...'). She might just as easily have said: **дрéвние хрáмы, стáрые теáтры** ancient churches, old theatres.

The Pushkin Museum of Fine Arts

Practise what you have learned

2

A tourist group is visiting three major cities in Russia and Ukraine. Unfortunately the programmes are all jumbled up. Listen to the tour guide and write down the places to be seen in each city. (Answers on page 162.)

(i) **Ки́ев** (ii) **Петербу́рг** (iii) **Москва́**

(a) **изве́стный па́мятник 'Ме́дный вса́дник'**
(b) **Крещáтик**
(c) **Храм Васи́лия Блаже́нного**
(d) **Софи́йский собо́р**
(e) **Не́вский проспе́кт**
(f) **Эрмита́ж**
(g) **музе́й Тара́са Шевче́нко**
(h) **дом-музе́й Достое́вского**
(i) **Донско́й монасты́рь**

New words:

изве́стный famous
храм church, temple
собо́р cathedral
па́мятник memorial, monument

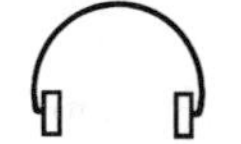

3

Volodya has found a holiday job showing tourists around Moscow. The trouble is that he knows next to nothing about the city! He hopes that total ignorance can be concealed by an abundance of superlatives. Listen to your recording, then fill in the missing words. (Answers on page 162.)

(i) **Кака́я э́то у́лица?**

Э́то .... у́лица в Москве́!

(ii) **Како́й э́то проспе́кт?**

Э́то .... проспе́кт в Москве́!

(iii) **Како́е э́то кафе́?**

Э́то .... кафе́ в Москве́!

(iv) **Кака́я э́то галере́я?**

Э́то .... галере́я в Москве́!

са́мый краси́вый the most beautiful
са́мый интере́сный the most interesting
са́мый изве́стный the most famous

Dialogues

4 *Some advice about the weather in Moscow*

Ira Éсли вы хоти́те прие́хать в Москву́, то вам, коне́чно, бу́дет интере́сно знать, кака́я здесь пого́да. Зимо́й у нас быва́ет и о́чень хо́лодно, но мо́жет быть и тепло́, и тогда́ появля́ется вода́ и снег та́ет. Ле́том пого́да обы́чно быва́ет дово́льно тёплая, но ча́сто дожди́. И поэ́тому я люблю́ отдыха́ть не в Москве́ ле́том, обяза́тельно на ю́ге, где тепло́. О́чень люблю́ тепло́.

Весна́ в Москве́ о́чень капри́зная. То со́лнце, то хо́лод. Поэ́тому мы весно́й предпочита́ем бо́льше сиде́ть до́ма.

появля́ется вода́ water appears
снег та́ет the snow melts
поэ́тому therefore
обяза́тельно definitely
капри́зный capricious
со́лнце sun
хо́лод the cold

- **прие́хать в Москву́** to come to Moscow
- **вам бу́дет интере́сно знать...** literally: 'it will be interesting *to you* to know...'. Similarly, 'it will be interesting to me...' is **мне бу́дет интере́сно...** By the way, leaving out **бу́дет** would put any such sentence into the present tense.
- **кака́я здесь пого́да** what the weather is like here. You only need to change your intonation to make this a question. And to find out what the weather will be like today, ask: **кака́я сего́дня бу́дет пого́да?**
- **быва́ет о́чень хо́лодно, но мо́жет быть и тепло́** it gets very cold, though it can be warm as well. Not of course necessary for a Russian winter, but in summer it can also be **жа́рко** hot.
- **пого́да обы́чно быва́ет дово́льно тёплая** the weather is usually fairly warm

Both **тёплый** and **тепло́** mean 'warm', but **тёплый** is an adjective and agrees with the noun, i.e. **тёплая пого́да** 'warm weather', whereas **тепло́** is used when no noun is mentioned, e.g. **Сего́дня тепло́.** It is warm today. Certain other words work in the same way, e.g.:
холо́дный день a cold day
Здесь хо́лодно. It is cold here.
жа́ркое ле́то a hot summer
Ле́том быва́ет жа́рко. It gets hot here in summer.

- **ча́сто дожди́** there is often rain. You will just as often hear the singular of this noun **дождь.**
- **отдыха́ть** to rest, take one's holiday
- **на ю́ге** in the south. The word for south is **юг**. The other points of the compass are: **се́вер** north, **восто́к** east, **за́пад** west.
- **то... то...** one minute... the next...
- **мы... предпочита́ем бо́льше сиде́ть до́ма** we prefer to sit at home. '*I* prefer' would be **я предпочита́ю**.

5 *One season is special*

Ira Но для души́ бо́льше прия́тна о́сень, пу́шкинская пора́, у нас её называ́ют золото́й о́сенью. Есть таки́е у Пу́шкина стро́ки:

Осе́нняя пора́! Оче́й очарова́нье!
Прия́тна мне твоя́ проща́льная краса́.
Люблю́ я пы́шное приро́ды увяда́нье.
В багре́ц и в зо́лото оде́тые леса́.

для души́ for the soul
пу́шкинская пора́ Pushkin's time (Pushkin loved this season particularly)
золота́я о́сень golden autumn (Fall)
стро́ки lines

- **для души́ бо́льше прия́тна о́сень** for the spirit autumn is nicer. It is more correct to say **бо́лее прия́тна**.
- **у нас её называ́ют золото́й о́сенью** we call it golden autumn (Fall). In Russian very often the third person plural of the verb (the 'they' form) is used *by itself* to mean 'people generally'. Another common verb used in this way is **говоря́т** 'they say'.
- **Осе́нняя пора́! Оче́й очарова́нье! ...** Ira makes a slight mistake in the first line of Pushkin's famous poem 'О́сень'. It should read: **Уны́лая пора́! Оче́й очарова́нье!** In D.M. Thomas' translation:

  Dejected season! enchantment to the eyes!
  Your elegiac beauty and your mourning
  Colours are dear to me: the sumptuous
  Fading of the woods in purple and gold...
  (Secker & Warburg Limited, 1982)

Turn over for the exercises based on these dialogues

A monument to Alexander Pushkin in Moscow

Practise what you have learned

4 Below are three pictures of different parts of the Russian Federation. As you see, the climate varies dramatically! Listen to your recording and match each prediction to the most appropriate picture. (Answers on page 162.)

(a) ....

(b) ....

(c) ....

5

Some friends are chatting about when and where they spend their holidays. Listen to the recording, then mark off the correct statements below. (Answers on page 162.)

(i) Nadya has her holiday in

- (a) summer ☐
- (b) spring ☐

(ii) She goes

- (a) north because the weather is better ☐
- (b) south because of Moscow's weather ☐

(iii) Sasha has holidays

- (a) in spring and winter ☐
- (b) in summer and winter ☐

(iv) He goes north because

- (a) he finds the cold invigorating ☐
- (b) he likes to ski ☐

The Kremlin, Moscow

6

You live in St. Petersburg. You will be asking questions about the weather in Moscow. As always, Andrei will prompt you.

Dialogues

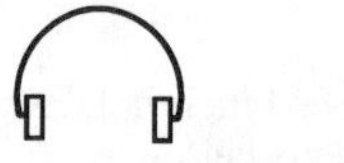

6 *Where do Larisa Alekseevna and her family spend their holidays?*

Boris Mikhailovich А где вы отдыха́ете?
Larisa Alekseevna О́тпуск мы, как пра́вило, прово́дим ле́тний на реке́ А́хтуба, а зи́мний о́тпуск мы прово́дим в Подмоско́вье, на турба́зе и́ли в до́ме о́тдыха.
Boris Mikhailovich А где располо́жен э́тот дом о́тдыха?
Larisa Alekseevna Дом о́тдыха располо́жен в Звени́городе на реке́ Москва́-река́. Э́то са́мое краси́вое ме́сто Подмоско́вья.
Boris Mikhailovich Там есть лес?
Larisa Alekseevna Там есть о́чень краси́вый лес.
Boris Mikhailovich Там есть кака́я-нибудь река́?
Larisa Alekseevna Там река́ Москва́-река́ протека́ет.
Boris Mikhailovich А ваш муж ло́вит ры́бу зимо́й?
Larisa Alekseevna Муж мой занима́ется рыба́лкой в зи́мнее вре́мя.
Boris Mikhailovich А э́то о́чень хо́лодно лови́ть зимо́й ры́бу?
Larisa Alekseevna Ну, он о́чень всегда́ тепло́ одева́ется.

как пра́вило as a rule
река́ river
турба́за tourist centre
дом о́тдыха holiday centre / sanatorium
лес forest

- **мы прово́дим ле́тний/зи́мний о́тпуск** we spend the summer/winter holiday. 'I spend' would be **я провожу́**.
- **где располо́жен...?** where is... located? This is a less common way of asking **где нахо́дится...?**
- **Подмоско́вье** the area around Moscow
- **там есть кака́я-нибудь река́?** is there a river there? Boris Mikhailovich evidently wasn't listening carefully since Larisa Alekseevna had just told him!
- **а ваш муж ло́вит ры́бу зимо́й?** does your husband fish in winter? Larisa Alekseevna's reply was a long way of saying 'yes'! **Занима́ться рыба́лкой** and **лови́ть ры́бу** both mean 'to fish'.
- **он о́чень всегда́ тепло́ одева́ется** he always dresses very warmly. The infinitive of this verb is **одева́ться** to dress oneself. 'I dress warmly' is **я одева́юсь тепло́**. 'To dress *lightly*' is, however, **одева́ться легко́**.

Practise what you have learned

7

Tamara asks some colleagues where they spend their holidays. Listen to your recording, then fill in the missing words (they are jumbled up in the box below). (Answers on page 162.)

Бори́с, где вы обы́чно .... (i) **?**

Я отдыха́ю обы́чно .... (ii) **на ю́ге. Я о́чень люблю́** .... (iii)

И́горь, где вы прово́дите .... (iv)**?**

Ле́тний о́тпуск мы .... (v) **на мо́ре, а** .... (vi) **мы отдыха́ем в до́ме о́тдыха, недалеко́ от Влади́мира.**

Там есть кака́я-нибудь .... (vii) **?**

Да, ... (viii) .... **располо́жен на реке́ Кля́зьма.**

тепло́	**река́**	**зимо́й**	**отдыха́ете**	**ле́том**
прово́дим	**дом о́тдыха**	**о́тпуск**		

Key words and phrases

To use

пока́зывать	to show
люби́мый, -ая, -ое	favourite
друг (pl. **друзья́**)	friend
гость (m.)	guest
парк, кото́рый нахо́дится...	the park which is located...
галере́я, кото́рая нахо́дится...	the gallery which is located...
зда́ние, кото́рое нахо́дится...	the building which is located...
недалеко́ от моего́ до́ма	not far from my home
быва́ть	to be (habitually, often)
я ча́сто быва́ю там	I am there often
приглаша́ть	to invite
приглаша́ем на экску́рсию...	we invite (you) on an excursion...
по Москве́	around Moscow
по Но́вгороду	around Novgorod
по са́мым па́мятным места́м столи́цы	around the most notable places of the capital
кака́я здесь пого́да?	what is the weather like here?
кака́я сего́дня бу́дет пого́да?	what will the weather be like today?
пого́да быва́ет тёплая	the weather is (usually) warm
пого́да бу́дет холо́дная	the weather will be cold
пого́да бу́дет жа́ркая	the weather will be hot
сего́дня тепло́	it's warm today
сего́дня бу́дет хо́лодно	it will be cold today
сего́дня бы́ло жа́рко	it was hot today
мне хо́лодно	I am cold
вам тепло́?	are you warm?
ча́сто дожди́/дождь	there's often rain
снег	snow
отдыха́ть (**я отдыха́ю**)	to rest, spend one's holiday
проводи́ть о́тпуск (**я провожу́, вы прово́дите**)**...**	to spend one's holiday...
на ю́ге (**юг**)	in the south (south)
на се́вере (**се́вер**)	in the north (north)
на за́паде (**за́пад**)	in the west (west)
на восто́ке (**восто́к**)	in the east (east)
река́	river
лес	forest

Grammar

Impersonal sentences

Some Russian sentences may at first sight appear telegraphic. This is mainly because there is no word in them for 'it is'. Thus:
Сего́дня хо́лодно. It is cold today.
Э́то о́чень интере́сно. That is very interesting.

Verb forms are, however, needed for 'it was' – **бы́ло** and 'it will be' – **бу́дет**, e.g.:
Сего́дня бы́ло тепло́. It was warm today.
За́втра бу́дет хо́лодно. It will be cold tomorrow.

If it is *Boris* who is, was or will be cold, the sentence will be:
Бори́су (бы́ло, бу́дет) хо́лодно. Boris is (was, will be) cold.
(Literally, this sentence means 'To Boris it is (was, will be) cold.)

Such sentences are very common in Russian when talking about feelings, opinions, etc. Here are some other examples:
Анто́ну интере́сно здесь. Anton finds it interesting here. (lit. To Anton it is interesting here.)
Ни́не бы́ло жа́рко. Nina was hot. (lit. To Nina it was hot.)
Мне на́до бу́дет рабо́тать. I will have to work. (lit. To me it will be necessary to work.)
Вам хо́лодно? Are you cold? (lit. To you cold?)

In these sentences, the noun or pronoun ('to me', 'to you', etc.) referring to the *person* involved has a dative ending. We introduced dative endings for pronouns on page 131. Names of people must also change.

Dative endings

There are really only three endings to learn:

Masculine & neuter singular nouns end in **-у** or **-ю**, e.g.:
Ви́ктору и Никола́ю интере́сно лови́ть ры́бу. Victor and Nikolai enjoy fishing.
Миха́илу Ива́новичу жа́рко. Mikhail Ivanovich is hot.

Feminine singular nouns normally end in **-е**, e.g.:
Ни́не хорошо́ здесь. Nina feels good here.
Татья́не Алексе́евне прия́тно чита́ть в па́рке. Tatyana Alekseevna finds it pleasant to read in the park.

In the plural, all nouns end in **-ам** or **-ям**, e.g.:
Экску́рсия по са́мым па́мятным места́м столи́цы Excursion around the most noteworthy places of the capital

Do not be put off by these endings. It is the pronouns you have learned in Unit 10 which you are more likely to *use*. The main thing is to *understand* such constructions.

8 Read and translate the following sentences. (Answers on page 162.)

(i) **Анто́ну хо́лодно сего́дня.**
(ii) **Ни́не на́до рабо́тать.**
(iii) **Мои́м друзья́м интере́сно знать, кака́я здесь пого́да.**
(iv) **Никола́ю бы́ло жа́рко.**
(v) **А́нне Степа́новне на́до говори́ть по-англи́йски на рабо́те.**
(vi) **Студе́нтам не о́чень интере́сно ходи́ть на конфере́нции.**

9 In the spaces below add the words in round brackets with the right endings. Make sure you understand each one. (Answers on page 162.)

(i) (Серге́й и Та́ня) **интере́сно ходи́ть в теа́тр.**
(ii) (Лари́са) **сего́дня тепло́, а** (Бори́с) **хо́лодно.**
(iii) (Студе́нт) **на́до мно́го рабо́тать.**
(iv) **Ва́шему** (друг) **интере́сно изуча́ть францу́зский язы́к?**
(v) (Ири́на Никола́евна) **бы́ло о́чень прия́тно обе́дать в рестора́не.**

Read and understand

10

Three tourists wrote notes in their diaries about the places they were visiting. Below are picture postcards which each one sent to a friend. If you read the diary entries, you will know who sent which postcard. (Answers on page 162.)

(i) **Сего́дня я ходи́л по Не́вскому проспе́кту и други́м проспе́ктам и у́лицам. Мне бы́ло так интере́сно! Я люблю́ ходи́ть по тем места́м, кото́рые опи́саны в рома́нах Достое́вского. Я ещё не ходи́л в Эрмита́ж, мо́жет быть, за́втра.**

Пого́да сейча́с дово́льно капри́зная: то со́лнце, то хо́лод, и ча́сто дожди́.

(ii) **Я ходи́ла по ста́рым у́лицам столи́цы, по у́лицам, кото́рые опи́саны в кни́гах Булга́кова, Толсто́го. Я за́втракала в кафе́, кото́рое нахо́дится недалеко́ от Кремля́, и ходи́ла в Музе́й Пу́шкина.**

Бы́ло о́чень хо́лодно, но я так люблю́ снег! В па́рке де́ти ката́ются на conька́х. Мне о́чень хорошо́ здесь!

(iii) **Пого́да здесь о́чень хоро́шая – тёплая, со́лнечная. Я о́чень люблю́ проводи́ть о́тпуск на реке́. Ка́ждый день я пла́ваю, загора́ю. Здесь о́чень краси́вый лес, мы ча́сто там быва́ем. У́тром я ловлю́ ры́бу и́ли ничего́ не де́лаю. О́чень прия́тно отдыха́ть здесь. Я ду́маю, э́то са́мое краси́вое ме́сто Подмоско́вья!**

(a)

(b)

(c)

Did you know?

Moscow and St Petersburg

A visitor may well have difficulty believing that these two cities are part of the same country. A few words about each city's past may help to explain the differences.

While Moscow does not date back to the earliest days of Kievan Rus', it is quite old, having been founded by Prince Yuri Dolgoruky in 1156. It was, however, one of the least important princedoms until the Tartar invasion of the 13th century and the fall of Kiev. Then its geographical location and a lack of fastidiousness on the part of Ivan Kalita (or 'Moneybags') in dealing with the invaders enabled Moscow to gain considerable power. This was further increased by the Metropolitan's decision to establish the Church centre in Moscow. Constantinople, the 'second Rome', fell in 1453. After the end of Tartar rule in 1480, Prince Ivan of Moscow declared himself Tsar, ruler of all Russia and of all Orthodox Christians. Moscow was to be the third Rome – there would be no fourth.

Moscow remained the capital of a burgeoning empire until the reign of Peter the Great (1672–1725). In supremely autocratic fashion Peter decided to build a new capital on the shores of the Baltic Sea. Undeterred by the marshy terrain and inauspicious climate, Peter used Swedish prisoners of war and Russian peasants to create St. Petersburg, a 'window onto Europe' ('Bronze Horseman' by Alexander Pushkin).

He also invited architects from abroad to create this 'Venice of the North'. The classical style of architecture, canals and bridges and the famous 'white nights' in June create a particular atmosphere which has fascinated writers and poets from Pushkin and Dostoevsky to the present day.

It was in this city, renamed from 1914 Petrograd, that the revolutions of February and October 1917 took place. In 1918, however, Lenin moved the capital back to Moscow. From 1924, following Lenin's death, up to 1991, the city was called Leningrad.

The Soviet period left its mark on both cities. The appearance of Moscow, historically more 'Russian', changed more, with many historical areas destroyed or converted into offices for the dozens of ministries centred in the city. Fifty years after the October 1917 revolution, fewer than half of Moscow's churches and monasteries remained standing.

St. Petersburg has altered less structurally. The problem here is that restoration and repair work have not kept pace with decay and many beautiful buildings are close to collapse.

St. Petersburg / Leningrad was also particularly ravaged by the Second World War. For 900 days the city was under siege, during which more than a million people died of starvation. To this day on one of the houses on Nevsky Prospect is a sign warning citizens of Leningrad that 'under gunfire this side of the street is more dangerous'.

Your turn to speak

11 In this exercise you will be talking about your own city or the place where you spend your holidays. Work out what you would like to say about it and try this out before listening to your recording. Remember that if your version is different from the recording, it is not *wrong*, just *different*! The following words may be useful:

у меня́ есть свои́ люби́мые места́	I have my own favourite places
парк, кото́рый нахо́дится...	the park which is located...
вам бу́дет интере́сно знать, кака́я здесь пого́да	you will be interested to know what kind of weather there is here
быва́ет хо́лодно	it gets cold
я предпочита́ю отдыха́ть в/на...	I prefer to take my holiday in...
са́мое краси́вое ме́сто Подмоско́вья	the most beautiful place in the area around Moscow

Answers

Practise what you have learned

Exercise **1**	(i) b (ii) a (iii) c
Exercise **2**	(i) b, d, g (ii) a, e, f (iii) c, h, i
Exercise **3**	(i) са́мая краси́вая (ii) са́мый изве́стный (iii) са́мое изве́стное (iv) са́мая интере́сная
Exercise **4**	(i) c (ii) a (iii) b
Exercise **5**	(i) b (ii) b (iii) b (iv) b
Exercise **7**	(i) отдыха́ете (ii) ле́том (iii) тепло́ (iv) о́тпуск (v) прово́дим (vi) зимо́й (vii) река́ (viii) дом о́тдыха

Grammar

Exercise **8**	(i) Anton feels cold today (ii) Nina has to work (iii) my friends are interested in knowing what the weather is like here (iv) Nikolai was hot (v) Anna Stepanovna has to speak English at work (vi) It's not very interesting for students to go to conferences.
Exercise **9**	(i) Серге́ю и Та́не (ii) Лари́се; Бори́су (iii) студе́нту (iv) дру́гу (v) Ири́не Никола́евне

Read and understand

Exercise **10**	(i) b (ii) c (iii) a

13 GIVING MORE INFORMATION ABOUT YOURSELF

You will learn

- to talk about how you spend your free time
- to describe your daily routine
- to describe the flat (apartment) you live in

and you will be given information about place names and the way they have changed

Study guide

- **Dialogues 1–3:** listen without the book
- **Dialogues 1–3:** listen, read and study one by one
- Practise what you have learned
- **Dialogue 4:** listen without the book
- **Dialogue 4:** listen, read and study
- Practise what you have learned
- **Dialogue 5:** listen without the book
- **Dialogue 5:** listen, read and study
- Practise what you have learned
- Study the **Key words and phrases**
- Study the **Grammar** section carefully
- Do the exercises in **Read and understand**
- Read **Did you know?**
- Do the exercises in **Your turn to speak**
- Listen to all the dialogues once again straight through

Dialogues

1 *Does Volodya take part in sport?*

Maria Dmitrievna Воло́дя, ты занима́ешься спо́ртом?
Volodya Да, о́чень люблю́ спорт.
Maria Dmitrievna А каки́м ви́дом спо́рта ты занима́ешься?
Volodya Пла́ванием.

пла́вание swimming

> **ты занима́ешься спо́ртом?** do you take part in sport?
> There are a number of verbs in Russian which are *always* followed by a certain case or ending. **Занима́ться** 'to occupy oneself with' is followed by *instrumental* endings (the ones explained in Unit 4). Here is how the nouns change:
> **спорт** → **я занима́юсь спо́ртом** I take part in sport
> **гимна́стика** → **вы занима́етесь гимна́стикой** you do gymnastics
> **цветово́дство** → **он занима́ется цветово́дством** he grows flowers
> You will learn more about the **-ся** ending of this verb in the grammar section on page 173.
>
> **каки́м ви́дом спо́рта ты занима́ешься?** what kind of sport do you engage in? The most common way of answering is with the verb **игра́ть в...** 'to play...', i.e. **я игра́ю в футбо́л, в баскетбо́л...**

2 *Sasha takes part in sport too, when he has the time*

Tanya А чем ты занима́ешься в свобо́дное вре́мя?
Sasha У меня́ о́чень ма́ло свобо́дного вре́мени. Я занима́юсь спо́ртом, хожу́ оди́н раз в неде́лю на бадминто́н игра́ть. Иногда́ ве́чером игра́ю с ребёнком.
Tanya У тебя́ сын?
Sasha Да. Ему́ пять лет.
Tanya Озорно́й?
Sasha Да, о́чень. С ним о́чень ве́село.
Tanya А в теа́тры хо́дишь?
Sasha О́чень ре́дко, потому́ что о́чень сло́жно купи́ть биле́ты на хоро́ший спекта́кль.
Tanya Жаль.

иногда́ sometimes
ребёнок child
(**с ребёнком** with a child)
озорно́й mischievous
ре́дко rarely
сло́жно complicated, difficult
жаль that's a pity

> **чем ты занима́ешься в свобо́дное вре́мя?** what do you do (lit. what do you *occupy* yourself with) in (your) free time?
>
> **у меня́ о́чень ма́ло свобо́дного вре́мени** I have very little free time. **Ма́ло** 'little', like its opposite **мно́го**, is followed by the genitive case.
>
> **оди́н раз в неде́лю** once a week. Twice a week would be **два ра́за в неде́лю**.
>
> **ему́ пять лет** he is five years old. Dative endings are used here too. However from two to four the noun for years is **го́да**. Thus:
> **у меня́ есть сын, ему́ два го́да**
> **у меня́ есть до́чка, ей три го́да**
> '*I* am 22 years old' would be **мне два́дцать два го́да**

➧ **с ним о́чень ве́село** it's fun with him. If he had a daughter, he would say: **с ней** with her.

➧ **о́чень сло́жно купи́ть биле́ты на хоро́ший спекта́кль** it is very difficult to get tickets for a good production

3 *How does Anna Ivanovna spend her free time?*

Ira А́нна Ива́новна, скажи́те, пожа́луйста, как вы прово́дите свобо́дное вре́мя?
Anna Ivanovna В свобо́дное вре́мя вечера́ми я занима́юсь чте́нием, смотрю́ телеви́зор и люблю́ вяза́ть.
Ira А в выходны́е дни?
Anna Ivanovna Выходны́е дни я провожу́ на да́че.
Ira Вы там отдыха́ете?
Anna Ivanovna Я и отдыха́ю, и занима́юсь цветово́дством, занима́юсь клубни́кой и куста́рниками.
Ira Вы там рабо́таете, я чу́вствую.
Anna Ivanovna Нет, мы э́то называ́ем акти́вный о́тдых!
Ira Но вы, наве́рно, хо́дите за гриба́ми?
Anna Ivanovna И по грибы́ хо́дим, да. О́чень я люблю́ собира́ть опя́та.
Ira О́чень интере́сно. Спаси́бо.

вечера́ми in the evenings
в выходны́е дни on days off
да́ча small cottage (see *Did you know?* in Unit 7)
цветово́дство flower cultivation
клубни́ка strawberries
куста́рник bush
наве́рно (or sometimes **наве́рное**) probably, I suppose
опя́та a type of mushroom

➧ **как вы прово́дите свобо́дное вре́мя?** how do you spend your free time? There is no difference between this question and **чем вы занима́етесь в свобо́дное вре́мя?**

➧ **я занима́юсь чте́нием.** A less common way of saying **я чита́ю** I read.

➧ **я смотрю́ телеви́зор** I watch television. The infinitive of this verb is **смотре́ть.**

➧ **вяза́ть** to knit. 'I knit' is **я вяжу́**.

➧ **я чу́вствую** I sense. Another common way of expressing an opinion is **мне ка́жется** it seems to me.

➧ **мы э́то называ́ем акти́вный о́тдых!** we call it active recreation!

➧ **ходи́ть за гриба́ми** to go mushroom-picking (a traditional Russian pastime!). Anna Ivanovna answers using a different, less common, preposition and ending **по грибы́**.

➧ **собира́ть опя́та** to collect a particular type of mushroom. Unless you have a specialist interest, it may be easier to say simply **собира́ть грибы́** to collect mushrooms!

Turn over for the exercises based on these dialogues.

Practise what you have learned

1 Larisa is telling a colleague how she spends her time. Listen to their conversation, then mark the correct answers. (Answers on page 178.)

(i) In the evenings Larisa likes to

- (a) read ☐
- (b) watch television ☐
- (c) knit or read ☐

(ii) She doesn't like to

- (a) listen to music ☐
- (b) watch television ☐

(iii) On Sundays she

- (a) always plays tennis ☐
- (b) sometimes goes mushroom-picking ☐

МАРШРУТЫ ГРИБНИКА

Наступает пора сбора грибов. Каждый мечтает вернуться из леса с полным лукошком, но далеко не всем известны заповедные грибные места.
Для москвичей, увлеченных «тихой охотой», Московское городское объединение «Турист» организует выезды за город на специальных поездах «Грибник».

2

Ina, a sports instructor stops a few people on the street and asks them some questions. Listen to their responses and write under each picture what sport the person plays, and how often. (Answers on page 178.)

New word: **бассе́йн** swimming pool

(i) ....

(ii) ....

(iii) ....

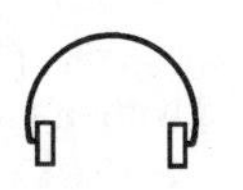

3

Your name is Syeva and you have a wide range of interests. Andrei will guide you

Dialogues

4 *Tamara doesn't seem to have <u>any</u> free time*

Tamara В моéй семьé четы́ре человéка: муж, сын и бáбушка. Я встаю́ óчень рáно, готóвлю зáвтрак и бегу́ на рабóту. В обéденный переры́в на рабóте я хожу́ по магази́нам. Пóсле рабóты я снóва хожу́ по магази́нам. Прихожу́ домóй, готóвлю у́жин, кормлю́ всех, мóю посу́ду, занимáюсь сти́ркой и пóздно вéчером ложу́сь спать.

бáбушка grandmother
в обéденный переры́в in the lunch break
снóва again
вставáть (я встаю́, вы встаёте) to get up
готóвить (я готóвлю, вы готóвите) to prepare
мыть (я мóю, вы мóете) посу́ду to wash the dishes
занимáться сти́ркой to do the laundry
ложи́ться (я ложу́сь, вы ложи́тесь) спать to go to bed (lit. to lie down to sleep)

- **в моéй семьé четы́ре человéка** there are four people in my family. If Tamara had a daughter as well, she might say: **двóе детéй** two children. Similarly **трóе детéй** three children and **чéтверо детéй** four children. For the moment you need only use these numbers with the word for 'children'. Some other members of a family:

отéц	father	**мать**	mother
брат	brother	**сестрá**	sister
дéдушка	grandfather	**бáбушка**	grandmother

- **я встаю́ óчень рáно** I get up very early. 'Very late' is **óчень пóздно**.
- **бегу́ на рабóту** I dash off to work. The verb **бежáть** 'to run' is usually followed by **в/на** and the accusative case. A more neutral verb here would be **идти́** 'to go', e.g.:
  я иду́ на рабóту I go to work.
- **ходи́ть по магази́нам** to go around the shops (in search of goods which are frequently unavailable). **Ходи́ть** is used for motion in more than one direction.
- **пóсле рабóты** after work. **Пóсле** after is always followed by the genitive case.
- **прихожу́ домóй** I come home. **Домóй** means '*to* home, homeward' and is used after verbs indicating movement. It should not be confused with **дóма** '*at* home'.
- **кормлю́ всех** I feed everybody

Practise what you have learned

4 On your recording you will hear three people describing their families. Listen carefully, then find the picture which corresponds below. (Answers on page 178.)

(a) .... (b) .... (c) ....

5 Valya and her neighbour have quite different lifestyles. The descriptions they gave of their daily routine are given below, but they are all jumbled up. Listen to your recording and then write down who does what in the correct order. (Answers on page 178.)

(i) Valya	(ii) Oleg
....	....
....	....
....	....
....	....
....	....
....	....
....	....

(m) **В обе́денный переры́в я хожу́ в кафе́.**

(e) **Я де́лаю ко́фе, но не за́втракаю.**

(b) **Я прихожу́ на рабо́ту по́здно.**

(a) **Я ложу́сь спать по́здно.**

(g) **Я встаю́ о́чень по́здно.**

(j) **Я встаю́ о́чень ра́но и гото́влю за́втрак.**

(h) **По́сле рабо́ты я занима́юсь спо́ртом.**

(c) **Пото́м я бегу́ на рабо́ту.**

(i) **Я прихожу́ домо́й по́здно.**

(k) **Там я гото́влю у́жин и кормлю́ всех.**

(l) **Пото́м я мо́ю посу́ду.**

(n) **Я ложу́сь спать ра́но.**

(d) **Иногда́ я хожу́ в теа́тр.**

(f) **В обе́денный переры́в я хожу́ по магази́нам.**

Dialogues

5 *Aleksandr Aleksandrovich describes his home*

Мы живём в но́вом райо́не Москвы́. Э́то дово́льно далеко́ от це́нтра, но ря́дом метро́. Живём мы в кооперати́вной кварти́ре, кото́рую купи́ли 20 лет наза́д. В э́той кварти́ре мы живём втроём, с до́черью. Ра́ньше у нас была́ госуда́рственная кварти́ра, но нам о́чень хоте́лось купи́ть со́бственную кварти́ру. Кварти́ра у нас трёхко́мнатная: гости́ная, спа́льня и для до́чери ко́мната. Небольша́я ку́хня. В гости́ной сте́нка, где храни́м кни́ги, посу́ду, журна́лы. Мы о́чень лю́бим чита́ть журна́лы. На стене́ большо́й ковёр и есть карти́ны.

дово́льно fairly
ря́дом next door
втроём three together
ра́ньше previously
со́бственный one's own
гости́ная living room
храни́ть to keep
спа́льня bedroom
ко́мната room
ку́хня kitchen
стена́ wall
ковёр carpet
карти́на picture

- **мы живём** we live. The verb **жить** is rather irregular: **я живу́, ты живёшь, он/она́ живёт, мы живём, вы живёте, они́ живу́т**. It does, however, conjugate normally in the past: **он жил, она́ жила́**.
- **в но́вом райо́не Москвы́** in a new district of Moscow. Every time a noun changes in Russian so do any adjectives describing it.
- **в кооперати́вной кварти́ре** in a cooperative flat
- **кото́рую купи́ли** which we bought. **Кото́рую** 'which' has an accusative ending since it is the direct object of **купи́ли**.
- **20 лет наза́д** 20 years ago. You will often also hear **тому́ наза́д**.
- **с до́черью** with (our) daughter. The word **дочь** daughter has very irregular endings.
- **нам о́чень хоте́лось...** another way of saying **мы о́чень хоте́ли...** we very much wanted...
- **трёхко́мнатная** three-roomed. You might also want to say: **однoко́мнатная** 'one-roomed' or **двухко́мнатная** 'two-roomed'. Note, however, that few Russians have a room used *only* as a living room and therefore they include any room which can be *lived* in.
- **небольша́я ку́хня** a smallish kitchen
- **сте́нка** a wall-unit including wardrobe, shelves, cupboards (cabinets) etc.
- **на стене́ большо́й ковёр** hanging on the wall is a big carpet. Russian flats are not normally carpeted, but it is very common to see a large Persian carpet decorating the wall.

Practise what you have learned

6 Listen to Vladimir Nikolaevich's description of his flat and then spot the mistakes in the following notes. (Answers on page 178.)

(i) They live in a new district, close to the centre.
(ii) They have a cooperative apartment which they bought 13 years ago.
(iii) There are four people: husband, wife, son and grandmother.
(iv) The apartment is three-roomed.
(v) They keep their clothes in a wall-unit in the bedroom.

7 Three people who are each hoping to exchange their own flat for another one are looking through the advertisements in the Bulletin of the Flat Exchange Office. Each finds one promising advertisement. Listen as they describe their present accommodation, and match each to the appropriate advertisement. (Answers on page 178.)

You will need to know the following phrase:

меня́ем (одну́ кварти́ру) на (другу́ю кварти́ру)
we will exchange (one flat) for (another flat).

(a)

МЕНЯЕМ
однокомнатную кооперативную квартиру в центре
на
однокомнатную кооперативную квартиру в новом районе Москвы.

(b)

МЕНЯЕМ
двухкомнатную государственную квартиру недалеко от центра
на
двухкомнатную государственную квартиру в новом районе Москвы недалеко от школы.

(c)

МЕНЯЕМ
одну двухкомнатную государственную квартиру в новом районе Москвы и одну однокомнатную государственную квартиру недалеко от центра
на
трёхкомнатную квартиру в старом районе Москвы недалеко от центра.

Key words and phrases

To use

занима́ться (я занима́юсь, вы занима́етесь)	to occupy oneself with
занима́ться спо́ртом	to take part in sport
(в) свобо́дное вре́мя	(in) free time
(в) выходны́е дни	(on) days off
смотре́ть телеви́зор	to watch television
проводи́ть (вре́мя) на да́че	to spend (time) at the dacha
ходи́ть за гриба́ми	to go mushroom-picking
собира́ть грибы́	to collect mushrooms
дво́е (тро́е, че́тверо) дете́й	two (three, four) children
встава́ть (я встаю́, вы встаёте) ра́но/по́здно	to get up early/late
ложи́ться спать (я ложу́сь спать, вы ложи́тесь спать)	to go to bed
бежа́ть (я бегу́, вы бежи́те)...	to run, dash...
идти́ (я иду́, вы идёте)...	to go...
на рабо́ту	to work
домо́й	home(ward)
ходи́ть по магази́нам	to go around the shops
гото́вить (я гото́влю, вы гото́вите)	to prepare, to cook
но́вый/ста́рый райо́н	new/old district
кооперати́вная кварти́ра	cooperative flat
госуда́рственная кварти́ра	state-owned flat
со́бственный	one's own
однoко́мнатная/двухко́мнатная/трёхко́мнатная кварти́ра	one-roomed/two-roomed/three-roomed flat
ко́мната	a room
гости́ная	a living room
спа́льня	bedroom
ку́хня	kitchen

To understand

чем вы занима́етесь в свобо́дное вре́мя?	what do you do in your free time?
как вы прово́дите свобо́дное вре́мя?/выходны́е дни?	how do you spend your free time?/days off?

Grammar

Verbs ending in **-ся**

The particle **-ся** is added to a verb to make it *reflexive*, i.e. to indicate that the subject is doing the action *to himself or herself*, or when there is no object after the verb. **Занима́ться** means 'to occupy *oneself* (with something)'. **Занима́ть** by itself means simply 'to occupy (a place, time etc.)'. You have seen other verbs ending in **-ся**, e.g.:

открыва́ться to open
Магази́н открыва́ется в 9 часо́в. The shop opens at 9 o'clock.

There is no *object* in this sentence – the shop 'opens *itself*'! However, the shopkeeper would say:

Я открыва́ю магази́н в 9 часо́в. I open the shop at 9 o'clock.

Some other important verbs which change in this way are:

закрыва́ть to close (something) | **закрыва́ться** to close
начина́ть to begin (something) | **начина́ться** to begin
конча́ть to end (something) | **конча́ться** to end
одева́ть to dress (somebody) | **одева́ться** to get dressed

Examples

Ва́ля начина́ет рабо́ту в 8 часо́в и конча́ет (рабо́ту) в 4 часа́.
Valya begins work at 8 o'clock and finishes (work) at 4.
В це́нтре магази́ны закрыва́ются по́здно.
In the centre shops close late.
Она́ всегда́ одева́ется легко́.
She always dresses lightly.
Он одева́ет сы́на, и они́ иду́т в парк.
He dresses his son and they go to the park.

There are other occasions when reflexive endings are used, but for the moment we suggest that you just try to remember the very common verbs mentioned here.

Endings

Do not be daunted by the new endings. The verb itself changes as you would expect (see page 119). To make it reflexive, you add **-ся** if the previous letter is a consonant or **-ь**, and **-сь** if it is a vowel. For example:

я занима́юсь | **мы занима́емся**
ты занима́ешься | **вы занима́етесь**
он занима́ется | **они занима́ются**

The past also follows this pattern:

он занима́лся, она́ занима́лась, они́ занима́лись

Turn over for the grammar exercises.

8

Fill in the missing verb. (Answers on page 178.)

(i) **Ресторáн .... в 11 часóв.** (открывáть (ся))

(ii) **Нúна Алексéевна .... магазúн ýтром.** (открывáть (ся))

(iii) **Я .... рабóту в 9 часóв.** (начинáть (ся))

(iv) **Фильм .... в 7.30.** (начинáть (ся))

(v) **В свобóдное врéмя я .... спóртом.** (занимáть (ся))

(vi) **Ковёр .... мнóго мéста.** (занимáть (ся))

(vii) **Мы .... ýжин óчень пóздно.** (кончáть (ся))

(viii) **Спектáкль .... в 7 часóв, и .... в 10 часóв.** (начинáть (ся), кончáть (ся))

9

In this exercise sometimes the verb is missing, sometimes the noun. (Answers on page 178.)

(i) **Чем вы .... в свобóдное врéмя?** (занимáться)

(ii) **Я занимáюсь .... и игрáю с ребёнком.** (спорт)

(iii) **Чем ты .... в выходны́е дни?** (занимáться)

(iv) **Я занимáюсь .... на дáче.** (цветовóдство)

(v) **Пóсле рабóты Тамáра занимáется ....** (стúрка)

(vi) **В свобóдное врéмя мы .... спóртом.** (занимáться)

Read and understand

The handwritten script

Up till now we have introduced only printed Russian. However, Russians *write* rather than print, and since you will probably wish to correspond with friends you make, it is worth spending some time becoming familiar with the handwritten script. Here is the alphabet with both printed letters and handwritten:

А	а	Л	л	Ч	ч
Б	б	М	м	Ш	ш
В	в	Н	н	Щ	щ
Г	г	О	о		ъ
Д	д	П	п		ы
Е	е	Р	р		ь
Ё	ё	С	с	Э	э
Ж	ж	Т	т	Ю	ю
З	з	У	у	Я	я
И	и	Ф	ф		
Й	й	Х	х		
К	к	Ц	ц		

Here are some common words, both printed and handwritten:

театр	*театр*
ресторан	*ресторан*
газета	*газета*
журнал	*журнал*
кофе с молоком	*кофе с молоком*

As you can see, some letters look quite different. Practise writing them and try forming whole words.

Now turn over for the exercises.

10

On retiring Natalya Aleksandrovna was given a card with the following signatures. Can you make out the names of her colleagues? (Answers on page 178.)

(i) Оля (ii) Татьяна Васильевна

(iii) Игорь (iv) Сергей Михайлович

(v) Мария Юрьевна (vi) Миша

(vii) Вера Павловна (viii) Катя

11

A young student called Tonya was asked to write a letter to a friend's brother who is studying Russian. Read her letter, then correct the mistakes in the statements below. (Answers on page 178.)

You will need to know: **Жду отве́та,** 'waiting for your reply'.

В моей семье 4 человека: мама, папа, бабушка и я. Мы живём в кооперативной квартире, которую купили 5 лет назад. Квартира двухкомнатная: у мамы и папы большая комната, а у нас с бабушкой маленькая.

Я студентка, и у меня мало свободного времени. Но я очень люблю читать, слушать музыку, и один раз в неделю я хожу в бассейн плавать. В выходные дни я люблю ходить за грибами или ничего не делать.

А где ты живёшь? Сколько человек в твоей семье? Чем ты занимаешься в свободное время?

Жду ответа,
Тоня.

(i) Tonya lives with her parents and sister.
(ii) They have a state-owned flat.
(iii) It is a three-roomed flat.
(iv) She likes to watch television and listen to music.
(v) She plays badminton once a week.
(vi) At the weekend she likes to go mushroom-picking or grow flowers.

Tonya asked some questions at the end of her letter. How would *you* answer them?

Did you know?

What's in a name?

The question may seem well-worn, but to Russians it is of immediate importance. Changing names of places, institutions etc. has taken on symbolic, as well as practical, significance.

In the first decades after the revolution of 1917, a large number of cities, towns, villages, streets etc. were renamed. Usually they were named after some revolutionary figure or group. Most famous is, of course, the city which Peter the Great founded. As you have read in Unit 12, from 1703 to 1914 it was called **St. Petersburg**. Then, in 1914, to make it sound more 'Russian', it was renamed **Petrograd**, only to be changed again in 1924 to **Leningrad**, in honour of Vladimir Lenin, who had just died. In 1991 a referendum on the question of the city's name was held and a majority voted for the restoration of the first name **St. Petersburg**. While officially the name is *Saint* Petersburg, Russians normally call it simply 'Petersburg'.

Under Stalin, renaming took on absurd proportions as the dictator and his retinue named squares, streets, towns and mountains after themselves.

The problem here was that when these people fell from favour, the names had to be changed yet again. Those reading about the famous Battle of Stalingrad, the turning point in the Second World War, may have been bemused to find no trace of the city on maps. This is because after the denunciation of Stalin in 1956 it was renamed **Volgograd**.

Only the most notorious in Stalin's following received the ignominious fate of having their names erased from history. The names of others, such as Zhdanov, were retained until late into the 1980s.

This form of self-worship did not end with Stalin's reign. Brezhnev also used it both for himself and as a reward for 'his' people.

Since the 1980s and particularly following the demise of the Union of Soviet Socialist Republics (USSR) at the end of 1991, many old names have been restored. Kalinin is now **Tver** once more, Gor'ky is **Nizhny-Novgorod**.

In Moscow many of the main streets have also reverted to the old names: **у́лица Го́рького** is again **Тверска́я**, and **проспе́кт Ма́ркса** is **Охо́тный Ряд**. It must be added that some names never really changed as far as the people were concerned. While authorities called the square close to Red Square **пло́щадь 50-ле́тия Октября́** (50th anniversary of October (revolution) square), Muscovites among themselves continued to use the old (and 'new'!) name **Мане́жная**.

All this means that asking may well be more efficient than trying to follow maps!

Your turn to speak

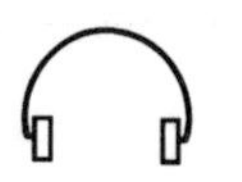

12

On a trip to Russia, you are introduced to a school teacher, Tatyana. Practise what you would say to her about your interests and pastimes, where you live, work etc. Once you have had a go, turn on the recording and listen to what *she* says about *herself*.

Useful phrases:

я (не) женáт, (не)зáмужем	I'm (not) married
у меня́ двóе детéй / нет детéй	I have two children / I don't have children
у меня́ есть сын/дочь (/дóчка)	I have a son/daughter
емý/ей два гóда / пять лет	he/she is 2 years old / 5 years old
я живý / мы живём...	I live / we live...
в двухкóмнатной квартúре	in a two-roomed flat
в госудáрственной / сóбственной квартúре	in a state-owned / one's own flat
я рабóтаю в/на...	I work in...
у меня́ мáло/мнóго свобóдного врéмени	I have little/lots of free time
я занимáюсь спóртом	I take part in a sport
читáть	to read
смотрéть телевúзор	to watch television
проводúть свобóдное врéмя...	to spend free time...
выходны́е дни	days off, the weekend
на дáче	in the holiday house
занимáться цветовóдством	to grow flowers
ходúть за грибáми	to go mushroom-picking

Answers

Practise what you have learned

Exercise **1**	(i) c (ii) b (iii) b
Exercise **2**	(i) swimming, 4 times a week (ii) basketball, 3 times a week (iii) badminton, once a week
Exercise **4**	(i) b (ii) c (iii) a
Exercise **5**	(i) j, c, f, i, k, l, n (ii) g, e, b, m, h, d, a
Exercise **6**	(i) old district (ii) 15 years ago (iii) three (no grandmother) (iv) two-roomed (v) keep books there
Exercise **7**	(i) c (ii) a (iii) b

Grammar

Exercise **8**	(i) открывáется (ii) открывáет (iii) начинáю (iv) начинáется (v) занимáюсь (vi) занимáет (vii) кончáем (viii) начинáется; кончáется
Exercise **9**	(i) занимáетесь (ii) спóртом (iii) занимáешься (iv) цветовóдством (v) стúркой (vi) занимáемся

Read and understand

Exercise **10**	(i) Óля (ii) Татья́на Васúльевна (iii) Úгорь (iv) Сергéй Михáйлович (v) Марúя Ю́рьевна (vi) Мúша (vii) Вéра Пáвловна (viii) Кáтя
Exercise **11**	(i) with parents and grandmother (ii) cooperative flat (iii) two-roomed (iv) likes to read and listen to music (v) swims once a week (vi) go mushroom-picking or do nothing

14 **STATING YOUR INTENTIONS**

You will learn

- to answer questions about holiday plans
- to talk about buying a flat
- to describe your work or studies
- to talk about plans for the future
- to invite somebody out

and you will read about life in a Russian city

Study guide

- **Dialogues 1, 2:** listen without the book
- **Dialogues 1, 2:** listen, read and study one by one
- Practise what you have learned
- **Dialogue 3:** listen without the book
- **Dialogue 3:** listen, read and study
- Practise what you have learned
- **Dialogues 4, 5:** listen without the book
- **Dialogues 4, 5:** listen, read and study one by one
- Practise what you have learned
- **Dialogue 6:** listen without the book
- **Dialogue 6:** listen, read and study
- Practise what you have learned
- Study the **Key words and phrases**
- Study the **Grammar** section carefully
- Do the exercises in **Read and understand**
- Read **Did you know?**
- Do the exercises in **Your turn to speak**
- Listen to all the dialogues once again straight through

Dialogues

1 *Where are Larisa Alekseevna and her family going on holiday?*

Boris Mikhailovich Лари́са Алексе́евна, куда́ вы пое́дете в о́тпуск?
Larisa Alekseevna В э́том году́ в о́тпуск мы пое́дем на рыба́лку, на ре́чку А́хтуба.
Boris Mikhailovich Как вы там бу́дете проводи́ть вре́мя?
Larisa Alekseevna Ну муж бу́дет ходи́ть на рыба́лку ра́но у́тром. Мы с до́черью бу́дем купа́ться, загора́ть, гото́вить уху́ и занима́ться люби́мыми свои́ми дела́ми.
Boris Mikhailovich А вы бу́дете там пла́вать?
Larisa Alekseevna Да, там о́чень тёплая, хоро́шая вода́.

рыба́лка fishing
ре́чка А́хтуба a (small) river, the Akhtuba
уха́ a particular type of fish soup
купа́ться / пла́вать to swim

- **куда́ вы пое́дете в о́тпуск?** where will you be going on your holiday? The verb **пое́хать** ends in exactly the same way as **е́хать** 'to go by vehicle'. The **по-** in front puts it into the future. Thus:

я пое́ду	I will go	**мы пое́дем**	we will go
ты пое́дешь	you will go	**вы пое́дете**	you will go (pl. or formal)
он/она́ пое́дет	he/she will go	**они́ пое́дут**	they will go

- **в э́том году́** this year
  в сле́дующем году́ next year
- **Как вы там бу́дете проводи́ть вре́мя?** how will you spend your time there? To say what you *will* be doing in Russian, you use, as appropriate, **я бу́ду, ты бу́дешь,...** followed by an infinitive verb, i.e. **я бу́ду чита́ть, а ты бу́дешь купа́ться** 'I shall read and you will bathe' (there is more about the future on page 189).
- **у́тром** in the morning. Other times of the day:
  днём during the day
  ве́чером in the evening
- **мы с до́черью** my daughter and I. Similarly: **мы с му́жем / с жено́й** my husband / wife and I. The verb takes the normal ending after **мы.**
- **занима́ться люби́мыми свои́ми дела́ми** to be occupied with our favourite pastimes

2 *Misha is going further away*

Tanya Ми́ша, а каки́е у тебя́ пла́ны на ле́то?
Misha Ле́том, я ду́маю, мы пое́дем со шко́лой, где я ра́ньше учи́лся, в Да́нию. Мы там бу́дем пока́зывать спекта́кль 'Наш А́ндерсен'. Мы там бу́дем жить в се́мьях в ма́леньком го́роде О́денсе.
Tanya А что ты хо́чешь там посмотре́ть?
Misha Ну, вообще́, про́сто о́чень интере́сно посмотре́ть другу́ю страну́.

спекта́кль show, performance
Да́ния Denmark
вообще́ in general
страна́ country

- **Каки́е у тебя́ пла́ны на ле́то?** what plans do you have for the summer? You can use this construction just to find out about somebody's plans for the evening, i.e. **каки́е у тебя́ / у вас пла́ны на ве́чер?**

- **со шко́лой, где я ра́ньше учи́лся** with the school, where I previously studied. The verb **учи́ться** means 'to study, to be a student'. The present tense is:

я учу́сь	**мы у́чимся**
ты у́чишься	**вы у́читесь**
он/она́ у́чится	**они́ у́чатся**

- **мы бу́дем жить в се́мьях** to live with a family. If he already knew the family he was staying with, he could say:
  мы бу́дем жить у друзе́й we will live with friends.
- **что ты хо́чешь там посмотре́ть?** what do you want to see there? If Misha had no particular idea, he might ask: **что мо́жно посмотре́ть?** what *is* there to see?
- **посмотре́ть** to look at *on a specific occasion*. This is the perfective form of **смотре́ть**. (See the grammar sections on pages 189 and 213.)

Practise what you have learned

1

Кто куда́? or Who is going where? Listen to your recording, then note the mistake in each of the following statements. (Answers on page 194.)

(i) Kolya is going with his brother to Tsarskoye Selo. He wants to see the lycée where Pushkin studied.
(ii) Olya and her school are going to England, where they'll put on their show: 'Our Pushkin'.
(iii) Yelena Dmitrievna and her husband are going east. They plan to swim and sunbathe.

2

You are going on holiday with your husband and daughter. You will be asked where you are going and what you'd like to do there. As always, listen for Andrei's prompts.

Dialogues

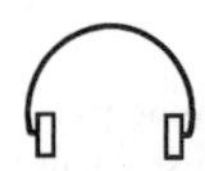

3 *Pavel is planning to buy a flat*

Tanya Ты снима́ешь кварти́ру?
Pavel Пока́ я живу́ с роди́телями, но собира́юсь купи́ть кооперати́в.
Tanya Оо... како́й?
Pavel Я хочу́ двухко́мнатный.
Tanya В но́вом до́ме?
Pavel Да, дом сейча́с стро́ится, но я наде́юсь, что че́рез год он бу́дет уже́ гото́в.
Tanya Ку́хня больша́я?
Pavel 12 квадра́тных ме́тров.
Tanya И балко́н есть?
Pavel Больша́я ло́джия. Там я собира́юсь разводи́ть да́же цветы́.
Tanya И как до́лго ждать?
Pavel Ну, я наде́юсь, что че́рез год я уже́ бу́ду в э́той кварти́ре жить.
Tanya Ну, наве́рно, э́то безу́мно до́рого?
Pavel Не о́чень. 12 ты́сяч рубле́й, и полови́ну мне даст в креди́т моё предприя́тие.

пока́ for the moment
кооперати́в another word for 'cooperative flat'
уже́ already
гото́в (f. **гото́ва**) ready
балко́н/ло́джия balcony
да́же even
безу́мно до́рого 'madly' expensive
че́рез год in a year

- **ты снима́ешь кварти́ру?** do you rent a flat? The infinitive is **снима́ть кварти́ру**.
- **с роди́телями** with my parents. The nominative – 'parents' – is **роди́тели**.
- **собира́юсь купи́ть кооперати́в** I plan to buy a cooperative flat. **Собира́ться** 'to plan, intend' is another way of expressing the future. It too is always followed by an infinitive verb.
- **дом сейча́с стро́ится** the block of flats (apartment block) is being built at the moment. **Дом** can refer to a simple 'house', but in cities it more often refers to a 'block of flats'.
- **я наде́юсь (, что...)** I hope (that...). The infinitive is **наде́яться**.
- **12 квадра́тных ме́тров** 12 square metres
- **разводи́ть цветы́** to grow flowers. A garden **сад** is no more than a dream for most Russian city dwellers, but one might also grow flowers in a garden, **в саду́**.
- **как до́лго ждать?** how long will you have to wait? (The word **на́до** 'necessary' is understood.)
- **полови́ну мне даст в креди́т моё предприя́тие** my firm will lend me half. **Предприя́тие** 'business, enterprise' comes at the end of the sentence as the most important element. This is a principle worth remembering when searching for the subject of a complicated sentence!

Practise what you have learned

3 Aleksei is answering some questions about his present and future homes. Listen to your recording, then choose the correct answers below. (Answers on page 194.)

(i) Aleksei and his wife are living with:

- (a) his wife's parents ☐
- (b) his parents ☐

(ii) They plan to buy:

- (a) a one-roomed flat with a big balcony ☐
- (b) a one-roomed flat with a big kitchen ☐

(iii) The flat is:

- (a) in a new block in a new district ☐
- (b) in a new block in the centre ☐

(iv) They should be there

- (a) in a year ☐
- (b) in two years ☐

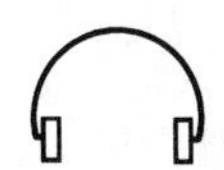

4 You will be talking about the flat you would like to buy.

МЕНЯЮ

3-х комнатную квартиру / 44 кв. м : 20 +I4+I0 /, комнаты изолированные, кухня 7,5 м,5 этаж 9-тиэтажного дома, рядом станция метро "Отрадное"

НУЖНО

- 2 отдельные квартиры

Возможны варианты

тел: 404 - 22 - 76

404 22 76 | 404 22 76 | 404 22 76 | 404 22 76 | 404 22 76 | 404 22 76

Many of those desperate to exchange their flats stick signs like this on lamp posts and any other available surface

Dialogues

4 *What is Kolya's ambition?*

Maria Dmitrievna Ко́ля, а кем ты хо́чешь стать?
Kolya Я мечта́ю стать космона́втом, но, наве́рно, полу́чится шофёром.

мечта́ть to dream, aspire
космона́вт astronaut
шофёр driver, chauffeur

- **кем ты хо́чешь стать?** what would you like to become? The verb **стать** 'to become' is followed by the same instrumental case endings as **занима́ться** (see page 164 and the grammar summary on page 211).
- **полу́чится шофёром** I'll end up a driver. Any noun after **получи́ться** 'to turn out' is also in the instrumental case.

5 *Dima asks Lyena whether she works or is studying*

Dima А вы что де́лаете, у́читесь и́ли рабо́таете?
Lyena Я и учу́сь, и рабо́таю. Я рабо́таю санита́ркой в больни́це, а ве́чером учу́сь в медици́нском учи́лище.
Dima Ой, я ду́маю, э́то о́чень тру́дно, учи́ться и рабо́тать.
Lyena Э́то о́чень тру́дно, коне́чно, но мне нра́вится. Коне́чно, иногда́ я о́чень устаю́, потому́ что заня́тия начина́ются в шесть, а зака́нчиваются в де́вять, а иногда́ да́же по́зже. Но мне нра́вится!
Dima Я ду́маю, заня́тия медици́ной тре́буют о́чень мно́го вре́мени. Вы хоти́те стать врачо́м?
Lyena Ну, я снача́ла ста́ну медици́нской сестро́й, а пото́м же, е́сли полу́чится, я попро́бую поступа́ть в медици́нский институ́т.
Dima Ну, я наде́юсь.
Lyena И *я* наде́юсь!

санита́рка hospital attendant
больни́ца hospital
медици́нское учи́лище medical school for nurses, midwives etc.
ду́мать to think
тру́дно difficult
заня́тия (pl.) lectures, studies
врач doctor
снача́ла first of all
медици́нская сестра́ (or **медсестра́**) nurse
пото́м же then

- **вы что де́лаете, у́читесь и́ли рабо́таете?** what do you do, study or work?
- **я и учу́сь, и рабо́таю** I both study and work. The easiest way to express 'both (... and...)' is by putting **и** before each of the two. Another example: **я хочу́ стать и инжене́ром, и балери́ной** I want to be both an engineer and a ballerina.
- **я рабо́таю санита́ркой** I work as a hospital attendant. Any occupation following **рабо́тать** has instrumental endings (i.e. the same endings as after **занима́ться**). Thus:
  рабо́тать врачо́м to work as a doctor
  рабо́тать инжене́ром to work as an engineer
  рабо́тать шофёром to work as a driver
  рабо́тать учи́телем (f. **учи́тельницей**) to work as a teacher
- **мне нра́вится** I like it (lit. 'it is pleasing *to me*'). The question 'do you like...?' begins **вам нра́вится...?**
- **иногда́ я о́чень устаю́** sometimes I get very tired. On any *particular* occasion, Lyena would say **я уста́ла** 'I'm tired', while a man would say **я уста́л**.
- **заня́тия начина́ются в 6, а зака́нчиваются в 9** lectures begin at 6 and end at 9. **Зака́нчиваться** is another word for **конча́ться**.

- **да́же по́зже** even later
- **заня́тия медици́ной тре́буют о́чень мно́го вре́мени** medical studies take a lot of time
- **е́сли полу́чится** if it works out
- **я попро́бую поступа́ть в медици́нский институ́т** I will try to get into a medical institute (for doctors). **Поступа́ть** is used with any educational institution, e.g. **поступа́ть в университе́т, в институ́т. Я попро́бую** 'I shall try' is important here since without connections the competition for tertiary (higher) education is fierce.

Practise what you have learned

5 'What would you like to be when you grow up?' is a question children will always willingly answer! Look at the pictures below and see if you can fill in the missing professions (with the right endings). (Answers on page 194.)

Professions
инжене́р
балери́на
космона́вт
учи́тель (m.) / **учи́тельница** (f.)
писа́тель (m.) / **писа́тельница** (f.) writer

(i) **Я мечта́ю стать** ....

(ii) **Я мечта́ю стать** ....

(iii) **Я мечта́ю стать** ....

(iv) **Я мечта́ю стать** ....

(v) **Я мечта́ю стать** ....

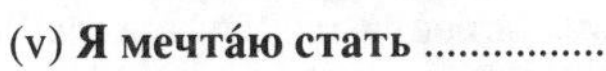

(vi) **Я мечта́ю стать** ....

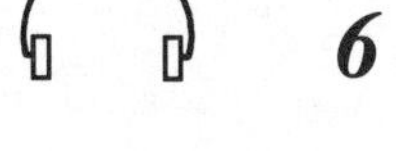

6 Vladimir Dmitrievich has met some of his ex-pupils at the school New Year concert and asks them what they do now. Listen to their replies, then match the statements in each list which go together. (Answers on page 194.)

New words:
педагоги́ческий институ́т teachers' training college
истори́ческий факульте́т history department

(i) **у́тром я рабо́таю в больни́це**
(ii) **я актёр**
(iii) **я учу́сь в педагоги́ческом институ́те**
(iv) **я учу́сь в университе́те**

(a) **я изуча́ю иностра́нные языки́**
(b) **а рабо́таю ве́чером в магази́не**
(c) **а ве́чером учу́сь в медици́нском учи́лище**
(d) **я рабо́таю в теа́тре в Москве́**

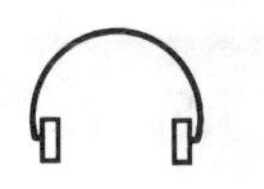

7 Your name is Dima, and, while working as a driver, you are studying at a medical college. Listen for Andrei's prompts.

Dialogues

6 *Dima invites Lyena to the theatre MKhAT*

Dima Ле́на, у меня́ есть два биле́та во МХАТ. Вы не хоти́те пойти́ со мной в теа́тр?
Lyena А на како́й спекта́кль?
Dima *Дя́дя Ва́ня* Че́хова.
Lyena Ой, я с удово́льствием пойду́.
Dima Замеча́тельно. А где мы встре́тимся?
Lyena У телегра́фа в 6.30.
Dima Мо́жет быть, лу́чше в пятна́дцать мину́т седьмо́го?
Lyena Ну, хорошо́. Как вам удо́бно.
Dima Договори́лись.
Lyena До встре́чи!
Dima До встре́чи!
Lyena Спаси́бо!

МХАТ Moscow Arts Theatre
замеча́тельно marvellous
как вам удо́бно as you wish
***Дя́дя Ва́ня* Че́хова** Chekhov's *Uncle Vanya*
договори́лись agreed
до встре́чи! until we meet!

- **вы не хоти́те пойти́ со мной в теа́тр?** would you like to come with me to the theatre?
- **со мной** with me. Other useful forms are: **с на́ми** with us, **с ва́ми** with you (formal or plural), **с тобо́й** with you (singular, informal).
- **на како́й спекта́кль?** to what production?
- **я с удово́льствием пойду́** I'll go with pleasure. The verb **идти́** 'to go by foot' also has a form used for specific future actions – **пойти́**. The endings are the same as for **идти́**:

я пойду́ I will go	**мы пойдём** we will go
ты пойдёшь you will go	**вы пойдёте** you will go (pl. or formal)
он/она́ пойдёт he/she will go	**они́ пойду́т** they will go

- **а где мы встре́тимся?** where shall we meet? The infinitive of this perfective verb is **встре́титься**.
- **у телегра́фа** by the telegraph office
- **лу́чше в пятна́дцать мину́т седьмо́го** better at a quarter past six

МХАТ
Сцена в проезде Художественного театра

Серия АА
Б/кн. №
000730

ПАРТЕР

8 ряд прав. № 20

Цена 3 рубля

27 ИЮЛЯ 1988

ОСНОВНАЯ СЦЕНА
ВЕЧЕР

Practise what you have learned

8 There must be something in the air... Three people have muddled their respective arrangements for going to the theatre. Listen to the dialogues on your recording, then look at the pictures below and explain the mistake each person has made. (Answers on page 194.)

(i) ....

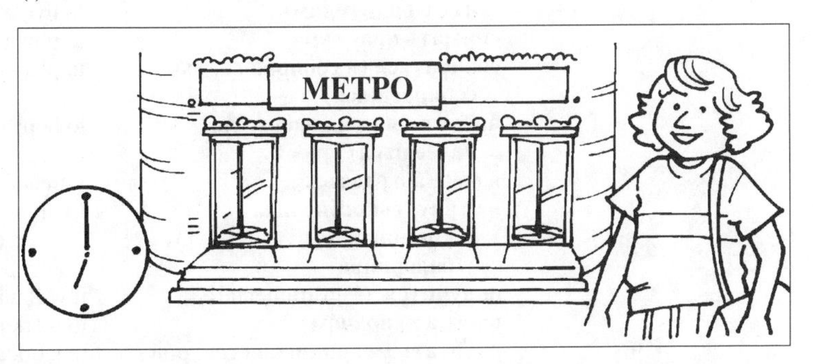

(ii) ....

(iii) ....

9 You are visiting Moscow and a new acquaintance has managed to obtain tickets to the theatre. Listen to Andrei's prompts.

Key words and phrases

To use

в э́том году́	this year
в сле́дующем году́	next year
пое́хать (я пое́ду, мы пое́дем) (perfective)	to go by vehicle (I will go, we will go)
пойти́ (я пойду́, мы пойдём) (perfective)	to go on foot (I will go, we will go)
я бу́ду, мы бу́дем...	I will, we will...
купа́ться	swim, bathe
гото́вить	cook
мы с до́черью	my daughter and I
у́тром	in the morning
днём	in the daytime
ве́чером	in the evening
учи́ться (я учу́сь, ты у́чишься)	to study
что мо́жно посмотре́ть?	what is there to see?
жить в се́мьях	to live with a family
жить у друзе́й	to live with friends
жить с роди́телями	to live with (one's) parents
снима́ть кварти́ру	to rent a flat
собира́ться (я собира́юсь, ты собира́ешься)	to plan, intend
наде́яться (я наде́юсь, ты наде́ешься)	to hope
я мечта́ю стать...	I dream of becoming...
я ста́ну, ты ста́нешь...	I will become, you will become...
космона́втом	an astronaut
балери́ной	a ballerina
полу́чится (+ instrumental)	it will turn out...
рабо́тать врачо́м	to work as a doctor
рабо́тать медици́нской сестро́й / медсестро́й	to work as a nurse
э́то о́чень тру́дно	it is very difficult
мне нра́вится...	I like...
устава́ть (я устаю́, ты устаёшь)	to get tired (I get tired, you get tired)
попро́бовать (я попро́бую, ты попро́буешь) (perfective)	to try (I will try, you will try)
поступа́ть в университе́т	to enter university
поступа́ть в институ́т	to enter an institute
мы встре́тимся...	we will meet...
у телегра́фа	by the telegraph office
как вам удо́бно	as you wish
договори́лись	agreed

To understand

куда́ вы пое́дете в о́тпуск?	where will you go for (your) holidays?
как вы бу́дете проводи́ть вре́мя?	how will you spend your time?
каки́е у тебя́ / у вас пла́ны...	what plans do you have...
на ле́то?	for summer?
на ве́чер?	for the evening?
кем ты хо́чешь / вы хоти́те стать?	what do you want to be?

Grammar

The future tense

To say that an action will be taking place, *or* that it will happen more than once, the future of **быть** (to be) is used, followed by an infinitive verb, e.g.:

я	**бу́ду чита́ть**	I will read
ты	**бу́дешь купа́ться**	you will bathe
он/она́	**бу́дет загора́ть**	he/she will sunbathe
мы	**бу́дем игра́ть в те́ннис**	we will play tennis
вы	**бу́дете рабо́тать**	you will work
они́	**бу́дут изуча́ть ру́сский язы́к**	they will study Russian

No indication is given as to whether the action will be *completed*; all the speaker indicates is that it will be *occurring*.

Even if you are not talking about an *action*, but rather a state, you still use the future of **быть**, for example:

Я бу́ду на рабо́те I will be at work
Кварти́ра бу́дет гото́ва че́рез год The flat will be ready in a year

A different form of the future is used, however, in order to talk about a *specific single action* in the future. Typical examples where such a form would be used are: 'I will finish that book tonight', 'He will set off for Moscow tomorrow', 'We will buy him a small present'. In Russian, this type of future action is expressed by the *perfective aspect* of the verb. It is most common for perfective verbs to be formed by adding **по-** to the verb, for example:

попро́бовать to try	**я попро́бую** I will try
пое́хать to go by vehicle	**я пое́ду** I will go by vehicle
пойти́ to go on foot	**я пойду́** I will go on foot
пообе́дать to have lunch	**я пообе́даю** I will have lunch
посмотре́ть to have a look	**я посмотрю́** I will have a look

You will see that the verb endings are those with which you are already familiar.

Without the prefix **по-** the form of the verb used is, in fact, the *imperfective aspect.*

Unfortunately not all these perfective forms begin with **по-**. There are a number of other possible prefixes and sometimes the verb itself changes. Compare the following:

чита́ть – прочита́ть to read
У́тром я бу́ду чита́ть кни́гу.
In the morning I will be reading a book.
Я прочита́ю кни́гу (и пойду́ в кафе́).
I will finish the book (and go to the café).

встреча́ться – встре́титься to meet
В Москве́ я бу́ду встреча́ться ка́ждый день с друзья́ми.
In Moscow I will meet with friends every day.
Где мы встре́тимся?
Where shall we meet?

There is also one exception (only one!) to the rule that adding **по-** makes a verb perfective. It is the verb 'to buy' where the form of the verb with **по-** is actually the *imperfective*, i.e. **покупа́ть**, while the *perfective* is **купи́ть**, for example:

Я бо́льше не бу́ду покупа́ть э́ту газе́ту. Она́ не о́чень интере́сная.
I won't buy that paper any more. It's not very interesting.
Я сего́дня куплю́ плато́к.
I will buy a scarf today.

Since it is rather a tall order to learn the perfective form of every verb, try to concentrate on becoming familiar with those which you are most likely to need.

Turn over for the exercises.

10

Irina Petrovna is trying to persuade a friend and her family to join a group heading to the river on holiday. In the box below is information about how each person normally spends his or her holiday. Bearing it in mind, fill in the missing verbs in the dialogue using the future tense. (Answers on page 194.)

(i) **Как мы там .... вре́мя?**

(ii) **Ну, мы с му́жем .... на рыба́лку.**

(iii) **Та́ня и Серёжа .... в те́ннис.**

(iv) **Ты, И́ра, ...**

(v) **Твой муж ....**

(vi) **О́ля .... с сы́ном.**

(vii) **Ба́бушка .... уху́**

(viii) **А вы, Алекса́ндра Никола́евна, ...**

мы с му́жем хо́дим на рыба́лку	**О́ля игра́ет с сы́ном**	**Алекса́ндра Никола́евна чита́ет**
И́ра купа́ется	**Та́ня и Серёжа игра́ют в те́ннис**	
ба́бушка обы́чно гото́вит уху́		**её муж загора́ет**

11

Pick the verb most appropriate for each of the following sentences. (Answers on page 194.)

(i) **Куда́ вы .... в о́тпуск в сле́дующем году́?** (бу́дете е́хать – пое́дете)

В о́тпуск мы .... на рыба́лку. (бу́дем е́хать – пое́дем)

(ii) **Куда́ ты .... по́сле рабо́ты сего́дня?** (бу́дешь идти́ – пойдёшь)

Наве́рно, я .... домо́й. (бу́ду идти́ – пойду́)

(iii) **Я обы́чно .... газе́ту в э́том кио́ске.** (бу́ду покупа́ть – куплю́)

Но сего́дня я .... её по доро́ге на рабо́ту. (бу́ду покупа́ть – куплю́)

(iv) **Я пообе́даю, ... газе́ту и пойду́ на рабо́ту.** (бу́ду чита́ть – прочита́ю)

Я бу́ду .... немно́го по-ру́сски ка́ждый день. (чита́ть –прочита́ть)

Read and understand

12

Что вы бу́дете де́лать, е́сли вам даду́т миллио́н рубле́й?
What will you do if you are given a million roubles? This question was put to some of the occupants of a communal apartment. Match the replies to the pictures. (Answers on page 194.)

(i)

Я больше не буду работать! Я куплю машину и поеду во Францию. Там я буду жить в лучшей гостинице. Я буду ужинать каждый вечер в хорошем ресторане и буду ходить в кино и в театр. Потом я поеду в Италию и в Испанию. Может быть, я куплю виллу и буду жить там летом. Я буду купаться, загорать и ничего не делать!

(a)

(b)

(ii)

Я куплю большую кооперативную квартиру с балконом. Там я буду разводить цветы. У нас будет большая спальня, и для дочери будет комната. Она будет там учить уроки и заниматься своими любимыми делами. Вечером мы будем сидеть дома и читать или ходить в театр и на концерты. Может быть, я куплю пианино, и муж будет играть на нём.

Continued...

(iii)

Я больше не буду ходить по магазинам и не буду стоять в очереди! Дома я не буду готовить. Мы, наверно, будем обедать в ресторане или в кафе. Я буду ходить на работу, только когда я хочу. Вечером я буду читать интересные книги и, может быть, буду изучать иностранный язык. Думаю, мы купим дачу на юге, где тепло и много фруктов. Я буду покупать очень много фруктов каждый день!

(c)

(d)

(iv)

Я куплю большую машину, компьютер и, конечно, квартиру. Я не буду жить в этой коммуналке и не буду ходить на работу. Я буду писать романы. Когда я напишу первый роман, я стану известным писателем и меня будут приглашать и в Англию, и в Америку. Может быть, я поеду в Англию и посмотрю, как живут люди там.

New words:

учи́ть уро́ки do homework
(игра́ть) на нём (to play) on it
о́чередь (f.) queue
стоя́ть в о́череди to stand in a queue
коммуна́лка communal flat, apartment

Before you leave this section, see if you can think of five things *you* would do if you had a million roubles, and express your ideas in Russian.

Did you know?

Life in a Russian city

While cities everywhere have difficulties providing accommodation, the problems faced in the Russian Federation are particularly acute.

These days foreigners looking for places to live, or for offices, are served by an ever-growing number of cooperative enterprises offering these and other services.

Russian citizens, unless they have a lot of foreign currency or 'connections', are less lucky. The official allocation of living space is 9 square metres per person, but in fact all over the Russian Federation millions live in less than this. Some live in hostels, others in communal flats, with a whole family often in a single room. Many wait in a 'queue' for housing for *years*.

Those who can afford it, or who, like Pavel, receive help from work, try to buy a cooperative flat. This is, however, expensive and out of reach for most people.

Жили́щная пробле́ма (the housing problem) has been a theme in literature, songs and anecdotes since 1917. The anecdotes are often extremely funny; however, it cannot be denied that the housing situation does have a very detrimental effect on people's lives, and especially upon the family.

Most newly married couples will continue to live with one or other's parents, sometimes without even a room of their own. This is perhaps one reason why the divorce rate is high and constantly rising.

Lack of adequate accommodation also deters women from having children, certainly from having more than one.

Perhaps there are some reasons for optimism. The city councils of many of the main cities have now not only acknowledged the problem, but have promised radical measures to try to improve the situation.

An advertisement for a new development of flats

Your turn to speak

13

You have won a considerable amount of money in the State lottery. Consider what you would like to do with it. You may find the words below useful. As usual, try it by yourself, before listening to one possible response on your recording.

я поéду в...	I'll go to...
я хочý посмотрéть...	I want to see...
я бýду купáться, читáть,...	I will bathe, read...
купи́ть (я куплю́)... (кварти́ру, дом, маши́ну,...)	to buy (I will buy) ... (an apartment, home, car...)

Answers

Practise what you have learned

Exercise **1**	(i) with a friend (ii) 'Our Shakespeare' (iii) going south
Exercise **3**	(i) a (ii) b (iii) b (iv) b
Exercise **5**	(i) писáтелем (ii) врачóм (iii) балери́ной (iv) учи́телем (v) инженéром (vi) космонáвтом
Exercise **6**	(i) c (ii) d (iii) b (iv) a
Exercise **8**	(i) an hour early (ii) meeting at telegraph office (iii) meeting outside underground station

Grammar

Exercise **10**	(i) бýдем проводи́ть (ii) бýдем ходи́ть (iii) бýдут игрáть (iv) бýдешь купáться (v) бýдет загорáть (vi) бýдет игрáть (vii) бýдет готóвить (viii) бýдете читáть
Exercise **11**	(i) поéдете; поéдем (ii) пойдёшь; пойдý (iii) бýду покупáть; куплю́ (iv) прочитáю; читáть

Read and understand

Exercise **12**	(i) c (ii) a (iii) d (iv) b

15

DISCUSSING WHAT YOU HAVE DONE

You will learn

- to talk about what you have done in the recent past
- to discuss previous holidays and trips abroad
- about a well-known newspaper
  and about changes in Russian society

Study guide

- **Dialogue 1:** listen without the book
- **Dialogue 1:** listen, read and study
- Practise what you have learned
- **Dialogues 2, 3:** listen without the book
- **Dialogues 2, 3:** listen, read and study one by one
- Practise what you have learned
- **Dialogue 4:** listen without the book
- **Dialogue 4:** listen, read and study
- Practise what you have learned
- **Dialogue 5:** listen without the book
- **Dialogue 5:** listen, read and study
- Practise what you have learned
- Study the **Key words and phrases**
- Study the **Grammar** section carefully
- Do the exercises in **Read and understand**
- Read **Did you know?**
- Do the exercises in **Your turn to speak**
- Listen to all the dialogues once again straight through

Dialogues

1 *How did Tanya spend her day?*

Tamara Та́ня, где ты сего́дня была́?
Tanya Ты же зна́ешь, как я люблю́ Булга́кова. Я сего́дня была́ в том до́ме, где он жил.
Tamara Там что, музе́й?
Tanya Нет, там нет музе́я, но лю́ди туда́ прихо́дят и оставля́ют на́дписи на стена́х, пи́шут цита́ты из его́ книг.
Tamara Ну, да́льше где ты была́?
Tanya Пото́м я реши́ла поброди́ть по места́м, где жи́ли, броди́ли геро́и Булга́кова. И бы́ло о́чень интере́сно.
Tamara А где приблизи́тельно ты была́ ещё?
Tanya На Патриа́рших пруда́х, ой нет, сейча́с они́ *Чи́стые* называ́ются. Ты по́мнишь рома́н *Ма́стер и Маргари́та*? Де́йствие как раз начина́ется на Патриа́рших пруда́х. Пра́вда, в том до́ме, отку́да улета́ла Маргари́та, я ещё не была́. Но собира́юсь.
Tamara Не ска́жешь, когда́ откро́ют музе́й?
Tanya Не зна́ю, но говоря́т, что ско́ро.

оставля́ть на́дписи leave inscriptions, graffiti
писа́ть (я пишу́, ты пи́шешь) to write
да́льше further; (here) next
приблизи́тельно roughly, approximately
рома́н novel
де́йствие как раз начина́ется... the action begins precisely...
пра́вда truth; (here) it's true

- **ты же зна́ешь, ...** you know (of course)... The particle **же** simply adds emphasis to the words it accompanies.
- **как я люблю́ Булга́кова** how I love Bulgakov. If the object of a sentence (the word in the accusative case) is a masculine noun referring to a *person*, the ending does change. Like the genitive, such nouns normally end in **-а** or **-я**: **Я люблю́ Пу́шкина, Го́голя**. Again, names which look like adjectives have adjectival endings , e.g.:
Я люблю́ Достое́вского, Чайко́вского.
- **в том до́ме, где он жил** in the house where he lived
- **лю́ди туда́ прихо́дят** people go (lit. come) there. The verb **приходи́ть (я прихожу́, ты прихо́дишь)** means 'to come', thus:
я прихожу́ в университе́т I arrive at the university
я прихожу́ на рабо́ту I arrive at work
- **пи́шут цита́ты из его́ книг** they write out quotations from his books
- **я реши́ла поброди́ть по места́м, где жи́ли и броди́ли геро́и Булга́кова** I decided to wander around the places where Bulgakov's characters lived and wandered. **Поброди́ть** is the *perfective* form of **броди́ть. По-** is often used to indicate that the action lasted a short time, e.g.:
почита́ть to read a little
поспа́ть to have a nap
- **где ты была́ ещё?** where else were you? The word **ещё** can be used to mean 'else', but in a negative sentence **ещё не/нет** means 'not yet'.
- **на Патриа́рших пруда́х, ... сейча́с они́ *Чи́стые* называ́ются** at the 'Patriarch's Ponds',... now they're called 'Clean ponds'. In fact this is not correct: until 1991 they had a different official name. Now they are once again 'Patriarch's Ponds'.

- **откýда улетáла Маргарúта** from where Margarita flew away (yes, literally!). The prefix **у-** is often used to indicate (going, taking...) *away*. The opposite (coming, bringing...) is **при**, e.g.:
  прилетáть to arrive by air
  улетáть to leave by air
  приходúть to arrive (on foot)
  уходúть to leave (on foot)
- **когдá открóют музéй?** when will they open a museum? **Откры́ть (я открóю, ты открóешь)** 'to open' is the *perfective* form of **открывáть**.
- **говоря́т, что скóро** they say soon

Practise what you have learned

1 Masha has had a very full day visiting places connected with literary or music figures. Listen to her account and mark out her route on the map below.

New words:
Цéрковь Вознесéния Church of the Ascension
венчáться to marry (in a church)
оттýда from there
óперный певéц Шаля́пин the opera singer Chaliapin

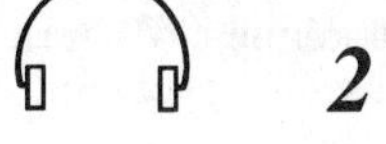

2 Below are the places Masha mentions, and the reasons each is of interest. The two lists have been jumbled up. Can you match them correctly? (Answers on page 210.)

(i) **Цéрковь Вознесéния**	(a) **где жúли Пýшкин и егó женá**
(ii) **Большáя Садóвая**	(b) **где жил Шаля́пин**
(iii) **Арбáт**	(c) **где венчáлся Пýшкин**
(iv) **ýлица Чайкóвского**	(d) **где жил Булгáков**

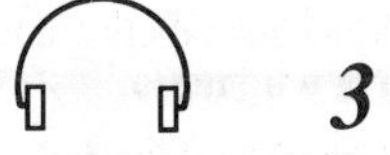

3 You will play the role of Seryozha, a lover of literature and music. You will be asked which writers you like: **какúх писáтелей вы лю́бите?**, and which composers: **какúх композúторов вы лю́бите?**

Dialogues

2 *Tanya can now read Bulgakov with her students*

Tanya Михаи́л Булга́ков. До́лгое вре́мя о нём не говори́ли. В шко́ле да́же не упомина́ли. И вот в после́днее вре́мя ста́ли выходи́ть знамени́тые рома́ны Булга́кова, *Ма́стер и Маргари́та*, по́весть *Соба́чье се́рдце*, *Роковы́е я́йца* и други́е. И да́же в шко́ле мы тепе́рь мо́жем вме́сте с ученика́ми чита́ть и *Бе́лую гва́рдию*, и *Соба́чье се́рдце*, говори́ть о ве́чных пробле́мах, о челове́чности. И э́то о́чень отра́дно, что э́то ста́ло возмо́жно.

до́лгое вре́мя for a long time
в после́днее вре́мя lately
знамени́тый famous
по́весть *Соба́чье се́рдце* the short novel *Heart of a Dog*
Роковы́е я́йца *Fateful Eggs*
тепе́рь now
вме́сте с ученика́ми together with the students
Бе́лая гва́рдия *White Guard*
отра́дно heartening
возмо́жно possible

о нём не говори́ли he wasn't talked about. The endings of pronouns after **о** (about) are:

обо мне	about me	**о нас**	about us
о тебе́	about you	**о вас**	about you (pl. or formal)
о нём	about him	**о них**	about them
о ней	about her		

не говори́ли..., не упомина́ли he wasn't spoken about..., he wasn't mentioned. Russian uses the third person plural (the **они́** form but *without* the pronoun) in both the present and past to express this passive meaning.

ста́ли выходи́ть... have begun to be published

говори́ть о ве́чных пробле́мах, о челове́чности to talk about eternal problems, about humanity. Any word following **о** (about) takes prepositional endings (the endings introduced in Unit 2).

3 *Yuri Bandura, deputy editor of* **Моско́вские но́вости,** *talks about his newspaper*

Yuri Bandura *Моско́вские но́вости* – еженеде́льник. Он выхо́дит раз в неде́лю, по сре́дам. У́тром уже́ продаётся в кио́сках, во всех. Э́то обще́ственно-полити́ческий еженеде́льник. Мы пи́шем, гла́вным о́бразом, о пробле́мах, кото́рые стоя́т пе́ред на́шей страно́й. Э́то экономи́ческие пробле́мы, полити́ческие, положе́ние в о́бласти культу́ры. На́ша газе́та издаётся на пяти́ языка́х. Э́то ру́сский, англи́йский, францу́зский, испа́нский и ара́бский.

обще́ственно-полити́ческий socio-political
еженеде́льник a weekly
гла́вным о́бразом in the main
экономи́ческие пробле́мы economic problems
положе́ние в о́бласти культу́ры the situation in the cultural sphere

он выхо́дит раз в неде́лю it comes out once a week. Many papers come out every day **ка́ждый день**, or twice a week **два ра́за в неде́лю**.

по сре́дам on Wednesdays. Similarly, **по понеде́льникам** on Mondays, **по вто́рникам** on Tuesdays etc.

- **продаётся в кио́сках, во всех** it is sold in all kiosks. Many verbs in Russian can be given a passive meaning by adding **-ся**. Other examples: **газе́та издаётся** the paper is published, **дом стро́ится** the house is being built.
- **кото́рые стоя́т пе́ред на́шей страно́й** which face our country
- **издаётся на пяти́ языка́х** is published in five languages. In two (three or four) languages would be **на двух (трёх, четырёх) языка́х**.

Practise what you have learned

4 Below are the titles of several Russian papers. Listen to your recording, and decide which paper is referred to in each snatch of conversation. (Answers on page 210.)

New word: **милосе́рдие** charity, compassion

(a) ***Аргуме́нты и фа́кты*** (b) ***Культу́ра***
(c) ***Литерату́рная газе́та*** (d) ***Милосе́рдие***

5 You have to be sharp to find a copy of many popular newspapers in Russian kiosks. To be ready, Kolya has found out when each of his favourite papers comes out, intending to make a note in his diary. Since he has forgotten, can you fill in the details? (Answers on page 210.)

(a) понеде́льник	(d) четве́рг ....
(b) вто́рник	(e) пя́тница ....
(c) среда́	(f) суббо́та ....
	(g) воскресе́нье ....

(i) ***Огонёк***
(ii) ***Аргуме́нты и фа́кты***
(iii) ***Литерату́рная газе́та***
(iv) ***Неде́ля***
(v) ***Культу́ра***

Dialogues

4 *Natasha spent her holiday last year in Sochi*

Mila Где вы отдыха́ли в про́шлом году́?
Natasha В про́шлом году́ мы отдыха́ли в Со́чи, я и моя́ семья́.
Mila Вы е́здили по путёвке?
Natasha К сожале́нию, нет, мы е́здили дикаря́ми. Путёвку о́чень тру́дно доста́ть, поэ́тому о́тдых у меня́ был неорганизо́ванный.
Mila Ну, а чем вы там всё-таки занима́лись?
Natasha Купа́лись. Я учи́ла своего́ сы́на пла́вать.
Mila А как вы устра́ивались с пита́нием?
Natasha В столо́вой.
Mila А фру́кты, о́вощи бы́ли?
Natasha На ры́нке покупа́ли фру́кты, пе́рсики, виногра́д.
Mila Ну, на сле́дующий год вы ещё раз пое́дете в э́то ме́сто? И́ли...
Natasha Ду́маю, что да.

в про́шлом году́ last year
Со́чи a popular resort town on the Black Sea
к сожале́нию unfortunately
поэ́тому therefore
о́тдых holiday, rest
неорганизо́ванный not officially organised
всё-таки all the same
столо́вая canteen
о́вощи vegetables
ры́нок market **на ры́нке** at the market
пе́рсики peaches
виногра́д grapes

- **вы е́здили по путёвке?** did you go on a pass? **Путёвка** gives one the right to eat and sleep in a particular rest home or sanatorium.
- **мы е́здили дикаря́ми** we travelled rough, i.e. without any accommodation organised. A family may simply rent a small room or part of one with no facilities or food provided. A single person would say **я е́здил(а) дикарём**.
- **е́здить** to travel by vehicle. **Е́здить** means to travel frequently or in more than one direction. In the past it can be just one journey *there and back*. **Ходи́ть** 'to go on foot' is used in exactly the same way.
- **путёвку о́чень тру́дно доста́ть** it's very hard to obtain a pass
- **я учи́ла своего́ сы́на пла́вать** I taught my son to swim. The endings of **свой сын** are accusative.
- **как вы устра́ивались с пита́нием?** what did you do about food?
- **на сле́дующий год** is another way of saying **в сле́дующем году́** next year
- **ещё раз** once again

Practise what you have learned

6 Victor asks some of his colleagues where they went on their holidays. Listen to the recording, then fill in their replies under the pictures below. (Answers on page 210.)

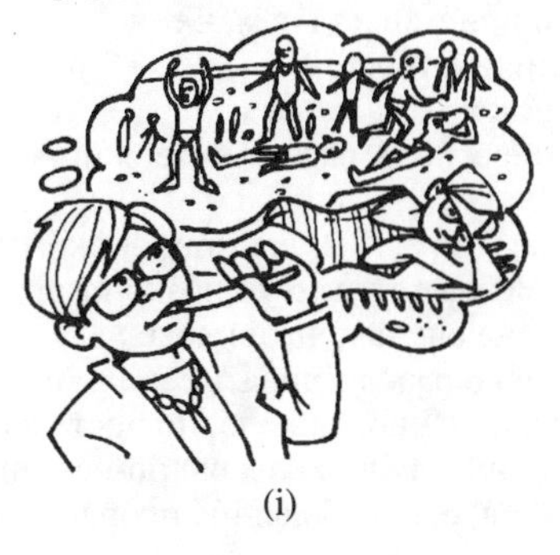

(i)

(ii)

(iii)

(i) **Ната́лья Ива́новна, где вы отдыха́ли в про́шлом году́?**

В про́шлом году́ мы ....
Вы е́здили по путёвке?
....

(ii) **Ви́ктор Фёдорович, где вы отдыха́ли в про́шлом году́?**

В про́шлом году́ мы ....
Вы е́здили по путёвке?
....

(iii) **О́ля, где ты отдыха́ла в про́шлом году́?**

В про́шлом году́ я ....
Ты е́здила по путёвке?
....

7 Your name is Dima and you spent your holiday in Sochi with your wife and son. Andrei as always will prompt you.

Dialogues

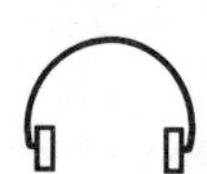

5 *Lyena asks Dima if he's ever been abroad*

·Lyena Скажи́те, вы бы́ли когда́-нибудь за грани́цей?
Dima Да, я неда́вно прие́хал из Герма́нии.
Lyena А вы там бы́ли как тури́ст?
Dima Нет, я там учи́лся.
Lyena Ой, о́чень интере́сно. А расскажи́те, я никогда́ не была́ за грани́цей.
Dima Я учи́лся в Ма́рбурге. Я изуча́л там эконо́мику. Мы жи́ли там в общежи́тии. Но я не то́лько учи́л эконо́мику, я путеше́ствовал по всей стране́. Мне о́чень понра́вилось.
Lyena А вам бы́ло легко́ разгова́ривать с людьми́?
Dima Снача́ла бы́ло, коне́чно, тяжело́, но постепе́нно я привы́к. Сейча́с я дово́льно-таки свобо́дно говорю́ по-неме́цки. Но, пра́вда, в после́днее вре́мя, есть небольши́е пробле́мы с пра́ктикой.

когда́-нибудь ever, at any time
за грани́цей abroad
расскажи́те tell me (about it)
эконо́мика economics
общежи́тие hostel **в общежи́тии** in a hostel
снача́ла at first
постепе́нно gradually
дово́льно-таки/дово́льно fairly

- **я неда́вно прие́хал из Герма́нии** I recently arrived (back) from Germany. **Из** 'from' is always followed by genitive endings. 'From Marburg' would be **из Ма́рбурга**.
- **как тури́ст** as a tourist
- **никогда́ не была́...** I've never been... **Никогда́ не** 'never' can be used in front of any verb.
- **учи́л эконо́мику** studied economics. **Учи́ть** if used with a subject means 'to learn, study'. If it's followed by a person it means 'to teach'.
- **я путеше́ствовал по всей стране́** I travelled around the whole country. Other useful phrases:
  путеше́ствовать по Росси́и to travel around Russia
  путеше́ствовать по всему́ ми́ру to travel around the whole world
- **мне о́чень понра́вилось** I liked it very much
- **вам бы́ло легко́ разгова́ривать с людьми́?** was it easy to converse with people? The opposite, i.e. 'difficult', is **тяжело́** or, more commonly, **тру́дно**.
- **я привы́к** I've got used to it. A woman would say **я привы́кла**.
- **я свобо́дно говорю́ по-неме́цки** I speak German fluently
- **есть небольши́е пробле́мы с пра́ктикой** there are some small problems with practice

Practise what you have learned

8

Aleksei chatted with some people at a party. Later he described his new acquaintances to a friend. Or thought he did... He has muddled the people and their accounts up. Listen to your recording, and readjust the order of the sentences below. (Answers on page 210.)

(i) **А́лла никогда́ не была́ за грани́цей.**
(ii) **Она́ жила́ в общежи́тии.**
(iii) **Она́ там изуча́ла францу́зский язы́к.**
(iv) **Ка́тя неда́вно прие́хала из Фра́нции.**
(v) **Са́ша неда́вно прие́хал из А́нглии.**
(vi) **Она́ неда́вно прие́хала из Ми́нска.**
(vii) **Она́ там рабо́тала. Она́ преподава́ла неме́цкий язы́к в университе́те.**
(viii) **Он там учи́лся.**
(ix) **Она́ жила́ у друзе́й и путеше́ствовала по всей Белару́си.**
(x) **Он дово́льно свобо́дно говори́т по-англи́йски.**

9

Dasha is talking to Lyudmila Nikolaevna, a professor of foreign languages. She doesn't even *attempt* to remember how many languages Lyudmila Nikolaevna reads with ease, how many she speaks fluently. Can you? (Answers on page 210.)

(a) **мне легко́ чита́ть**	(b) **я свобо́дно говорю́**
(i)	(iv) ....
(ii)	(v) ....
(iii)	

A demonstration in late 1989. The banner reads 'It's impossible to live like this'.

Key words and phrases

To use

приходи́ть (я прихожу́, ты прихо́дишь)	to arrive on foot (I arrive, you arrive)
броди́ть – поброди́ть (perfective)	to wander – to take a (short) wander
писа́ть (я пишу́, ты пи́шешь)	to write (I write, you write)
о рома́не Булга́кова	about Bulgakov's novel
о поли́тике	about politics
о ве́чных пробле́мах	about eternal problems
газе́та выхо́дит...	the paper comes out...
по сре́дам	on Wednesdays
по понеде́льникам	on Mondays
е́здить (я е́зжу, ты е́здишь)	to go by vehicle (I go, you go) (see the grammar section)
по путёвке	with a pass to a sanatorium or resort
дикарём (sing.) / **дикаря́ми** (pl.)	(travelling) rough
тру́дно доста́ть...	it is hard to obtain...
покупа́ть (я покупа́ю, ты покупа́ешь)	to buy (I buy, you buy)
прие́хать (я прие́ду, ты прие́дешь) (perfective)	to arrive by vehicle (I will arrive, you will arrive)
из Герма́нии	from Germany
из Ло́ндона	from London
путеше́ствовать (я путеше́ствую, ты путеше́ствуешь)	to travel (I travel, you travel)
по всей стране́	around the whole country
легко́	(it is) easy
тру́дно / тяжело́	(it is) difficult
разгова́ривать с людьми́	to converse with people
свобо́дно говори́ть по-неме́цки	to speak fluently in German
пробле́мы с пра́ктикой	problems with practice

To understand

где вы отдыха́ли в про́шлом году́?	where did you spend your holiday last year?
чем вы там занима́лись?	what did you do there?
вы бы́ли когда́-нибудь за грани́цей?	have you ever been abroad?

Grammar

Verbs of motion

A word of caution

There are a large number of verbs of motion in Russian, and it is easy to become bogged down in choice and not move at all! The following should give you some useful information and hints. You may well, however, want to concentrate on certain common usages and make sure you are quite confident with them.

The verb 'to go'
Since there are four verbs in Russian which can be translated as 'to go', it is necessary to be clear about the differences between them. They fall easily into two categories:

идти́ / ходи́ть to go on foot (or to the theatre, cinema etc.)
е́хать / е́здить to go by vehicle

How to choose between ***идти́*** *and* ***ходи́ть****?*
Идти́ is normally used when you are talking about a specific occasion in a single direction, e.g.:

– **Куда́ вы идёте сего́дня ве́чером?**
– Where are you going this evening?
– **Я иду́ на конце́рт/домо́й.**
– I am going to a concert/home.

Ходи́ть is used for frequent movement, and for more than one direction. You will often use this when talking about the past (since you *have* been in at least two directions – there and back!), e.g.:

Я ча́сто хожу́ в теа́тр.
I often go to the theatre.
Вчера́ я ходи́ла на *Дя́дю Ва́ню*.
Yesterday I went to *Uncle Vanya* (and came away again).

The same principle applies to **е́хать** (like **идти́**) and **е́здить** (like **ходи́ть**). Here are some examples:

Она́ *обы́чно* е́здит на рабо́ту на метро,
She *normally* goes to work by underground,
но *сего́дня* она́ е́дет на авто́бусе.
but *today* she is going by bus.
Он *обы́чно* хо́дит в магази́н у́тром,
He *normally* goes to the shop in the morning,
но *сего́дня* он идёт в магази́н ве́чером.
but *today* he is going to the shop in the evening.

The future tense
Only the single-direction verbs **идти́** and **е́хать** have *perfective* forms which are used in the future:

идти́ → **пойти́** (**я пойду́** I will go, **ты пойдёшь** you will go)
е́хать → **пое́хать** (**я пое́ду** I will go by vehicle, **ты пое́дешь** you will go by vehicle)

По́сле рабо́ты я пойду́ в кафе́.
After work I'll go to a café.

Continued...

Ле́том мы поéдем на юг.
In summer we'll go south.

Very often, however, the present tense (**идти́** and **е́хать** *only*) is used even when you are talking about the future, e.g.:

я иду́ за́втра на конце́рт.
I'm going to a concert tomorrow.

The past tense
Both **пойти́** and **пое́хать** can be used in the past also, but they imply *that the action is still in effect.*

Где То́ша? – Он пое́хал в А́нглию. He's gone to England.

The past of **пойти́** is rather irregular: **он пошёл, она́ пошла́, они́ пошли́**:

Где Ла́ра? – Она́ пошла́ на рабо́ту. She's gone to work.

Compare:

Воло́ди нет до́ма. Он пошёл на рабо́ту.
Volodya isn't here. He's gone to work.
Та́ня, где ты была́? – Я ходи́ла на ры́нок.
Tanya, where were you? – I went to the market (– but obviously I've come back!).
Здра́вствуй, Се́ва! Я ду́мал, что ты пое́хал в Клин.
Hello, Syeva! I thought you'd gone to Klin (i.e. I didn't expect to see you here).
Здра́вствуй. Нет, я е́здил в Клин в понеде́льник.
Hello. No, I went to Klin (and returned) on Monday.

10

Fill in the missing verbs in the following sentences. (Answers on page 210.)

New words:
ма́мы нет до́ма mother's not at home
о́зеро Байка́л Lake Baikal

(i) **Я .... сего́дня в музе́й.** (иду́, хожу́)

(ii) **По сре́дам он .... в клуб.** (идёт, хо́дит)

(iii) **Вы ча́сто .... в кино́?** (идёте, хо́дите)
Не о́чень ча́сто. Но сего́дня мы с жено́й .... на но́вый фильм. (идём, хо́дим)

(iv) **Ма́мы нет до́ма. Она́ .... в институ́т.** (пошла́, ходи́ла)

(v) **Мы вчера́ .... на конце́рт.** (пошли́, ходи́ли)

(vi) **Я сейча́с поза́втракаю и .... на рабо́ту.** (пойду́, хожу́)

(vii) **Куда́ вы .... в о́тпуск в про́шлом году́?** (пое́хали, е́здили)
В про́шлом году́ я .... в Ки́ев (пое́хал, е́здил)

(viii) **Я обы́чно .... в о́тпуск на по́езде.** (е́ду, е́зжу)

(ix) **В суббо́ту я .... в А́нглию.** (е́ду, е́зжу)

(x) **Как вы сего́дня .... на рабо́ту – на метро́ и́ли на авто́бусе?** (е́дете, е́здите)

(xi) **В сле́дующем году́ вы ещё раз .... в Я́лту?** (пое́дете, е́здите)
Ду́маю, что нет. Скоре́е всего, мы .... на о́зеро Байка́л. (пое́дем, е́здим)

Read and understand

Read the following letters, written by some Russians who have recently returned from their holidays. Find out how *they* like to spend their holiday, what they are interested in. Imagine the sort of holiday you would pick and the letter you would write to *them*.

Здравствуй, дорогой Володя!

Я решил рассказать тебе о своей поездке. Мы со школой ездили в Англию. Как ты знаешь, я никогда раньше не был за границей, и мне было так интересно! Мы жили в семьях в маленьком городе, не очень далеко от Лондона. Мы довольно часто ездили на поезде в Лондон. Нам показывали известные музеи, галереи, Трафальгарскую площадь, Вестминстер. Мне всё очень понравилось.

Ты знаешь, что больше всего на свете я люблю театр. В Лондоне я ходил несколько раз в театр и даже видел своего любимого актёра!

Мы были не только в Лондоне. Мы с английскими друзьями ездили по всей стране. И, самое главное, я ездил в Страдфорд-на-Эйвоне, где родился Уильям Шекспир. Было здорово!

бо́льше всего́ на све́те more than anything
са́мое гла́вное most important
здо́рово amazing

Здравствуйте, дорогие друзья!

Мы с семьёй недавно приехали из отпуска. Мы ездили по самым старым городам России. Мы были в Новгороде, Пскове и Ростове Великом. Вы были когда-нибудь в этих городах? Они такие красивые! Если не были, то обязательно поезжайте!

Во Пскове мы жили несколько дней. Я думаю, вы можете догадаться, куда мы ездили. Конечно, в Михайловское! Вы же знаете, как мы все любим Пушкина. Мы видели дом, в котором он жил, леса и поля, по которым он бродил, и его могилу.

А куда вы ездили в отпуск?

обяза́тельно поезжа́йте! definitely go there!
догада́ться to guess
Миха́йловское family estate of Alexsander Pushkin
леса́ и поля́ forests and fields
моги́ла grave

Здравствуй, дорогая Наташа!

Куда ты собираешься поехать в отпуск в этом году? Если ты ещё не решила, то я рекомендую поехать в Ялту. Я совсем недавно приехала из Ялты, где я отдыхала две недели.

Путёвку, конечно, я не достала, поэтому ездила дикарём. В Ялте я снимала маленькую комнату в одном доме. С питанием, правда, было немножко сложно, но там хороший рынок, и каждый день я покупала персики, виноград, арбуз.

Трудно сказать, чем я занималась. Ну, много купалась и загорала. Читала журналы, иногда играла в теннис. В общем, отдыхала и, самое главное, совсем не думала о работе, о Москве и проблемах там!

Думаю, что в следующем году я ещё раз поеду в Ялту. Может быть, поедем вместе?

сло́жно complicated
арбу́з watermelon
в о́бщем in general
совсе́м absolutely

Did you know?

'Ру́кописи не горя́т' – 'Manuscripts don't burn'

These words, from Bulgakov's novel *The Master and Margarita* (spoken by the Devil as he restores the master's apparently destroyed novel), have taken on a particular resonance since the mid 1980s.

It is easy to understand why, if one looks back a little. From the days of the Russian tsars, the State has tried to control its writers and artists. In the Russian Empire most 'dangerous' were those who called for political change or asserted nationalist claims. After the revolution, the net was widened. Particularly under Stalin thousands of writers and artists shared the fate of millions: arrest, torture, summary execution or labour camp. Writers had to be very careful, and often memorised works or entrusted them to friends.

After Stalin's death, most of those who had survived the camps were released. However, until well into the 1980s there were cases of writers being sent to labour camps or psychiatric hospitals.

Since about 1986 the situation has changed dramatically. All the works suppressed for many years have been published. Some of the greatest writers of the Soviet period have been 'returned' to the reading public: Mandel'shtam, Bulgakov, Platonov, Grossman, Solzhenitsyn, Pasternak and many many others.

This new freedom or **гла́сность** (openness) has not been confined to literature. For many years the mistakes of the past, social and economic problems and national conflict were simply denied. While there are people continuing to take this line, it has become possible to read truthful accounts, listen to hard-hitting speeches and form one's own opinion. The process is continuing, and it is a painful one, but the change is marked: people now speak out, and believe that they have a right to be heard.

A photo from the newspaper Россия, August 1991

Your turn to speak

11

You have just returned from Russia. You'll want to tell your friends where you have been, what you did and generally share your impressions. You may want to look over the notes about the past tense in Unit 11. The following words and phrases will help you to begin, but there will be a lot of other things *you* will want to say!

я неда́вно прие́хал(а) из...	I have recently returned from...
я путеше́ствовал(а) по всей стране́	I travelled around the whole country
я е́здил(а) в...	I went to...
мне о́чень понра́вилось	I liked it very much
я ходи́л(а) ...	I went...
в музе́и	to museums
на вы́ставки	to exhibitions
в дом, где жил...	to the house where... lived
мне бы́ло тру́дно / легко́ разгова́ривать с людьми́	it was difficult / easy to speak with people

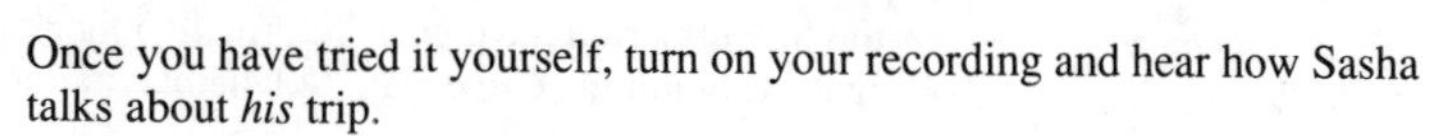

Once you have tried it yourself, turn on your recording and hear how Sasha talks about *his* trip.

Answers

Practise what you have learned

Exercise **2**	(i) c (ii) d (iii) a (iv) b
Exercise **4**	(i) c (ii) d (iii) a (iv) b
Exercise **5**	(i) f (ii) b (iii) c (iv) e (v) b, d, g
Exercise **6**	(i) отдыха́ли в Я́лте, мы е́здили дикаря́ми (ii) отдыха́ли в Со́чи; у нас была́ путёвка (в дом о́тдыха) (iii) я отдыха́ла в Ки́еве; я жила́ у друзе́й
Exercise **8**	iv, iii, ii, v, viii, x, i, vi, vii, ix
Exercise **9**	(i) по-францу́зски (ii) по-испа́нски (iii) по-неме́цки (iv) по-англи́йски (v) по-неме́цки

Grammar

Exercise **10**	(i) иду́ (ii) хо́дит (iii) хо́дите; идём (iv) пошла́ (v) ходи́ли (vi) пойду́ (vii) е́здили; е́здил (viii) е́зжу (ix) е́ду (x) е́дете (xi) по́едете; пое́дем

Grammar summary

Below you will find a brief summary of the main grammar points occurring in this course. Some important grammatical terms will also be explained.

NOUNS	A noun is the name of a person or thing, e.g. Tanya, magazine, time. Nouns are either masculine, feminine or neuter. In most cases it is possible to tell the gender of a Russian noun from its ending. Most masculine nouns end in a consonant. Feminine nouns normally end in **-а** or **-я**. Nouns ending in **-ь** may be masculine or feminine – the dictionary entry will tell you which. The majority of neuter nouns end in **-о** or **-е**. There are no words for 'the' and 'a' in Russian. (See grammar on page 17.)
Cases	Nouns also have other endings depending upon their *function* in a particular sentence. There are six 'cases' in Russian to cater for such functions.
Nominative case	The case required for the *subject* of the sentence; this is the form mentioned above and the one you will find in the dictionary, e.g.: **По́езд опа́здывает.** The train is late. **Медсестра́ уста́ла.** The nurse is tired. (See grammar on page 17.)
Accusative case	The case required for the *object* of a sentence, e.g.: **Я чита́ю кни́гу / журна́л.** I am reading a book / journal. When the object is a singular 'inanimate' noun, i.e. a thing, only the feminine changes. With 'animate' nouns (people etc.), masculine nouns also change, e.g.: **Я люблю́ Пу́шкина и Достое́вского.** I like Pushkin and Dostoevsky. (See grammar on page 44.)
Genitive case	The case used after most numbers, after the prepositions **до** (up to), **для** (for), **без** (without) and some others. It is also used after **нет** to mean 'there is no...', e.g.: **три биле́та до Москвы́** three tickets to Moscow **молока́ нет** there is no milk (See grammar on pages 93 and 105; for other references see index.)
Dative case	The case required for the *indirect object*, used after verbs such as **дать** (to give) (**да́йте мне...** give me...), **пока́зывать** (to show). It is also used to give somebody's age and in talking about feelings etc., e.g.: **Я пока́зываю Ни́не кни́гу.** I show Nina the book. **Серге́ю хо́лодно здесь.** Sergei feels cold here. **Тама́ре два́дцать лет.** Tamara is 20 years old. (See grammar on page 159.)
Instrumental case	Used after **с** meaning 'with', and after certain verbs, e.g. **занима́ться** (to occupy oneself with) and **стать** (to become), e.g.: **бутербро́д с колбасо́й** salami sandwich **занима́ться спо́ртом** to take part in sport **Она́ ста́ла инжене́ром.** She became an engineer. (See grammar on page 57 and pages 164 and 184.)
Prepositional case	Used after **в/на** meaning 'in/at', and **о** meaning 'about', e.g.: **Он живёт в Москве́.** He lives in Moscow. **Она́ рабо́тает на заво́де.** She works at a factory. **Мы говори́м о литерату́ре.** We talk about literature. (See grammar on page 31 and page 198.)
Learning case endings	There are a lot of endings here. We have found that the best approach is to learn particular – useful – phrases. For example, if you remember: **я чита́ю кни́гу** (I read a book) and that the accusative is used, you will know the ending for other feminine nouns in the singular.

PRONOUNS

Pronouns (I, you, he, she, etc.) stand for a noun, e.g. *Ivan met Sergei, and showed **him** the room.* In Russian, pronouns also have different endings depending upon their function in the sentence.

Most useful are the pronoun as subject (the nominative case), as object (the accusative case) and as indirect object (the dative), e.g.:

Я ру́сский. *I* am Russian.
Вы меня́ понима́ете? Do you understand *me*?
Покажи́те мне, пожа́луйста, э́ту кни́гу. Show *me* that book please.

Here are the other pronouns:

Nominative	Accusative	Dative
я	**меня́**	**мне**
ты	**тебя́**	**тебе́**
он	**его́**	**ему́**
она́	**её**	**ей**
мы	**нас**	**нам**
вы	**вас**	**вам**
они́	**их**	**им**

(See grammar on page 131.)

ADJECTIVES

Adjectives are words such as *interesting* or *beautiful* which describe a person or thing. An adjective must have the same gender (masculine, feminine or neuter) and number (singular or plural) as the noun it refers to, e.g.:

краси́вый костю́м a beautiful suit
краси́вая кварти́ра a beautiful flat
краси́вое пла́тье a beautiful dress

Any adjective in Russian must also have the same *case* as the noun. The endings, unfortunately, are not the same as for nouns. We suggest at this stage you simply note and try to remember the words you have seen here.
(See grammar on pages 17 and 81.)

PREPOSITIONS

Prepositions are words such as *to*, *from*, *in* etc. In Russian, prepositions take a certain case (never the nominative). Thus nouns following **до** (to) or **без** (without) have genitive endings.

Some prepositions may take two different cases depending on their meaning. **В** and **на** can mean 'in' or 'on'. If so, they are followed by nouns in the prepositional case. They can also mean 'to' if used with a verb indicating movement. Any nouns following will be in the accusative case.

– **Где вы живёте?**
– **Я живу́ в Москве́, но е́ду в Ло́ндон.**
– I live in Moscow, but I'm going to London.
– **Я живу́ в Ло́ндоне, но е́ду в Москву́.**
– I live in London, but I'm going to Moscow.

(See particularly grammar on pages 31 and 105; for other references see index.)

VERBS

A verb is a word denoting action or being, e.g. *she **reads**, he **was***. The simplest part of a verb is the infinitive **чита́ть** (to read), **быть** (to be). This is the form you find in a dictionary. However, in any particular sentence the ending will change depending on who is the subject of the verb. There are two main types of verb endings. The infinitive of one type ends in **-ать** (or **-ять**), and the infinitive of the other ends in **-ить** (or **-еть**):

рабо́тать to work	**говори́ть** to speak
я рабо́таю	**я говорю́**
ты рабо́таешь	**ты говори́шь**
он/она́ рабо́тает	**он/она́ говори́т**
мы рабо́таем	**мы говори́м**
вы рабо́таете	**вы говори́те**
они́ рабо́тают	**они́ говоря́т**

	Sometimes verbs in Russian have **-ся** attached to these endings. Such verbs are either *reflexive*, that is they refer to an action which the subject of the verb is doing to him or herself, or they do not have an object, e.g.: **Я занимáюсь спóртом** I take part in (lit. I occupy myself) with sport **Магазúн открывáется в 8 часóв** The shop opens at 8 o'clock (See grammar on pages 119 and 173–4.)
Past tense	Talking about what you were doing in the past is very easy in Russian. There are only four endings depending on whether the subject of the verb is a masculine, feminine, neuter or plural noun. Thus: **он(я, ты) рабóтал, онá (я, ты) рабóтала, онó рабóтало, онú (мы, вы) рабóтали**. (See grammar on page 143.)
Future tense	It is also straightforward to talk about what you *will be* doing in the future. The future of the verb 'to be' **быть** is used, followed by the appropriate verb in the infinitive, e.g.: **я бýду рабóтать** **ты бýдешь рабóтать** **он/онá бýдет рабóтать** **мы бýдем рабóтать** **вы бýдете рабóтать** **онú бýдут рабóтать** (See grammar on page 189.)
Imperfective / Perfective	Most Russian verbs have two *aspects* – 'imperfective' and 'perfective'. To talk about an action in general, or one that will go on for some time, perhaps be repeated, the *imperfective* is used. This is the one used in all the examples under the verb entries above and it is probably the more common. However, to focus on one specific occasion, or on the result of a future or past action, the *perfective* must be used. Perfective verbs are often, though not always, formed by attaching a prefix to the imperfective verb, e.g.: imperfective **читáть** perfective **прочитáть** A perfective verb has only two tenses – past and future. **Я прочитáю журнáл** means 'I shall read (and finish) the journal'. **Я прочитáл журнáл** means 'I finished the journal'. All perfective verbs are noted in the glossary. (See grammar on page 189.)
Verbs of motion	Russian has a lot of them! There are separate verbs depending upon whether the travel is on foot (**идтú, ходúть**) or by vehicle (**éхать, éздить**). The choice between **идтú** (or **éхать**) and **ходúть** (or **éздить**) is generally clear: **идтú** is used about movement in a specific direction, normally on a specific occasion. **Ходúть** implies more than one direction, and is therefore used to talk about going somewhere frequently and about having gone somewhere – and come back, e.g.: **Я идý сегóдня в кинó. Я чáсто хожý в кинó.** I am going to the cinema today. I often go to the cinema. **Вчерá я ходúл в теáтр.** Yesterday I went to the theatre (and came back again!).

Vocabulary

а but/and
а́вгуст August
авиаконве́рт airmail envelope
авто́бус bus
а́дрес address
актёр actor
актри́са actress
америка́нец/америка́нка American man/woman
англи́йский, -ая, -ое English
англича́нин/англича́нка Englishman/Englishwoman
А́нглия England
апре́ль (m.) April
аппети́т; **прия́тного аппети́та!** appetite; bon appetit!
апте́ка chemist (pharmacist)

ба́бушка grandmother
бадминто́н badminton
балери́на ballerina
бале́т ballet
балко́н balcony
бар bar
бассе́йн swimming pool
бежа́ть (я бегу́, ты бежи́шь) to run (I run, you run)
безалкого́льный, -ая, -ое non-alcoholic
бе́лый, -ая, -ое white
бензи́н petrol (gasoline)
библиоте́ка library
биле́т ticket
бифште́кс beefsteak
благодари́ть; благодарю́ вас to thank; thank you
ближа́йший, -ая, -ее nearest, next
блу́зка blouse
блю́до dish
боль (f.); **головна́я боль** pain; headache
больни́ца hospital
бо́льше more
большо́й, -а́я, -о́е big
борщ borshch (beetroot soup)
брат brother
броди́ть (я брожу́, ты бро́дишь) to wander (I wander, you wander) – **поброди́ть** (perfective) to wander a little
брю́ки (pl.) trousers (pants)
бу́дьте добры́/любе́зны be so kind, please
бутербро́д sandwich
буфе́т buffet
быва́ть to be (frequently)
бы́стро quickly
быть (я бу́ду, ты бу́дешь) to be (I will be, you will be)

в in, at; to
валю́та foreign currency
вам (dative of **вы**) to you
вас (accusative and genitive of **вы**) you
ваш, ва́ша, ва́ше your
вегетариа́нец/вегетариа́нка vegetarian man/woman
ведь you see, you know; after all
весна́; весно́й spring; in spring
ве́чер; ве́чером evening; in the evening
ве́чный, -ая, -ое eternal
взять (я возьму́, ты возьмёшь) (perfective) to take (I will take, you will take)
взять напрока́т to hire (rent)
вид view; kind (of)
ви́деть (я ви́жу, ты ви́дишь) to see (I see, you see)
вино́ wine
вку́сно tasty
вку́сный, -ая, -ое tasty (*adjective*)
вода́ water
во́дка vodka
во́здух air
возмо́жность possibility
вокза́л railway station
во-пе́рвых first, first of all
восемна́дцать eighteen
во́семь eight
во́семьдесят eighty
воскресе́нье Sunday
восто́к east
восьмо́й, -а́я, -о́е eighth
вот here (is)
врач doctor
вре́мя; ско́лько сейча́с вре́мени? time; what is the time?
все everyone
всегда́ always
всего́ in all
всё everything
встава́ть (я встаю́, ты встаёшь) to get up (I get up, you get up)
встреча́ться to meet – **встре́титься** (perfective) to meet on a specific occasion

вто́рник Tuesday
второ́й, -а́я, -о́е second
вход entrance
вчера́ yesterday
вы́пить (perfective) to drink
вы́ход exit
выходи́ть (я выхожу́, ты выхо́дишь, они́ выхо́дят) to go out (of a place) (I go out, you go out, they go out)
выходно́й (день) day off

газе́та newspaper
галере́я gallery
га́лстук tie
гарни́р garnish, vegetables
гастроно́м grocer's
где where
Герма́ния Germany
говори́ть (я говорю́, ты говори́шь) to speak (I speak, you speak)
год year
головна́я боль headache
го́род city
горя́чий, -ая, -ее (boiling) hot
гости́ная living room
гость (m.) guest
госуда́рственный, -ая, -ое state
гото́вить (я гото́влю, ты гото́вишь) to prepare, to cook (I prepare, you prepare)
гриб (pl. **грибы́**) mushroom
грузи́нский, -ая, -ое Georgian
гуля́ть to stroll
– **погуля́ть** (perfective) to take a stroll

да yes
далеко́ (от + genitive) far (from)
дать (perfective); **да́й(те)...!** (imperative) to give; give...!
да́ча holiday house outside the city
два (две with f. noun) two
два́дцать twenty
двена́дцать twelve
две́сти two hundred
дво́е; на двои́х two; for two (people)
двухко́мнатный, -ая, -ое two-roomed
де́вушка young woman
девяно́сто ninety
девятна́дцать nineteen
девя́тый, -ая, -ое ninth
де́вять nine
дежу́рная (по этажу́) woman on duty (on floor of hotel)
де́йствующий, -ая, -ее functioning
дека́брь (m.) December
деклара́ция declaration
де́лать to do, make
день (m.) **(два дня, пять дней)** day (two days, five days)
день рожде́ния birthday
де́ньги (pl.) money
десе́рт dessert
деся́тый tenth
де́сять ten
де́ти (pl.) children
дие́та diet
дикарём (sing.); **дикаря́ми** (pl.) (travelling) rough
дискоте́ка discotheque
для (+ genitive) for
днём during the day
до́брый, -ая, -ое good, kind
до (+ genitive) to, up to
договори́ться (perfective); **договори́лись** to come to an agreement; agreed
дождь (m.) rain
дое́хать (до + genitive) to reach, to get to
до́лго for a long time
до́ллар dollar
дом house, block of flats (apartments)
до́ма at home
домо́й home(ward)
доро́га road
до́рого it is dear, expensive
дорого́й, -а́я, -о́е dear
до свида́ния goodbye
доста́ть (я доста́ну, ты доста́нешь) (perfective) to obtain with difficulty (I will obtain, you will obtain)
до́чка / дочь daughter
друг (pl. **друзья́**) friend
друго́й, -а́я, -о́е other
ду́мать to think
душ shower
душа́ spirit, soul

е́здить (я е́зжу, ты е́здишь, они́ е́здят) to travel (in more than one direction (I travel, you travel, they travel)
его́ him; his

её her
е́сли if
есть; у вас есть...? there is, there are; do you have...?
е́хать (я е́ду, ты е́дешь, они́ е́дут) to go by vehicle (in specific direction) (I go, you go, they go)
ещё still, yet

жа́ркий, -ая, -ое hot
жа́рко it is hot
ждать (я жду, ты ждёшь, они́ ждут) to wait (for), to expect (I wait, you wait, they wait)
жела́ть to wish, to desire
жена́ wife
жена́т married (about man)
жизнь (f.) life
жить (я живу́, ты живёшь, они́ живу́т) to live (I live, you live, they live)

за for; behind
заброни́рован booked
заво́д factory
за́втра tomorrow
за́втрак breakfast
за́втракать to have breakfast – **поза́втракать** (perfective)
загора́ть to sunbathe
за грани́цей abroad
зака́з an order
заказа́ть (perfective) to order
закрыва́ть(ся) to close
заку́ска hors d'oeuvre
за́мужем married (about woman)
занима́ться (+ instrumental) to be occupied with
за́пад west
зда́ние building
здесь here
здра́вствуйте, здра́вствуй hello
зелёный, -ая, -ое green
зима́; зимо́й winter; in winter
зи́мний, -яя, -ее winter (*adjective*)
знать to know
зовут; как вас зову́т? called; what is your name?

и and
игра́ть to play
идти́ (я иду́, ты идёшь, они́ иду́т) to go, to be going (on foot in specific direction) (I go on foot, you go, they go)
из (+ genitive) from
изве́стный, -ая, -ое famous
извини́те excuse me
изда́тельство publishing house
изуча́ть to study
икра́ caviare
и́ли or
и́менно specifically
инжене́р engineer
иногда́ sometimes
иностра́нный, -ая, -ое foreign
институ́т institute
интере́сно (it is) interesting
интере́сный, -ая, -ое interesting
их them; their
ию́ль (m.) July
ию́нь (m.) June

ка́ждый, -ая, -ое each
ка́жется it seems (to me)
как how
како́й, -а́я, -о́е what kind of
кани́кулы (pl.) (school, university) holidays (vacations)
ка́рточка; креди́тная к. визи́тная к. card; credit card, business card or guest's card (in hotel)
карто́шка (/ карто́шечка) potatoes
ка́сса cashier's desk
ката́ться на лы́жах to ski
ката́ться на конька́х to skate (on ice)
кафе́ café
ка́ша porridge
ка́шель (m.) (genitive sing. **ка́шля**) cough
кварти́ра flat (apartment)
килогра́мм kilogram
кино́ cinema (movies)
кио́ск kiosk (stand)
кла́дбище cemetery
ключ key
когда́ when
когда́-нибудь ever, at any time
колбаса́ salami
ко́мната room
коне́ц; в оди́н коне́ц end; one way
коне́чно of course
конча́ть(ся) to end
кооперати́вный, -ая, -ое cooperative
копе́йка (две копе́йки, пять копе́ек) copeck (two copecks, five copecks)

космона́вт astronaut
кото́рый, -ая, -ое which
ко́фе coffee
краси́вый, -ая, -ое beautiful
кра́сный, -ая, -ое red
круглосу́точно around-the-clock
кто who
купа́ться to bathe, to swim
купи́ть (я куплю́, ты ку́пишь) (perfective) to buy (I will buy, you will buy)
ку́хня kitchen; cuisine

легко́ easy, easily
ле́тний, -яя, -ее summer (*adjective*)
ле́то; ле́том summer; in summer
лифт lift (elevator)
ложи́ться спать (я ложу́сь спать, ты ложи́шься спать) to go to bed (I go to bed, you go to bed)
лу́чше всего́ best of all
люби́мый, -ая, -ое favourite
люби́ть (я люблю́, ты лю́бишь) to love, to like (I love, you love)
лю́ди (pl.) people

магази́н shop
май May
ма́ленький, -ая, -ое small
ма́ло a little
ма́рка (postage) stamp
март March
ма́сло butter
матрёшка 'matryoshka' doll
мать/ма́ма mother
маши́на car
медици́нская сестра́ / медсестра́ nurse
ме́дленно slowly
меню́ menu
меня́ть to change
ме́сто place
метро́ underground (subway)
мечта́ть to dream
мину́та/мину́точка minute (time)
мно́го much, many
моги́ла grave
мо́жет быть perhaps
мо́жно it is possible
мой, моя́, моё my
молоко́ milk
моро́женое ice cream
москви́ч (m.), **москви́чка** (f.) Muscovite
мочь (я могу́, ты мо́жешь, они́ мо́гут) to be able (I am able, you are able, they are able)
муж husband
музе́й museum
мы we
мя́со meat

на at, on; to
наде́яться (я наде́юсь, ты наде́ешься) to hope (I hope, you hope)
на́до it is necessary
наза́д back; ago
нале́во to the left
напи́ток a drink
напра́во to the right
наприме́р for example
напрока́т; взять напрока́т hire; to hire (rent)
на́сморк head cold
находи́ться to be located
начина́ть(ся) to begin
наш, на́ша, на́ше our
не not
недалеко́ not far
неде́ля week
немно́го a little
нет no
но́вый, -ая, -ое new
но́мер number, room
ноя́брь (m.) November
ну well
ну́жен, нужна́, ну́жно necessary
нра́виться to please
– **понра́виться** (perfective)

о (об) (+ prepositional) about
обе́д lunch, middle meal of day
обе́дать to have lunch
– **пообе́дать** (perfective)
обменя́ть to change
обра́тно; туда́ и обра́тно back; there and back
одева́ться to get dressed, to dress
оди́н, одна́, одно́; на одного́ one; for one (person)
одноко́мнатный, -ая, -ое one-roomed
октя́брь (m.) October
опа́здывать to be (running) late
о́пера opera
опя́ть again
о́сень (f.); **о́сенью** autumn; in autumn (Fall)
остано́вка stop

от (+ genitive) from
отде́л section
отдохну́ть (perfective) to have a rest
отдыха́ть to rest, to take one's holiday (vacation)
оте́ц father
открыва́ть(ся) to open – **откры́ть(ся)** (perfective)
откры́тка postcard
о́тпуск leave, holiday (vacation)
о́чень very
о́чень прия́тно pleased (to meet you)
о́чередь (f.) queue

па́мятник monument
па́мятный, -ая, -ое memorable
парк park
пе́рвый, -ая, -ое first
переры́в break
перехо́д subway, crossing, underpass
писа́ть (я пишу́, ты пи́шешь) to write (I write, you write)
письмо́ (pl. **пи́сьма**) letter
пла́вать to swim
план plan
плати́ть to pay
плато́к (pl. **платки́**) scarf
платфо́рма platform
пла́тье (pl. **пла́тья**) dress
пло́хо badly
пло́щадь (f.) square
по (+ dative) around
по-англи́йски in English
побо́льше a little more, bigger
повтори́ть (perfective) to repeat
пого́да weather
погуля́ть (perfective) to take a stroll
подеше́вле a little cheaper
подру́га (female) friend
по́езд train
пое́хать (я пое́ду, ты пое́дешь) (perfective) to go (by vehicle) (I will go, you will go)
пожа́луй perhaps, probably
пожа́луйста please
поза́втракать (perfective) to have breakfast
пойти́ (я пойду́, ты пойдёшь) (perfective) to go (on foot) (I will go, you will go)
по́здно late
поздравля́ть to congratulate
по́зже later
пока́зывать to show – **показа́ть** (perfective); **покажи́те** show (me)
покрупне́е a little bigger (about fruit etc.)
покупа́ть to buy
поли́тика politics
полови́на half
получи́ть (perfective) to receive
получи́ться (perfective) to turn out
поме́льче a little smaller (about fruit etc.)
поме́ньше a little less, smaller
помидо́р tomato
по́мнить to remember
понеде́льник Monday
по-неме́цки in German
пообе́дать (perfective) to have lunch
попро́бовать (я попро́бую, ты попро́буешь) (perfective) to try (I will try, you will try)
порекомендова́ть (я порекоменду́ю, ты порекоменду́ешь) (perfective) to recommend (I will recommend, you will recommend)
по-ру́сски in Russian
после́дний, -яя, -ее last
послеза́втра the day after tomorrow
посмотре́ть (я посмотрю́, ты посмо́тришь) (perfective) to take a look (I will take a look, you will take a look)
поступа́ть to enter
потому́ что... because...
поу́жинать (perfective) to have dinner
по-францу́зски in French
почём? (colloquial) how much?
почему́? why?
по́чта post office
пра́ктика practice
предложи́ть (perfective) to offer, to suggest
приглаша́ть to invite
прие́хать (я прие́ду, ты прие́дешь) (perfective) to arrive by vehicle (I will arrive, you will arrive)
принести́ (я принесу́, ты принесёшь) (perfective) to bring (I will bring, you will bring)

приня́ть (perfective); **приму́те...** (imperative) to take; take
приобрести́ (perfective) to obtain, to purchase
приходи́ть (я прихожу́, ты прихо́дишь) to arrive on foot (I arrive, you arrive)
прия́тный, -ая, -ое pleasant
пробле́ма problem
проводи́ть (я провожу́, ты прово́дишь) to spend (I spend, you spend)
прое́хать (perfective); **как прое́хать...?** to get to by vehicle; how do I get to...?
пройти́ (perfective); **как пройти́...?** to get to on foot; how do I get to...?
прости́те excuse me
про́сто simply
про́шлый, -ая, -ое past
пря́мо straight
путеше́ствовать (я путеше́ствую, ты путеше́ствуешь) to travel (I travel, you travel)
пятна́дцать fifteen
пя́тница; в пя́тницу Friday; on Friday
пя́тый, -ая, -ое fifth
пять five
пятьдеся́т fifty
пятьсо́т five hundred

рабо́та; на рабо́те work; at work
рабо́тать to work
рад (m.), **ра́да** (f.) pleased, happy
разгова́ривать to chat
разме́р; како́го разме́ра? size; which size?
разреши́те (пройти́) allow me (to pass)
райо́н district
ра́но early
рейс flight
река́ river
реши́ть (я решу́, ты реши́шь) (perfective) to decide (I will decide, you will decide)
рестора́н restaurant
роди́тели (pl.) parents
роди́ться (он роди́лся, она́ родила́сь) (perfective) to be born (he was born, she was born)
ро́зовый, -ая, -ое pink
рома́н novel

Росси́я Russia
руба́шка shirt
рубль (m.) (**два рубля́, пять рубле́й**) rouble (two roubles, five roubles)
ру́сский, -ая, -ое Russian (*adjective*)
ру́сский, ру́сская a Russian man, a Russian woman
ры́ба fish
рыба́лка fishing
ря́дом next door, next to

са́хар sugar
све́жий, -ая, -ее fresh
свини́на pork
свобо́дно freely, fluently
свобо́дный, -ая, -ое free
свой, своя́, своё one's own
сда́ча change
сде́лать (perfective) to make
се́вер north
сего́дня [sivódnya] today
седьмо́й, -а́я, -о́е seventh
семна́дцать seventeen
семь seven
се́мьдесят seventy
семья́; жить в се́мьях family; to live with a family
сентя́брь (m.) September
сестра́ sister
си́ний, -яя, -ее dark blue
сказа́ть (perfective); **скажи́те...** (imperative) to say; tell (me)...
ско́лько how many
сле́дующий, -ая, -ее following, next
слу́шать (+ accusative) to listen to
смотре́ть (я смотрю́, ты смо́тришь) to look (I look, you look)
– **посмотре́ть** (perfective) to take a look
снег snow
снима́ть (кварти́ру) to rent (a flat)
собира́ть to collect
собира́ться to plan to
со́бственный, -ая, -ое own
сове́т advice
сок juice
со́рок forty
спа́льня bedroom
спаси́бо thank you
спать (я сплю, ты спишь) to sleep (I sleep, you sleep)
специа́льность (f.) profession, job

спорт sport
среда́; в сре́ду Wednesday; on Wednesday
сре́дний, -яя, -ее medium
срок term, period
ста́нция (**метро́**) (underground/subway) station
ста́рый, -ая, -ое old
стать (я ста́ну, ты ста́нешь) (perfective) to become (I will become, you will become)
сто a hundred
сто́ить to cost
сто́лик table (in restaurant)
страна́ country
страхо́вка insurance
счастли́во! all the best!
суббо́та; в суббо́ту Saturday; on Saturday
суп soup
су́тки (pl.) twenty four hours
счёт bill
сын son
сыр cheese
сыт (m.) **сыта́** (f.) full, replete
сюда́ (to) here

табло́ board (showing arrivals/departures)
такси́ taxi
там there
теа́тр theatre
телеви́зор television
телегра́ф telegraph office
телефо́н telephone
те́ннис tennis
тепло́ heat, warmth; (it is) warm
тёплый, -ая, -ое warm
тогда́ then
то́же also
то́лько only
то́чно exactly
трамва́й tram
тре́тий, -ья, -ье third
трёхко́мнатный, -ая, -ое three-roomed
три three
три́дцать thirty
трина́дцать thirteen
три́ста three hundred
тро́е; на трои́х three; for three (people)
тролле́йбус trolleybus
тру́дно (it is) difficult
тру́дный, -ая, -ое difficult
туда́ (to) there
турба́за tourist centre
тяжело́ difficult, tough

удо́бно comfortable
удово́льствие; с удово́льствием pleasure; with pleasure
уже́ already
у́жин dinner, evening meal
у́жинать to have dinner – **поу́жинать** (perfective)
украи́нец a Ukrainian (man)
у́лица street
уме́ть (я уме́ю, ты уме́ешь) to be able to, to know how to (I am able to, you are able to)
универма́г department store
университе́т university
устава́ть (я устаю́, ты устаёшь) to get tired (I get tired, you get tired)
у́тро; у́тром morning; in the morning
учи́тель (m.) **/ учи́тельница** (f.) teacher
учи́ть (я учу́, ты у́чишь) to learn; to teach (I learn/teach, you learn/teach)
учи́ться (я учу́сь, ты у́чишься) to study (I study, you study)

фами́лия surname
февра́ль (m.) February
фило́лог linguist

хлеб bread
ходи́ть (я хожу́, ты хо́дишь, они́ хо́дят) to go on foot (more than one direction) (I go, you go, they go)
хо́лодно; мне хо́лодно (it is) cold; I feel cold
холо́дный, -ая, -ое cold
хоро́ший, -ая, -ее good
хорошо́ well, good
хоте́ть (я хочу́, ты хо́чешь, они́ хотя́т) to want (I want, you want, they want)
ху́же worse

цвет; како́го цве́та? colour; what colour?
цветы́ (pl.) flowers
цветово́дство flower-growing
центр centre

чай tea
час (**два часа́, пять часо́в**) hour; one o'clock (two o'clock, five o'clock)
ча́сто often
ча́шка/ча́шечка cup
челове́к (pl. **лю́ди**) person
че́рез (+ accusative); **че́рез неде́лю, че́рез доро́гу** across, through; in a week, across the road
чёрный, -ая, -ое black
четве́рг Thursday
че́тверо; **на четверы́х** four; for four people
четвёртый, -ая, -ое fourth
четы́ре four
четы́реста four hundred
четы́рнадцать fourteen
чита́ть to read
чте́ние reading
что what
что́-нибудь something, anything

шестна́дцать sixteen
шесто́й, -а́я, -о́е sixth
шесть six
шестьдеся́т sixty
шко́ла school

экску́рсия excursion
электри́чка suburban train
эта́ж floor
э́то this is
э́тот, э́та, э́то this

ю́бка skirt
юг south

я I
язы́к; **на ру́сском языке́** language; in Russian
янва́рь (m.) January

Index

Breakthrough Language Packs

Complete self-study courses

Each Breakthrough Language Pack is designed as a complete self-study course using audio cassettes and a course book. Each Pack contains:

* Three 60- or 90-minute audio cassettes
* The course book

Breakthrough Language Packs available:

Breakthrough Arabic	ISBN 0–333–56692–0
Breakthrough French	ISBN 0–333–58511–9
Breakthrough German	ISBN 0–333–56730–7
Breakthrough Greek	ISBN 0–333–48714–1
Breakthrough Italian	ISBN 0–333–48179–8
Breakthrough Russian	ISBN 0–333–55726–3
Breakthrough Spanish	ISBN 0–333–57105–3
Breakthrough Further French	ISBN 0–333–48193–3
Breakthrough Further German	ISBN 0–333–48189–5
Breakthrough Further Spanish	ISBN 0–333–48185–2
Breakthrough Business French	ISBN 0–333–54398–X
Breakthrough Business German	ISBN 0–333–54401–3
Breakthrough Business Spanish	ISBN 0–333–54404–8

* CD Packs are also now available for:

Breakthrough French	ISBN 0–333–58513–5
Breakthrough German	ISBN 0–333–57870–8
Breakthrough Spanish	ISBN 0–333–57874–0